CHEN, S   A year in upper Felicity:

951.18   7/12

9/02

Please renew/return this item by the last date shown.

So that your telephone call is charged at local rate,
please call the numbers as set out below:

	From Area codes 01923 or 0208:	From the rest of Herts:
Renewals:	01923 471373	01438 737373
Enquiries:	01923 471333	01438 737333
Minicom:	01923 471599	01438 737599

L32b

A YEAR IN UPPER FELICITY

A YEAR IN UPPER FELICITY

Life in a Chinese Village During the Cultural Revolution

JACK CHEN

Illustrations by the Author

HARRAP   LONDON

First published in Great Britain 1973
by GEORGE G. HARRAP & CO. LTD.
182-184 High Holborn, London, WC1V 7AX

© Jack Chen, 1973

ISBN 0 245 52100 3

First published in Great Britain 1973

Printed by Redwood Press Limited, Trowbridge
Made in Great Britain

To Yuan-tsung

Contents

❧ INTRODUCTION   xiii

Winter

❧ A ·TIME OF PREPARATION

Arrival	3
Our Cottage	7
Lao Man and His Wife	13
Our Stove	16
Cadres for Remolding	20
Our Hamlet	34
Neighbors' Cottages	42
Secrets	44
Cooking and Vegetables	48
Raising Capital	55
Little Pig	57
Old Ideas Change, New Ideas Grow	60
The Seasons of the Year	61
The Commune Center	65
Pestle and Bell	67
Vegetable Supplies	68
Midwinter Days	70

Betrothal and Marriage   72
Fleeing Flood and Drought   88
No More Fear of Flood or Drought   96
Former Landlords and Rich Peasants   99
Bringing Up the Children   104
Our Old, Sick, and Disabled Team   107
Spinning, Weaving, Making Clothes   111
How Lao Man Went Cooperative   115
Upper Felicity Crops and Animals   119
Deep-Digging   122
Greetings and a Watch   124

Spring

✤ A TIME OF GERMINATION

Spring Festival Preparations   129
A Story of the Past   130
The Brigade Secretary   135
Spring Festival   146
Big Pig Goes to Market   154
Work-Points and Allocations   156
Tractor Repair Shop   165
Wage Earners   169
Bachelor Life   171
Honored Families   174
Spring Comes and a "Barefoot Doctor"   175
What We Wear   178
Raising Chicks   183
Spring Building   186
Spring Really Comes   195
Tragedy   199
Ox, Horse, and Tractor   201
Changeable Weather   202
Home Gossip   203
Schooling the Youngsters   205

Deep-Well-Digging   208
How We Ate in Spring   220
Movies and Operas   222

Summer

❧ A TIME OF GROWTH AND MATURING

Harvesttime   229
Summer Wear   243
On the Threshing Floor   244
Summer Storm   248
Summer Heat   249
Between Harvest and Sowing   252
First Aid and Beansprouts   253
Of Pig and Sunflowers   254
The Old Men   255
Summer Food   257
Summer Nights   262
Wind and Cloud Battles   262
Heat and Storm   265
Family Tiff   266
The "Cat" Problem Solved   269
Transport Team   270
Beating the Flood   272
After the Rain   279

Autumn

❧ A TIME OF RIPENING AND REJOICING

Autumn Tiger   283
Discussing State Affairs   286
Cottage Architecture   287

On the Road   289
County Town   292
Remolding at the Cadre School   298
Late Summer, Early Autumn   304
Art Criticism   305
Foreign Affairs as Seen from a Ditch   307
Apotheosis of Pig   309
Au Chiu   310
Autumn Harvest   311
Evening   314
Year's End Fruits   315
Mao's Way   315
The Communist Party   321
The People's State   328
The Revolution in the Countryside   332
The Cultural Revolution in Felicity   360
Farewell to Upper Felicity   365

POSTSCRIPT: Felicity Revisited   369

APPENDIX A: The Huang Fu Brigade   379

APPENDIX B: Conversion Table   383

Illustrations

Our cottage   8, 9
Map of Upper Felicity   36
Cutting turnips for drying   49
Workers   100
Ta Sao weaving   112
Ta Hsiang spinning   113
Reeling cotton   114
Second Team's stable   121
Spring Festival on the threshing floor   148, 149
At the mill   158
Our Third Team goes out to work   160
The baby next door   173
Peasant women   180
Important business   187
Spring building   190, 191
Digging the deep well   210, 211, 212, 214
The First Team's scythe and reaper team   230, 231
Harvest   232, 234, 235, 237
Team meeting   326, 327

I spent almost a year in the North China village of Upper Felicity, living and working, as much as I was able, with the peasants there. Nothing stupendous happened. Nothing, that is, that hit the headlines. It was a workaday life we all led, the ordinary, everyday life of China's seven hundred million peasants who live on the land. But one day I got to thinking and said to my wife: "Yuan, nearly a fifth of mankind is living the way Upper Felicity is living, and the rest of the world knows very little about it. I think I should tell them." She agreed, and that is how this book came to be written.

I cannot call Upper Felicity "typical" of China's villages; I do not know what such a typical village would be like. There are mountain villages and seacoast villages, villages in oases in the middle of deserts, moving villages of yurts on the lovely slopes of the Mountains of Heaven. Upper Felicity is a village on the Yellow River plain in North Honan Province. This was an abysmally poor region before the Liberation, and sad to say, its achievements during the twenty-one years since the People's Republic was established are if anything somewhat below average. So I suppose that makes Upper Felicity a typical subaverage commune in a poor plain area.

I have seen many other commune villages where political, economic, and social developments and standards of living are considerably higher. Not long ago I visited a commune on Peking's outskirts where the peasants are raising over 1000 jin of grain per mu (or 7500 kg. per hectare). In Kwangtung Province, where farmers get three full harvests a year, they are doing far better than that. Upper Felicity is working hard now to reach an average yield of 400 jin per mu, that is, around 2000 kg. a hectare. The famous Tachai Brigade in arid northern Shansi is raising 6600 kg. a hectare, up from 630 kg. before the Liberation in 1949.

Quite a bit has been written about the pacesetter communes and farm brigades, places like Tachai or Yangtan in Shansi Province, the farms around Shanghai or the famous Red Star Commune in the Turfan oasis in Sinkiang. These are the ones that thousands visit to learn how socialist methods are being used to get record yields. But little has been written about average or subaverage farms, which are the majority. Upper Felicity is one of them. This book tells a bit about its history, its present, and its hopes, which I am sure will be realized. The villagers are modest, but in their unassuming way, as I learned by living with them, they are pertinacious, hard-working folk when they really set their minds on something.

Are they socialists? I know most readers will ask. The short answer is that the socialist ideals that are the guidelines for running everything in China are, so far as they understand them, their day-to-day rules of thumb. Some, like the Party secretary, may be fully articulate about them. Ta Sao, Elder Sister, with whom we lived, did not "know" much about them, but lived them. If you knew the old China, the China of pre-liberation days, warlord, Kuomintang China, then as you read this book you will see that already socialist ideas, ideals, and methods have succeeded in transforming the life of these seven hundred million farmers in a way that nothing in Chinese history for the previous two thousand years succeeded in doing. Some things are utterly transformed. An electric pump pours water from a deep well where only a decade or so ago peasants sweated and strained at ineffectual treadle pumps draining capricious surface wells. Other things, such as the present marriage customs, are in slow, strange stages of transition, as the new overlays and transforms the old. But change there is in everything, and the pattern that is emerging is socialist.

How did I, an overseas Chinese journalist from Trinidad, come to live in Upper Felicity longer than any other outside journalist or writer has ever lived in any Chinese commune? I got there via London, Moscow, Paris, and New York by a combination of happenstance and desire. I had got caught up in the tumultuous events of the Cultural Revolution, and with all the excitement, I was not feeling well. So when I was given the chance of going to Upper Felicity for a working holiday, I quickly accepted the proposal. For some time before the Cultural Revolution I had been asking the offices concerned to let me see more of the communes. I had written *New Earth,* a study of the cooperative farms in China's Chekiang Province, in 1956–57, and I very much wanted to see how the co-op farms had developed into communes and how they were getting on. I had lived for a fortnight at the famous Yangtan Commune Farm Production Brigade in Shansi Province and written a feature story and report on that, but I wanted to take a good, hard, close-up look at a commune. Here was the opportunity.

Upper Felicity is a real place with that name, but I have altered the name of the commune by putting Great in place of Upper, to avoid confusion between the commune center and the hamlet. I have also changed the names of all the people mentioned in this book. I take the responsibility for any misquotations. The interpretation of events in China and in Upper Felicity is my own. Possibly others who were there may have different interpretations.

Winter 1973

Winter

A TIME OF PREPARATION

*N*orth, east, and south stretched the vast North China plain of bare yellow-brown loess earth. The trees were leafless. Sparse sprouts of winter wheat were the only spots of green. Over all was the translucent blue of a sky without a single fleck of cloud. On three sides the horizon was a sharp, flat line of brown on palest purple haze. To the west it was a serrated mist—the Taihang mountain range.

We arrived in Upper Felicity in the last days of November 1969, soon after *Hsiao Hsueh,* the time of Little Snow. It was nearly lunchtime on a bright winter's day when a truck from the county town deposited me, my wife, and our small son at the big gate of the Great Felicity Commune.

We clambered out, our arms filled with the usual bundles, packages, and string bags that one collects at the last moment on such moves. Someone handed down our three suitcases from the truck. We had arrived.

The young man who received us was talkative and helpful. We learned later that he was one of the "educated youth" sent from the county town to help the commune for a few months. He said we should wait a moment for a handcart to put our baggage on and meanwhile gave us our bearings. Inside the arched gateway of the commune's central office compound he pointed out the post office with its little green postbox hung on the wall. Next door was a branch of the People's Bank, commune offices, and meeting rooms and, at the far side, one- or two-roomed homes of some of the commune officials, usually called cadres. A large commune like this has frequent visitors, officials from the county or provincial Party committees and governments, and from the supply and marketing cooperatives and trade bureaus. Right then a number of cadres, or office workers from Peking and other cities, were also spending time at the commune. Like the young man who had received us, some of them had come to help the commune in any way they could, but mainly they had come to remold their ways of thinking and their outlook on life by living and working with, and learning from, the peasants.

It was a neat, newly built complex, really two compounds of grey brick and red tiles, one behind the other, occupying an area about two-thirds the size of a football field. Trees and vegetables grew in the open spaces between the pathways in the center of the compounds. The rooms were heated by stoves, and there were small dumps of coal outside a few doorways. There was electric lighting and two tall masts supported a radio aerial. Painted on a wall facing the gate was a large portrait of Chairman Mao. Many slogans taken from his *Selected Works* decorated the pillars of the veranda that ran around the compounds. Over the archway of the entrance was written in molded characters "Serve the people." On one side was a nameboard: Revolutionary Committee of Great Felicity Commune.

Since I had been spending quite a bit of time in bed nursing colds and flu, I had inquired particularly whether there was a doctor in the vicinity, and had been told that the commune had its own clinic and hospital. The young cadre pointed this out to me just across the road from the commune office. It too was a new, one-story building, with an eighty-foot frontage, housing the hospital, clinic, pharmacy, and offices. Behind it was a large quiet compound with wards, dormitories, rest rooms, and stores on the other three sides. The saplings growing around were still only beanpoles crowned with tufts of small branches.

After this quick look around we piled our suitcases and various packages onto the handcart and, the cadre pulling and me pushing, trundled it up the road, which was the commune's main street and also the highway from the county town to the next county. On both sides were farmers' houses surrounded by somewhat dilapidated farmyard walls of tamped earth. We passed a big new brick grain-storage compound. Here, we were told, we could buy our rations of rice, kaoliang, maize, wheat flour, and vegetable oil. Then we came to a small snackshop selling noodle soup and steamed bread, meat, and *yo-bing*, a sort of griddle cake fried in deep fat. But we hardly looked at this. Since we came as cadres to the village we had been told that it would not be proper for us to frequent this local snackshop. It would put too much strain on its slender resources and disrupt the local economy.

We turned north straight through the heart of the commune center. This was not very attractive in the leafless bareness of November. Like all northern country villages, it was built mostly of sun-dried bricks faced with adobe, the friable yellow loess earth of the North China plain mixed with clay and straw. Among the older houses only the landlord's grey mansion was built of brick. There were numerous ponds from which the loess building material had been dug. The houses were all built on different levels, giving the village a rather untidy appearance. It was very clean despite its simple rural looks, but bare. The year-old saplings planted alongside the road and around the ponds still had that scrawny look of adolescents.

I did not notice much else at the time. I was too busy trying to keep up with the cart. I remember the young cadre striding along, pointing north (by this time we had turned sharp east again) to a long new brick building with blue shutters and throwing out, "That's the co-op shop." Then, "That's the school," pointing to a large earth-walled compound to the south with several rows of long brick buildings inside it. He called out that the red-tiled roof showing over the barren limbs of a grove of trees was the tractor-repair workshop.

We crossed a road that ringed the commune center, passed a tree nursery with a dense growth of saplings, went down hill and then up, and reached the little hamlet of Upper Felicity, which for the next year we were to call home.

I visited many hamlets in the neighborhood. I never saw one that was more attractive to the eye than ours. I grew to love it, but my preference for it is not partisanship. Even in winter our hamlet is attractive. In summer, bowered in green and with its shining big pond enclosing it wholly to the east, it is enchanting.

In many ways it is like thousands of other hamlets on the North China plain above the Yellow River. Its houses are just like those in the nearby commune center, but somehow the way they lie up and down, facing this way and that without any plan, so far as I could see, the setting of their trees, all has a natural harmony that immediately pleases the eye.

Setting us down at the old landlord's house, which serves as office for the Third Production Brigade to which the whole hamlet belongs, the cadre introduced us to the brigade chairman, another youngish man, and then went off to fetch our host, the commune member in whose farmyard we would stay. While he was gone, the chairman made the usual polite inquiries: How was the journey? Were we tired? He pointed out our new home. This was some fifty yards away, four farmyards down Upper Felicity's main lane. Then our host came hurrying up to escort us over to his home.

He was a middle-aged man of medium height, strongly built. He wore black padded trousers, a jacket of black cotton homespun, and scuffed, homemade cotton shoes. His head, shaved bald, shone in the winter sunlight. I liked the enormous, good-natured smile of welcome that creased his sunburned face in wrinkles. Hardly waiting for the introductions to be over, he seized our biggest bag, slung it on his shoulder, and was off with a long stride, with us trailing after. This, we found, was typical of Lao Man. If there was something to be done, he did it. As our little procession went up the lane a number of farmers and their wives, looking stout in their padded black cotton winter outfits, glanced at us curiously but politely from their yards and doorways.

Our Cottage 🌿

A farmer's dwelling usually consists of several buildings: bedrooms and living rooms, grouped together in a u-shape or square with a separate outside kitchen for use in the spring, summer, and autumn; a tool- and store-shed; a manure pit, a large pigsty, and a chicken coop and run. Sometimes the whole complex is enclosed by a sun-dried loess brick wall; sometimes, as with our farmyard, there is no wall at all.

In Upper Felicity there are no private plots attached to the household, but in its own courtyard a family may grow its own trees, including fruit trees, shrubs for making brooms, sunflowers, tobacco, peppers, and the like. Nearly every family tries to grow a large shade tree in its courtyard. This makes a big difference to one's comfort in the hot summer days. The size of the average farmyard is not large—about fifty by sixty feet.

The time-honored form for grouping the household's buildings is to start with a single three-room house. A "room" is a unit about eight feet by ten. A three-room house may actually contain only one or two rooms, but have an area equal to three. This main cottage is usually divided into two-thirds and one-third by an inside wall. The large room is the center of family life. The big portrait of Chairman Mao is over the long altar table where the ancestral tablets were once kept. And usually around the portrait are photographs of members of the family, particularly absent ones.

When more funds are available, a second similar but slightly smaller or lower building is built at right angles to the

first. Then comes another one, facing it. A wall is then built to join the backs of these houses, then a wall and arched gateway are set up to complete the home rectangle at the front. The farmers like to decorate their front gateways with some bricks carved with a traditional floral or scroll design. Pigsty, chicken coop, outside kitchen, and outhouses for storing implements go up wherever convenient inside the farmyard enclosure.

Of course, it is best for a house in these latitudes to face south so that the winter sun warms the rooms throughout the day. The prevailing cold winter winds blow impotently against the thick, windowless north wall. In summer, the afternoon breeze cools the house off quickly for the night. The morning, midday, and afternoon sun falls into the rooms obliquely so that they are cool when east- and west-facing rooms are baking hot, and light when north-facing rooms are shadowed.

Lao Man led us to a large, south-facing cottage of three rooms in a two-cottage farmyard. He and his wife and children lived in the eastward-facing cottage. This was the main one, of the same size but built on a higher foundation. The door of our cottage was open. Inside it was whitewashed, clean-swept, and empty of everything except a wooden bed, with fresh straw strewn on its rope cradle, and a pile of fresh green cabbages in a corner—a welcoming gift from the brigade. It was divided by an inside wall into a large living room and a small bedroom. The north wall was made of baked brick and the other walls of tamped earth and sun-dried brick on a low, knee-high, kiln-made brick foundation.

There was plenty of headroom—ten feet under the eaves to ten and a half in the middle of the curved, smoke-darkened wattle that formed the ceiling. Good hardwood rafters and kaoliang stalk wattle supported the roof covering of loess mixed with lime and straw to form a smooth, rainproof covering. I noticed that the roof beam, a good foot and a half in diameter, had a small oblong of red paper stuck to it when the house was built with the character "fu" for happiness written on it.

The two paper-covered lattice windows and the latticed space over the two-leaved door let in plenty of light. Later

I replaced the paper with sheets of transparent plastic and this solved the daylight lighting problem completely. With the door ajar—and it usually was when we were at home, winter or summer, except when it was blowing very cold or raining very hard—there was no problem. When the door was closed, the plastic let in ample light for reading and even for drawing or painting.

The floor was of tamped earth, quite dry, we found, even in the rainy season. We used to sweep it daily. This took off a bit of the top along with the stray bits of fluff, paper, and what-not that had fallen on it. But where it was worn down or pitted with holes, it was a simple matter to throw some muddy loess on the spot and stamp it down flat. This made the floor as good as new.

We had brought down our bed, and this, with our suitcases and a box for storing our quilts, sweaters, and other winter clothes in summer, filled the little bedroom. The large room was winter kitchen and living room, dining room, and studio combined. The picture I made of it gives the general layout. In the northeast corner (nobody ever says "left" or "right" except for politics in this compass-oriented land), I put my divan. This was the bed that was in the room when we came. It was a wooden stretcher on tall legs with a web of rope in place of the usual canvas covering. I covered this over com-fortably with straw and a kaoliang mat woven in criss-cross pattern that I bought in the local co-op for a few mao (the price of three or four packets of cheap cigarettes). South of that, along the wall was our crockery and food cupboard, and next to that, the cupboard for our pots and pans filled the southeast corner. Under this was our store of coal piled behind a board by the stove which extended westward almost to the doorway.

On the other side of the doorway was a corner for our tools and the big, half-broken water jar that we used for making our stove fuel, a mixture of coal dust, powdered clay, and water. Here in the west wall was the doorway to our bedroom. We covered this archway with a curtain made from the thick-meshed linen I paint on. Next to the door on the same west wall was a wooden packing case on its side. We covered this with a sheet of green plastic. Underneath was a useful cupboard and on top were our washbasin and toilet things. Next to that was the large pail we kept our water in, filled daily from the well. My wife, Yuan-tsung, and I enjoyed this joint chore as it gave us a chance to bid good day to all our neighbors on both sides of the lane.

The northwest corner and half of the north wall was our vegetable store. I built a rack of bamboo poles here, and within a week it held many pounds of turnips and carrots and a mountain of cabbage. Then came three suitcases stacked one on top of the other. Covered with a piece of folk weave I had bought in Sinkiang, these formed a handy shelf. Next to it was our Peking tallboy with our clothes, and then the divan corner. The tallboy was crowned with our clock in its glass case to keep the dust out and muffle its raucous ticking, several jars of homemade pickles and preserved duck eggs, and my paintbrushes. Above it we hung our colored print of Chairman Mao waving from the top of the Tien An Men rostrum. No home is complete without a portrait of the Chairman.

In the center of our room, near the divan, was the dining table with two chairs and a small brown stool. That, with my large wooden easel, completed the furnishings. Later on we acquired two spades, a hoe, a sickle, and a large jar with a cover, in which we kept our store of rice, corn, and wheat flour. We were always careful to keep the food jar covered for fear of rats. But we soon acquired a little mouse who made his home at the back of the stove and fed on the scraps that we swept into the stove hold overnight.

When everything was shipshape, the stove giving off the warmth, and the kettle whistling, ready for tea, our cottage was a cozy home, one of the nicest in Upper Felicity.

But long before that, indeed from the time we first reached the village, we had begun to enjoy the warmth of its hospitality. When we arrived we had seen leaflets stuck to walls and trees: "Welcome to the cadres coming to the countryside!" Not long afterwards we returned the compliment by painting a slogan in whitewash on a cottage wall: "Learn from the poor and lower-middle peasants!" The peasant family with whom we lived took us to its heart immediately. As I sit in this busy foreign metropolis and write about them now, I am seized by a feeling of nostalgia for their innocence and kindness.

How they would tremble for us, living in a society where a car can knock down a woman and child and never even stop; where there are saloons with women wearing transparent clothes or nothing on top or bottom either, where muggings and armed robberies are taking place practically every day of the week, where "live shows" are the latest sensation and gambling is legalized. . . . If I told them about all this I do not think they would believe it possible.

Lao Man and His Wife

*L*ao Man and his wife, Su-tsung (Virtuous Beloved), made us part of the family from the very first, and so we remain today. No one could have been more attentive or tactful. The whole of that first day we depended entirely on them, for our food, furniture, and fuel had not yet arrived. They threw their cottage open to us. "We are all one family," said Lao Man. And what's more, he meant it.

Still tense as I was after months in the midst of the tumult of the Cultural Revolution in Peking, the quiet of the country-side and the unassuming, unaffected goodness of these two was balm to the soul.

Mrs. Man gave us large wheaten pancakes to eat for lunch with stewed cabbage and pickles. We all ate together. Lao Man and I, as the elders, sat at the table; the others wherever they liked. In the evening, we each had some pickled vegetables and an enormous bowl of millet porridge. It was more than I could finish at one meal, and I ate the rest for breakfast the next morning. We exchanged information about our families. I presented my small son, Hsiao Di (Small Younger Brother), who immediately became Au Di ("Hsiao" becoming "Au," rhyming with "how" in the local dialect). Lao Man told me he had a grown-up son, Ching Chun (Celebrate Spring), who was eighteen years old and in the last class of the commune's middle school. He also had a daughter, Ta Hsiang (Elder Fragrance) in school. His two youngest, a boy and girl, who hung around the door looking shyly but inquisitively at the guests, were called Au Chiu (Small Autumn) and Hsiao Ching (Small Brightness). They were seven and five.

Our first impression of Lao Man was the same as our last impression a year later. He wore well. Always good-natured, he threw himself into work—any work—with the same natural enthusiasm as a tree pushes out its leaves in spring. Work, for him, was something to be done, and done right away. In those first few days I was busy putting our cottage in order: repairing the bed that had been broken on the journey; fixing up cupboards and racks for the vegetables, and finding a place to put the coal. Coming back from the fields after a long day's work and seeing me hard at it, Lao Man would pitch in without a moment's thought and, when the job was done, go off without waiting for or expecting thanks.

We soon learned that his generosity was proverbial in the village. He had a venerable sheepskin coat, an essential for long-distance carting in the winter. One early morning a friend came to the farmyard and called not "Will you lend me your sheepskin?" but "Lao Man! Who has your sheepskin?" His sheepskin was practically team property.

At forty, he no longer had the bounce and spring of youth, but he moved with energy, was full of muscle and endurance. He said he had never in his life been really ill, yet by all accounts before liberation he had suffered from chronic undernourishment, exposure, and outright starvation. Later we heard that he had been ill once. Back in 1961, toward the end of the "three difficult years," life had been tough in this part of Honan. Mismanagement of the new commune, due to inexperience, had been compounded by vile weather, continuous downpours, sodden fields, and blight. No one had starved,

but there was a lot of undernourishment. It had been hard
going for the Man family. (I think this partly accounted for
Ta Hsiang's diminutive size.) Lao Man's uncle, who lived
next door but one, had gotten sick and needed a blood transfusion. Lao Man, though in a weak state himself, offered
without hesitation to donate blood. Unfortunately, the young
doctor who gave the transfusion was inexperienced and took
too much blood from Lao Man. Making his way home after-
ward he felt dizzy, then stumbled like a drunken man. He
just made it to the cottage door and fainted. Mrs. Man said
that he was half unconscious for three days, his body bathed
in sweat.

Lao Man had dismissed the whole incident from his mind.
The past only showed on his face, which was deeply lined.
His generation had lived a hard life and they still toiled hard.
Naturally it was not from him that I learned he was a "Red
Flag Commune Member." The title, signifying that he was a
model socialist-farmer, had been conferred on him by unani-
mous vote of his brigade.

Mrs. Man was just a few years younger than Lao Man and
just a shade shorter. Lao Man had a well-shaped head, but he
was far from good-looking. He had an enormous mouth, and
when he grinned he showed all his teeth and gums. Mrs. Man
even now was pretty, and in her young days must have been
quite a beauty. She had a light, rosy complexion, finely shaped
nose and mouth, and white small teeth. She was always neatly
dressed and combed. Her hair, still jet black and always
washed and oiled, hung in heavy tresses to her shoulders. It
was an unusual style for a peasant woman. Most of the women
of her age wear chignons or shorter bobs. She wore black
homespun cloth which she made herself. Unlike the younger
girls who wore slacks, she tied the ends of her black trousers
around the ankles with white tape. You usually found her
half-smiling, as if enjoying some secret joke. She was not the
worrying sort but the kind of person who, when faced with a
difficulty, does not waste time complaining but sets about
overcoming it.

She had borne six children in all. Two had died. In preliberation days she had had her full share of troubles, including wars and the perennial flights from drought or flood, and she had experienced the alarms of postliberation land reform and other campaigns as well. But she carried the past lightly on her shoulders. She was always active, always doing something. Usually it was some household task—spinning, weaving, making shoes or clothes, cooking, washing, cleaning, pickling, feeding the hens or pigs; or she was out working in the fields. My wife called her Ta Sao—Elder Sister, a traditional courtesy title for an older woman addressed by a younger. I used this form of address too, even though Lao Man did not think it quite correct, because he was younger than I, so my wife and I took precedence over him and his wife.

Our Stove

The day we arrived, Ta Sao said almost nothing. Lao Man did the honors and the talking. We sat around the table and ate with Lao Man. Ta Sao brought the dishes and resolutely refused to let my wife help her. But when we had eaten, Yuan-tsung would not take no for an answer and helped her clean up. This began and cemented their friendship, and she was completely won over when Yuan-tsung insisted on calling her Ta Sao.

We only really got to know her, however, a few days later when Lao Man was out at work and we were battling with our stove.

Our stove bulked large in our life. At first it amazed us with its cussedness. Sometimes it went out seemingly without cause. Sometimes, after we had given it up for dead and turned our backs on it, it suddenly sprang to life again. It was built under our living-room window and stood two and a half feet high, four feet long, and two and a bit wide. Most of this volume of sun-dried brick and daub was to give working space on top for pots and pans and the broad board we used for rolling dough and cutting up vegetables, meat, and fish.

The fuel burned in a central, flask-shaped chamber whose round mouth, as big as a saucer, was cut in a square metal plate let into the top of the stove. A smaller opening at its base led to the front of the stove through a six-inch-long tunnel. This was for raking it out or giving it, when needed, a blast with the bellows. Its bottom was a metal grate over a hole opening wide to the front of the stove. This gave a good draft, and was big enough to collect the ash and cinders of a whole day's burning as well as the sweepings off the floor. Our stove burned coal or, more usually, coal balls made of coal dust and powdered clay mixed two to one with water to the consistency of a thick paste. This fuel was put in at the top.

For two days I surveyed the stove in pleasant expectation of its warmth and cheer. But the coal had not yet arrived and this area had little firewood. Meanwhile Ta Sao fed us thrice a day with corn (maize) porridge, corn pone (*wawatou*), flat-cakes (pancakes) and cabbage, sometimes with pickles, and this kept us going. Varied with carrots (usually eaten raw) and turnips (also eaten raw, but sometimes boiled or pickled) this was the Mans' usual winter fare six days of the week. Sometimes they made steamed bread (*mantou*) and had a bit of meat or eggs. They had enough to eat, but their diet was clearly deficient in proteins. We ate what the Mans ate but in the mornings I drank malted milk that I brought down from Peking for elevenses. I also had a couple of large pats of butter which I put on Ta Sao's pancakes in the privacy of our cottage. It tasted fine but I could not help feeling a twinge of conscience at first. This sort of clandestine luxury would definitely interfere with my remolding. But more about food later.

The Mans had two stoves. One, like ours, was in their living room. But since this only burnt coal, which was expensive for them, they only used it when the weather was very cold. The other stove, in the outside kitchen, of fanciful shape, burned kaoliang stalks and dried corncobs, which they fed into its front opening and kept blazing by working a bellows whose nozzle was set into the side of the stove. They lit this stove to cook each meal and it created vast amounts of acrid smoke. This soon filled the little kitchen and then billowed out through the door. One day I thought I would help Ta Sao ply her bellows. In a few minutes I was driven out into the fresh air, my eyes streaming.

When the Mans fired their inside stove, an exact replica of ours, this too belched out smoke that filled the room and laid a dusty film everywhere. I set about thinking how to confer a lasting benefit on Upper Felicity by designing a better stove. Soon my plans were laid: I would fix a zinc chimney over the stove's mouth and lead the smoke out through a hole which I would make in the wall or the window latticework. Once the fire was lit, the chimney could be swung aside out of the way. It was the lighting of the stove that was the trouble. Once it was going it was quite efficient and economical.

But I was forced to postpone my innovation. My cadre friends told me that such a radical alteration involving stove and window would indicate dissatisfaction with my host's arrangements and would not be polite. So I dropped this idea for the time being. Later on I found that a short length of chimney got the fire blazing quickly and gave a good draft, and that the smoke soon dispersed among the rafters and then drifted out of the cottage.

I carried out the second part of my plan with disastrous results. The coal had arrived. I would light my stove. I found it filled to the top with clinkers. I wondered at this for a moment. The clinkers were all largish and there was no small ash at the bottom of the grate. However, my scientific mind was not to be deterred. I raked out all the clinkers and built my fire in the approved London way: a layer of loosely crumpled paper; small slivers of wood and shavings followed by larger pieces of firewood; smallish lumps of coal on top. When all this was blazing merrily, I threw on some larger lumps of coal . . . and the whole thing collapsed and burned out.

Scientifically, of course, this should not have happened. Perhaps the wood was wet? I repeated the process, this time soaking the wood in kerosene. The fire blazed and then subsided. I smashed a box and stuffed the slivers in the stove. It was no use: all I had was a roomful of smoke and frustration.

I had also used up my slender stock of firewood and wasted kerosene.

In this crisis, Ta Sao, seeing the billowing waves of smoke pouring out of the room and evidently fearing a fire, came in and without more ado took over. Seeing the pile of clinkers before the stove, she took in the situation at a glance. This later became one of the jokes of the village—"One man took all the clinkers out of the stove!" and this would be followed by gales of good-natured laughter. "Ah, these intellectuals!"

Ta Sao cleared the grate and then put most of the clinkers back in again. From her house she brought a handful of twigs for firewood and corncobs and a large box bellows whose snout fitted snugly into the small front opening of the stove. She lit one long piece of wood and thrust this into the top of the stove among the clinkers. When this had caught well, she added another and then another, each about a foot long, to form a sort of cone-shaped cradle. Then she threw in corncobs and two or three pieces of hard tree root. When all this was burning fiercely she put in some lumps of coal, covered the stove's mouth with a short length of chimney, and began to ply the bellows. Clouds of smoke filled the room, but soon we could hear the crackling of real fire within and the smoke grew less. The fire had caught. "*Tsung-la* (That'll do!)," she exclaimed triumphantly. It had all taken just a few minutes with peasant science.

When the stove was burning hot she plastered the hungry mouth with a generous blob of coal dust mixed with clay and water. This sizzled and corked up the opening. Then she made three holes in the crust with the poker, pushing the poker down to the bottom of the grate. Blue flames shot up through these three chimneys. The stove thus stoppered would burn unattended for five or six hours. Later we learned to damp it down in this way so that it burned steadily the whole night through.

Ta Sao also taught us how to make coal balls, the usual day-time fuel for the fire. Before making my first fire I had spent the morning outside the cottage laboriously trying to roll coal balls by hand. It was easy to mix the coal dust and clay with water, but rolling this paste into balls was another matter.

Nothing remotely resembling a ball emerged—only bits of chaos. Ta Sao had seen me doing this but had said nothing. Too polite, she evidently thought I knew what I was doing. But now she threw a large blob of coal and clay mud down onto the top of the stove, cut it roughly with the spade into squares, separated them and left them to dry. They were not round, but they were perfectly good coal balls, and took no time at all to make.

When we finally mastered it, we found that the Upper Felicity stove was an efficient and economic contraption. All it needed was a removable chimney for lighting. But it still took us several days to master it, to judge just what was a good fire, when it needed coddling, when it had to be fed hard, and just how much to rake it and not have the whole blazing bottom and all the clinkers fall out. We complained one day to Ta Sao: "This stove is like a baby with loose bowels. We feed it at the top and it all comes out right away at the bottom!" Ta Sao liked this humor, and the joke soon went the rounds of the village.

Mastering that stove and having it purring under our hands made us feel really at home. It was warm; we had a constant supply of hot, boiled water in our three thermos bottles, and we began to cook. Our neighbors' solicitous "How is your fire?" of a morning gave place to great admiration of our prowess with the local stove. Later we were cited approvingly at a public meeting for our zeal in learning from the poor and lower-middle peasants.

Cadres for Remolding 🔅

*J*t was the stoves that brought us together with our cadre friends.

"Cadre" is a translation of *gan bu*—a doer in management or administration—but that is not a broad enough definition.

All kinds of office workers and professionals are cadre—a doctor in the health service, a nurse, an editor, a journalist, a typist. A minister, an ambassador, and a trade-union leader are cadres, and so are a county head and a peasant who has been elected to a commune's managing revolutionary committee.

Our cadre friends did various jobs in a Peking translation and publishing bureau. There were department heads, artists, translators, several of the technical staff, bookkeepers, and typists. The six couples who were with us in Upper Felicity had all come to live and work there among the peasants and to be remolded. All the husbands and three of the wives worked in the translation bureau. Two wives were housewives. One worked in another organization but had elected to come with her husband; in this case he might have elected to go with her to the place where her organization was sending its cadres to be remolded. My wife and I joined in with these six families to form the Old, Sick, and Disabled Team attached to the Third Brigade of Great Felicity Commune.

Since 1969–70 hundreds of thousands of urban cadres have gone down to the countryside. Like many other things in New China, this mass move of cadres to the grass roots is multipurpose.

At this stage of the Cultural Revolution a number of difficulties had to be overcome to clear the way for further advance. Beginning in 1966, many leading cadres had been accused by the rank-and-file in the bureau of being dyed-in-the-wool followers of Liu Shao-chi, the deposed President, and trying to lead the bureau along the road to capitalist restoration. This was bad enough, but sometimes investigation into their activities had uncovered doubtful passages in their past and further charges were added of an even more serious nature. Some were said to have been guilty of corruption or embezzlement, to have betrayed the Party and the people, and even to have collaborated with the enemies of the Revolution, the Chiang Kai-shek Kuomintang and the imperialist powers.

In the further course of the Revolution such cadres were "struggled against" and criticized. They were asked to answer the charges and, if at fault or guilty, make a self-criticism.

During this period, if the charges were serious, they were usually taken off their jobs and given manual labor to perform, cleaning the offices and the compounds or helping in the canteen. For a time some of the most seriously criticized lived under strict discipline and supervision.

If a cadre could prove that the charges against him were groundless, that was an end to the matter. In other cases, if he conscientiously performed the various tasks given him and showed through self-criticism that he realized what his mistakes or misdeeds were and sincerely desired to atone for them by service to the people, then he was "liberated." An assessment of him was written up by the revolutionary committee in charge of the office, and he was allowed to return to normal work.

Most leading cadres had in fact carried out the Liu Shao-chi line in one way or another (after all, he had been virtually in charge of the Party and government), but many had done so in good faith, thinking that whatever their own private opinions, they should carry out what they believed to be Party orders that seemed to them reasonable. Some cadres had previously worked long and sacrificed much for the Revolution, and once they had acknowledged their mistakes as unwilling or unwitting followers of Liu Shao-chi, they were rated "good men who had made mistakes" and liberated. It was cadres like these who had been co-opted into the revolutionary committees that now ran the offices. These new tripartite leading groups were made up of the leaders of the revolutionary mass organizations that had seized power (from the Liu Shao-chi "capitalist roaders"), representatives of the People's Liberation Army's Mao Tse-tung Thought Propaganda Teams that had come to help the revolutionary left in the offices, and the best of the old leading cadres.

Unfortunately, a number of cases involving cadres, both leading and rank-and-file, could not be solved and were hung up because of conflicting evidence or other causes. Some special cases did not seem to be covered by any of the Party instructions for handling cadres' problems.

In some departments feeling still ran high between mem-

bers of the various revolutionary groups* that had contended
for power in the early and middle stages of the Revolution,
and these conflicts were reflected in stalemated decisions about
cadres supported by one or the other group. Then there were
the cadres who had been labeled counterrevolutionaries. This
was a serious matter and such cases had to be reviewed by
higher administrative and Party organizations. In 1969 some
of these organizations had not yet been fully reconstituted,
and so there was a bottleneck, cases were hung up, and it was
difficult to form really efficient new managements, which had
to include all the best of the old cadres.

Under these circumstances it was felt that a cooling-off
period might be in order. The Party published Chairman
Mao's suggestion that it might be a good idea to try settling
matters in a third of an organization first and then going on
from there. It was also common knowledge that many Peking
offices were top-heavy with staff. It was felt that this would
be a good opportunity to gently transfer some cadres to other
organizations. (Premier Chou stated in 1970 that the number
of officials in central government administration had been cut
from 60,000 to 10,000 during the Cultural Revolution drive
to streamline administration.)

But the main issue was that every urban cadre and intellectual should go to learn from the revolutionary peasants and
rid himself of elitist attitudes. In November it was announced
that groups of the offices' staff should go in turn to the countryside to live and work among the poor and lower-middle
peasants, staunchest allies of the revolutionary working class
in the villages, and there steel themselves through labor and
remold their ideology, their world outlook, stained or cor-
rupted by feudal, bourgeois (capitalist), or revisionist ideas.
The commune peasants would teach them and help them
develop a truly socialist outlook. After that they would return
to their city jobs and carry on the Cultural Revolution better.

* The mass revolutionary organizations took very militant-sounding
names such as the Red Flag Corps, Red Guard, or Proletarian Revolutionary Fighting Detachment.

In the meantime their offices would pay them all the same wages they were getting in Peking.

On these terms, everybody expressed his willingness and even eagerness to go to the villages. A list of names of those selected to go in the first group was posted by the bureau's revolutionary committee. Those going were not told how long they would stay in the countryside; it was understood that they would live there indefinitely until recalled.

There were thus three groups of cadres in and around Upper Felicity. In the first category was the largest group in one place, unmarried young men or women, or married people without their spouses or families, living in the bureau's May Seventh Cadre School. This was housed in a former state farm and the cadres farmed the several hundred mu of land attached to it. They studied the works of Marx, Engels, Lenin, and Stalin and the development of their ideas and teachings in Mao Tse-tung's *Selected Works*. They had regular current affairs courses and discussions. They continued to carry on the Cultural Revolution. They criticized the revisionist ideas of Liu Shao-chi and his followers, repudiated selfish, individualistic attitudes, analyzed the events of the Revolution and their part in them, and discussed how to carry out the final stages of the movement, clearing up outstanding problems and putting all work on a new firm basis along the lines of the good suggestions put forward during the Cultural Revolution. This was all called "grasping revolution and promoting production." The May Seventh School was one of thousands so named because they were modeled on the instructions that Chairman Mao issued for the reform of education on May 7, 1966. In those instructions he had advised that education should serve socialist policies, that is, the political aims of the proletariat, and be combined with productive labor. Government offices, ministries, the artists', writers', musicians', actors', and film workers' associations, research institutes, universities, and other similar organizations had all set up May Seventh Schools in the rural areas, and here their cadres were being tempered and remolded, group by group.

In nearby villages were groups, large and small, of the second category of cadres. These were all fairly able-bodied cadres with their wives and children. Unlike the May Seventh School cadres, who traveled light, with just their clothes, sleeping things, and some books, these cadres and their families had brought down their household goods and furniture just as I had. They and their families were also expected to learn from the peasants. The discipline in this category was not so strict, but they were expected to observe "the discipline of the movement" in a conscientious way. Bad discipline here as there was cause for criticism and self-criticism.

The six families in Upper Felicity composed the third category. These cadres were all either old (over sixty as I was), sick, or disabled, and therefore in need of special consideration. Like the second category of cadres, they went to the village to live. When and if they were required, they would return to their offices in Peking. But they had all been told not to think of recall, as this would inevitably interfere with their remolding.

A number of cadres had been given the choice of leaving the organization entirely if they wished. In that case they would receive a lump sum in severance pay (one month's wage for every year of work) or get a pension if they were entitled to one. Men could retire at the age of sixty and women at fifty-five and receive 75 or 80 per cent of their monthly wage, depending on how many years they had worked. In some cases it was hoped that they would go back to their native villages, and a few had gone to live as commune members with their families in the villages where they came from. But most preferred to remain with the translation bureau and take a chance that their stay in Upper Felicity would be temporary, though prolonged perhaps for a year or two, and that they would eventually return to Peking. All of these rusticated cadres, except for those who had taken severance pay or were pensioned, received their usual salaries while they were in the countryside. All did some kind of work in the farms and, while they worked with the peasants, studied and existed as a separate organized unit. Their children attended school and, like all the village children, worked in the fields when the work needed them.

The other six families in our village all arrived at the same time we did, so there was much bustle and excitement in the village that week. Several horse-drawn carts brought in our baggage and furniture. Most had packed up all they possessed for the move. It was not a great deal in any case. None had more than two rooms provided by their office in one or other of its buildings, and most shared a kitchen or bathroom, so that they brought with them only bare essentials: beds, chairs or stools, a table, a wardrobe or chests for linen and summer or winter clothes, a few suitcases, some books and knick-knacks, a radio. Three brought bicycles.

In Peking very few cadres bothered to furnish their flats much. Most did not have the money to do it, and they were exhorted to hold themselves ready at any time to "go to the countryside." Besides, there had been a couple of invasion scares, once during the Korean War and later during the Vietnam War. No one wanted to be burdened with a lot of household furniture. Most of them had already gone once or twice for many months to the countryside, to help with the land reform in 1952, to help with the socialist education movement in 1964 or 1965, or simply to be "remolded." Anyway, if they had set about acquiring property and preoccupying themselves with home comforts, this would have led to criticism for showing bourgeois tendencies. In Peking they all lived rather simply.

So materially speaking and in comparison with Peking, they were not so badly off in the village. Old Tang, over sixty years old and a senior leading cadre, and his wife earned between them about 320 yuan a month ($106 U.S.), but here in the village they could spend only about 100 yuan a month. Conspicuous consumption was not allowed to cadres in the village, or how could they integrate with the peasants and remold themselves? So they were able to put a couple of hundred yuan in the savings bank every month at 2½ per cent interest. All their children were grown up and economically independent.

On the other hand, Ling, a middle-aged artist, was the only wage earner in a family of four. And he, poor chap, had only one lung. His wife, a motherly sort, looked after the house. In Peking she had earned pin money doing sewing in a neighborhood housewives' co-op, but here they depended entirely on Ling's wage. Their two children were in primary and middle school.

You may wonder how a family of four can live on 100 yuan a month—$200 Hong Kong or $40 U.S. a month. Hong Kong resettlement housing is built to accommodate poor families earning under $600 H.K. a month. But Ling was by no means rated poor in Peking. A small, reasonably clean room in Hong Kong today can command a rent of $50–60 U.S. In Peking a cadre pays about 1 yuan or less (U.S. $0.40) in an old-style house, and perhaps double that in a new block of flats. Water, heating in winter, and lighting may cost less than that. A single person can eat all his meals in an office canteen for about 15 yuan a month. School fees are minimal, almost token. Clothes are cheap. No one is ashamed to go out in clean, patched clothes; in fact they are a sign of commendable thrift and frugality. A single visit to a doctor in Hong Kong will cost you $50 H.K. A cadre in China is wholly covered by the national health scheme. His wife and children pay half the cost of treatment. But children in school will come under various free health services for children. And anyway, if Ling were really in financial difficulties, he could apply for a grant from the office staff association and would surely get it.

With an income of around 100 yuan a month, the Lings still had to be frugal both in Peking and in Upper Felicity. Ling had been offered severance pay and permission to return to his native village near Wuhsi, but he had not accepted the offer. He had not seen his own village for three decades and felt no particular attachment to it. In his condition, field work as a regular commune member was out, but of course he could do clerical work for the commune and use his skill as an artist in commune cultural activities, or perhaps as a teacher or in some handicraft project. But Ling was reluctant to try out something so new and preferred to rusticate a bit in the hope of eventually returning to Peking. He, like many others faced with similar choices, calculated that with the expansion of industrial and other activities in China, Peking's offices and bureaus would eventually need his services again.

The Lins were also a bit pinched for funds. Only old Lin worked, and he was not well. He had stomach ulcers. He had joined the Party in the lean days of war before liberation, and the hard living had told on his health. He had joined the revolutionary work as a peasant activist and been transferred after liberation to work in Peking, and with no special trade or profession, he earned little more than Ling the artist. His wife, also an old Party member and also not in good health, was now a housewife and earned no salary. They had three children. The two girls were in kindergarten and primary school. The boy, however, was more or less independent. He had not completed his middle-school education but had volunteered to go and work on a state farm in the northeast. He earned little more than his keep at the moment but would soon be earning more, and like all good Chinese boys would contribute what he could to the rest of the family.

Like Ling, the Lins had been offered a choice of getting severance pay and going back to their native village. But they too wondered what they would do there once their savings were spent. Could they really settle down forever in the village? They only had distant relatives there "back home," and had lost contact even with them. So they too preferred to take a chance and hope that they would once again be recalled to Peking, where Lin worked in the general affairs department of the office.

The cadres discussed each other's affairs quite freely. There was never any secret about what anybody earned, and such matters as how many there were in the family, what the children were doing, where the family came from and so on were public knowledge. In one way or another, these facts had come out in the frequent group discussions in the office. Most people agreed that a general expansion of work and production would see everyone back in Peking within a few years, except for those completely incapacitated by age or sickness. This applied even to Lin, who was probably the most expendable of cadres. Any youngster with an education could take on his job, which involved such things as dispatching letters and parcels and seeing to office supplies and the general maintenance of the office rooms. But he was a completely honest Party member and so was his wife, loyal and dependable. These are qualities the Party values highly. So his chances of returning to Peking were rated high.

Old Tang was so certain that his stay in Upper Felicity was only temporary that he never unpacked all his baggage. They had two beds, but he and his wife slept most uncomfortably on one. They never even bothered to stack up their boxes and suitcases properly. After ten months they were still strewn around the floor haphazardly, just as they had been left on the first day of arrival.

Tan and his wife were a pair apart. Tan had rheumatism and was near sixty. His wife was a bustling forty-plus. Their two boys were grown and working. One was in the People's Liberation Army and the other on a state farm. Tan had a good knowledge of English and his wife was a bookkeeper. Their combined wages were close to 200 yuan a month. They were pretty certain that she would eventually be recalled to work, and since he would go back too, a job would certainly be found for him. They regarded their stay in Upper Felicity as an interlude that had to be lived through, and they banked their spare cash against the day. It would be a nice nest egg when they got back to city life.

The Yuans were the youngest couple among us. He was there because he had suffered from ulcers and had had most of his stomach cut out—at least that was how he phrased it. His wife was a fine-looking girl, energetic and in robust health. She worked in another organization but had elected to accompany him to Upper Felicity. They had their oldest boy with them, a child of eleven. Their youngest child lived with his grandparents in Canton. Yuan didn't like living in cold

Peking, and he had been offered the opportunity, long sought, of being released from his office with severance pay. He had hoped to fulfill a long-held wish and go south to join his parents and take another job there. But precisely at that time, Canton, like Shanghai and Peking, decided to curb its rapidly growing population. It had simply stopped giving registration or residence permits for people wishing to come there. In the circumstances, the Yuans had elected to come down to Upper Felicity and wait until conditions changed and they could either go on to Canton or back to Peking. Their combined wages were about the same as the Tans', so they were fairly well off. Both of them were university graduates.

Finally the Tsangs. Tsang was very tall and lanky. He was in fairly good health but tired easily. Mrs. Tsang had a liver complaint picked up during an earlier stay in the countryside, and this had left her a chronic invalid. She was a Party member and a good one. Whatever they both could do, they did— and more. They had volunteered to come down to the village and took their responsibilities seriously. University graduates, they earned somewhere over 150 yuan a month. Everyone liked them. Of course they knew that they would eventually return to the work in Peking, but since they had been enjoined, like everyone else, to put this idea out of their heads and concentrate on the job of settling down in the village, they did just that. They fitted up their little cottage room to make it livable, but avoided any ostentation; they threw themselves into their new life in the team and never talked about going back to Peking. There wasn't a hint of priggishness about their goodness.

No one in our Old, Sick, and Disabled Team expected or wished to settle in the countryside, but there were a few among the other cadres who were genuinely determined to settle down. One old librarian, getting on to a hale and hearty seventy, had opted for retirement on his pension. The commune had given him a cottage, and with his 180-yuan-a-month pension he was well off. His wife, who was much younger, was not too happy about the move, but their two children throve. He was a Cantonese and very stubborn. He gave voluble and impassioned speeches at meetings and was firmly

convinced that what he spoke was good Mandarin (the standard Peking dialect). It was only with the greatest difficulty
that he was persuaded to allow a fellow Cantonese to trans-
late his orations into real Mandarin. The Felicity people, who
spoke North Honan dialect, were astounded by his language,
of which they did not understand a word, and tended to treat
him at first like some rare bird. However, they appreciated his
unfailing good humor, which triumphed over every misunder-
standing, and after a few months he became something of a
village character of whom Felicity people boasted when they
went to other communes.

We heard about another pensioner, a retired engineering
professor, also very aged, who had settled in a nearby commune. He received a considerable pension, in excess of 300
yuan a month. His college had got the commune to build him
a new cottage of brick and tile. He had brought down all his
furniture and books and, in retirement, continued work on
some pet project that he expected would make a useful contribution to the nation's economy.

I said that the stoves brought us and the cadres together.
Lighting the stoves and keeping them alight was the main
preoccupation of us all during those first days in Upper Felicity. It was a lively topic of conversation among the villagers.
How long would it take us to master this key housekeeping
job? Who would do it first?

Doing this simple chore showed up the characters of all
seven families. Old Tang's stove was always going out. He
had a theory that a good ruddy-looking glow on the top of the
fire was a sign of good health. When it glowed that way he
refused to put coal on. Actually it was like the false bloom
on the cheeks of a tubercular. It masked a rapid decay within,
and no sooner had he turned his back on the patient than it
promptly died on him. He tried to keep his constant failures
secret, but of course his hostess, a pretty young grass widow
with three children, soon told all. Only he did not know that
it was the talk of the village. Apparently this was also the
way he worked in his office, and that was why he had been
criticized.

Ling, the artist and old-style intellectual, left everything that concerned household chores to his wife. This included the stove. Whenever she went out, so did the fire. Ling then abandoned hearth and home and went to have his meal with the Yuans.

Tan's chronic rheumatism was sometimes so bad that he could hardly hold a pen to write. For some weeks until his wife joined him, he lived alone, but so complete was his disdain for household labor that he resolutely refused to learn to keep his fire going or relight it when it went out. When the stove went out at night he would freeze till morning. You knew this because he set his face in a mask of suffering that told the bitter truth to everyone as he stood outside his cottage. He would stand on a small eminence that dominated the entrance to the village, hands firmly clasped over his belly and his face raised to the distant horizon. Wordlessly he told the world: "I, Tan, am suffering. I am sick and cold. But it is a heroic suffering. I am carrying out the behest of the Party and State to come down to the countryside to learn from the poor and lower-middle peasants!"

The lack of practical sense displayed by Old Tang, Tan, and Ling and their clumsiness with their hands is characteristic of a certain type of Chinese intellectual of the older generation. The privileged classes of preliberation, semifeudal society considered manual labor "lower" than mental labor and felt that an intellectual lost caste if he soiled his hands doing "menial" work. Something of this attitude still remained in the minds of intellectuals brought up in the old society even twenty years after liberation. The practice of *hsia fang*—going back to the grass roots—was aimed to eradicate such prejudices. By and large it succeeded.

The Tsangs' fire also often burned out, but for another reason. They would bank it down well and go out, but become so engrossed in a meeting they were attending or in another task that the stove would lose patience and die. Then Tsang would come rushing over to get some live coal from us and apologize profusely because he had no time to light the fire with wood. There was another meeting to attend and they simply must eat quickly. . . . Everyone liked the Tsangs and were very good-natured about this; all except the Tans, who grudged giving away even a few burning coals. Nevertheless Tsang became convinced that the constant death of his fire reflected a lack of conscientiousness on his part, some defect in ideology. He grew painfully embarrassed whenever he came to borrow live coals, no matter how heartily we gave them. To solve this problem it became a custom for anyone passing the Tsangs' cottage to look in to see how their stove was doing and feed it up if it looked weak.

Lin's fire never went out, or if it did, no one ever heard of it. He was usually ailing and needed the fire and its warmth. Mrs. Lin was an exemplary housewife, and as a woman brought up in the countryside she was of course well accustomed to country stoves.

The Yuans told all and sundry: "Our fire never goes out unless we want it to!" This was true. But young Yuan grew so proud and possessive about the stove—he insisted on doing all the cooking—that finally he would not even let his wife touch it. This led to words, estrangement, and a threat of divorce that was only averted by the combined efforts of the other six families.

As for my wife and me, once we had learned how to light and keep our fire going, I left it mostly to my wife while I did my drawing. We kept it going for three weeks. I boasted about this all over the village and got completely arrogant about it, even worse than Yuan. Then one day when my wife was away I threw on too much coal and it went out. My wife, who has lived with me through worse things than that, bore this silently.

If I poke fun at our cadre friends, I hope they will not take this amiss. We all had our human weaknesses and we all needed remolding. But they were in many ways typical of the good white-collar cadres of China. It must not be forgotten that they were all skilled workers, in many cases highly skilled. Yet inspired by the Communist Party's exhortation and example, they were working hard and well and for the most part uncomplaining under conditions of considerable discomfort and at very little pay, and all to "serve the people."

Our Hamlet 🎋

*N*ow more about Upper Felicity itself. The Great Felicity People's Commune today numbers some 28,000 souls. They live and work in forty production brigades. Our brigade, the Third, has 1600 mu of land round about the hamlet and nearly a hundred families, 480 persons all told, divided into three production teams. Half of these families were formerly poor peasants. That is, at the time of the land reform in 1952 they were classified as poor peasants because they owned very little or no land or other property and had to rent land at exorbitant rates or work for others in order to make a living.

At that time, thirty-five households were classified as lower-middle peasant families. These owned a bit more land and were just a shade better off than the poor peasants.

Eleven families were middle peasants. These had sufficient land and implements and enough of other property to make a tolerable living. They worked their own land and did not exploit hired labor.

The three rich peasant families had more than the average holding of land and implements. They all worked their land themselves, but they engaged in a bit of usury and hired farm hands to help them run their farms. This made them exploiters of labor and set them off from the rest of the peasants.

Only the landlord was completely parasitical. Although members of his family tilled the land, he himself lived like a gentleman without "soiling his hands" with manual labor. He regularly hired labor for household and farm tasks (our Lao Man had been one of his hired laborers), rented out land, and engaged in usury at high rates of interest as a regular source of income. Like most landlords thereabouts he took upwards of 50 per cent of the crop as rent for his land. (This was not unusual in Old China. In some cases landlords demanded as much as 70 to 80 per cent of the crop.) In the old

days he lived in the large old brick house that is now used as
the brigade's office. He could afford to own horses and cattle
and pigs and chickens, and he regularly ate meat and other
delicacies. Since his house stood on the highest plot of ground
in the village, he never had to leave it even in severe floods.
Ample reserves of grain and money left him immune even in
times of drought. He sent his children not only to primary
and middle school but even to college. He dressed soberly
but well and was not ostentatious of his wealth. This was not
a moral question. It was simply common sense in a time of
grasping warlords, marauding soldiery, and often desperate
and starving peasants.

Now this landlord is living in an ordinary cottage to the
south of the hamlet. His land and some other property, like
implements and houses, were confiscated during the land reform and distributed among the needy peasants. It was only
in the Cultural Revolution in late 1967 that his last house and
surplus furniture were taken from him and handed over to
the brigade. At this time it was felt that the earlier lenient
treatment of him had not been in accordance with the proletarian line, the revolutionary way of doing things, but
smacked of Liu Shao-chi's reformist, revisionist line.

Thus, everyone in this village except the three rich peasant and landlord households had lived in a state of indigence,
ignorance, and misery. By the standards of a developed country even the middle peasants here would have been classified
as living under the poverty line. Perhaps 5 per cent of the
community—just some members of the landlord's household
and the rich peasants—were literate. Rags were normal wear
for most. Undernourishment was common, starvation frequent. Meat was a luxury. Many ate it only during the big
New Year Festival and perhaps at Ching Ming in April, and
some could not afford it even then. In the winter months,
most families could only afford to eat salted pickles with their
monotonous diet of mealy porridge. Even today most Upper
Felicity folk do not drink tea. They long ago lost the taste for
it and consider it a luxury they can do without.

In the land reform all the landlord's property was requisi-

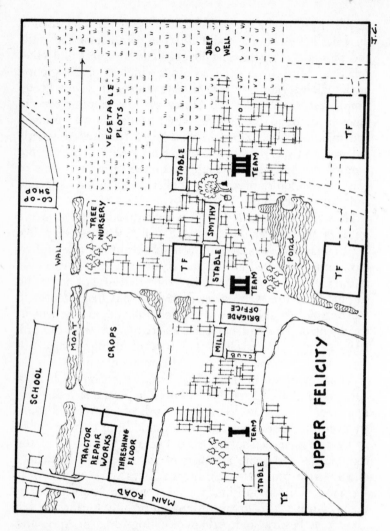

tioned. This pool of land was then divided up among all those who lacked land, so that everyone in the village had roughly three mu. The landlord and his family got a similar share. Surplus tools were also divided up as equitably as possible. The poorest and most in need got first choice. This sharing of the land has not led to the growth of individual farms as some Old China hands prophesied. On the contrary, as Lao Man described it to me, the Communist Party made it the basis of the peasants' new collective life and well-being.

Upper Felicity's hundred families live in the cluster of cottages around the western edge of the big pond. The accompanying sketch map gives a rough idea of the layout of the hamlet or brigade and its constituent teams.

At the south end are the households of the First Production Team; in the middle and to the west are those of the Second Production Team; and strung out to the north are those of the Third Production Team to which my wife and I belonged along with Old Tang and his wife and the Tans. The brigade's land surrounds the hamlet on all sides, but most of it is to the north, northwest, and east. The fifty-meter belt of tree nurseries and some vegetable plots lie directly to the west between the hamlet and the Great Felicity Commune center and village. The land to the south was being farmed for the time being by a group of young county-town cadres who had come to the country to be "steeled through labor." Though they worked on the First Team's land, they lived in the commune center, where more vacant rooms were available. These southern fields were good, fertile soil, in fact the best the Third Brigade had, but were on several different levels. The cadres were not only raising crops of wheat and maize but were leveling the land and arranging its irrigation system under the direction of the First Team. They worked on this project a whole year, raised a record crop, and left the land a flat, level area, well drained and, like the rest of the brigade's land, suitable for mechanized farming. This was a big help to the First Team, which was short of manpower.

The land to the north and northwest nearest the hamlet was divided among the three teams as home vegetable plots. Here they raised rape seed for oil, red flower (a valuable herbal medicine), spinach, lettuce, and onions, *tcho tsai,* a sort of onion plant, eggplant, cucumbers and various kinds of squash, pumpkins, and melons, early maize and sweet potato, cabbages, carrots, turnips, radishes and such for their members' own consumption. Whatever surplus there was they sold either to the marketing co-op or at local fairs where other brigades and teams also sold their surplus of vegetables and fruit or handicraft products.

Except for a sandy patch that they had tried a year before to plant to peanuts, all the land beyond the vegetable gardens was sown by the brigade's three teams to their main crops: wheat, barley, maize, kaoliang, beans, and cotton. Each team has its own share of this land and each has its own threshing floor. The First Team's floor is at the southeast extremity of the hamlet. The Second Team has one floor to the west and one to the east of the hamlet. The Third Team's floor is at the hamlet's northeast corner, north of the big pond.

Lao Man told me how the three teams had been formed and how they had become a brigade of the commune. After the peasants got their share of land in the land reform of 1952, most of them found that it was not easy for a single household working in isolation to cultivate its land properly. Families with many children but perhaps with only two able-bodied adults found it difficult. The old or sick found it well-nigh impossible. This was the main reason they had taken up the idea spread by the Communist Party of setting up work-exchange groups. These had developed by stages into seasonal and then permanent mutual-aid teams linking up groups of neighboring households. These groups were small and comprised usually no more than half a dozen households. Later on, in the mid-fifties when they had got more experience in collective organization of farming, the mutual-aid teams in the north of the hamlet formed Upper Felicity's first elementary cooperative farm with each member household pooling its land and larger farm animals and tools as shares in the co-op. At this stage use of the land was planned in common, but each household received a share of the crop based on the amount of land and other property, such as draft animals or implements, it had put in as its share. This arrangement was an improvement on the mutual-aid team but was not very satisfactory. It gave insufficient incentive to labor. That is why they went on to organizing an advanced co-op in which the crop was divided up according to the amount of work each

member put in. This was calculated in work-points. Each job
—plowing one mu, ditching so many meters, weeding, pruning, and so on—carried a fixed number of work-points. At
year-end accounting, that part of the harvest set aside for
work-points, after deducting reserves, welfare, and capital
construction funds, was divided by the total number of work-
points allocated, and each worker received his share according
to the number of work-points earned.

The households at the southern end of the hamlet and
those in the center similarly evolved into two other co-ops.
When in 1958 the whole hamlet voted to enter the big commune based on Great Felicity, it became that commune's
Third Production Brigade, and the constituent co-ops became
the three teams of the brigade.

This gradual development of the commune facilitates planning. Each team has learned more or less what its potentiali-
ties in land and labor are, and each brigade knows pretty well
what each of its teams can do. It is not difficult then to coordinate this knowledge at the commune level. Each team of
the Upper Felicity Brigade owns its share of the land, does
its own accounting, and is responsible for its own gains and
losses. But it is by no means an entirely independent unit.
It is linked by planning with the brigade and the commune;
it shares in collective brigade and commune undertakings,
such as the brigade mill and smithy, and water conservancy
works, such as the mechanized deep wells; it shares in the
commune-run hospital, tractor and tools pool and repair works,
the primary schools and middle school, and in the big water
and soil conservancy works organized by the commune itself
and in combination with other communes. The prosperity
and hopes of each team are thus inseparable from those of its
brigade and commune.

Just as the provincial administration (the provincial revolutionary committee) gets its production plan and quotas from
the Central Government planning organs, and the county
administration (revolutionary committee) gets its planning
figures from the provincial administration, so the commune
gets its plan, or at least the orientation figures for its plan,

from the county. These figures tell it how much wheat, kaoliang, maize, cotton beans, and oil seeds it is expected to raise,
and on the basis of past performance it works out what each
brigade should contribute. The brigade passes down the plan
and their projected quotas to the teams. The team members
then discuss their plans in detail and amend the quotas where
they think necessary. The brigade may set a quota for more
cotton, for instance, than a team may consider it possible to
raise. On the other hand, a team may find ways and means
of increasing its quota and will so inform the brigade. The
new figure will go up and will most probably be accepted.

The Upper Felicity teams have some more land that I have
not mentioned. This is part of a huge thirty-thousand-mu
expanse of alkaline flats that spreads to its south, southeast,
and southwest. Some experimental work has been done on
this wasteland, access roads have been built into and across
it and some tree belts planted. But most of it is still unculti-
vated and uncultivatable. The old state farm whose buildings
the May Seventh Cadre School now inhabits was tackling this
problem but finally packed up and moved elsewhere, after
showing that exploitation of this area is possible but will require
a major and long-term effort involving considerable investment
of labor and capital. Irrigation and drainage channels and
ditches will have to be cut, large quantities of water be brought
in to leach out the salts, more windbreaks must be planted, and
the soil gradually enriched with humus and fertilizer. All this
will require an investment in labor and capital that even a single commune, much less a brigade or team, cannot afford. The
several communes fringing and owning the area will have to
coordinate their efforts. This sort of intercommune cooperation is quite common. The building of three large reservoirs
and the deepening and straightening of the course of the Wei
River and the raising of its dikes have been accomplished this
way. It was in big-scale undertakings of this kind that the
communes first demonstrated their advantages over the smaller
co-op farms and collectives that preceded them. Communes
all along the Wei valley have cooperated to improve the course
of that river all along its several hundred miles to the sea. This
has been a major means of ending floods in North Honan.

Throughout the time I was in Upper Felicity I saw the preparations going ahead for the big work of opening up this wasteland. Experimental crops were being sown. Teams were drilling down to find water. My own Number Three Team planted a trial crop. Although it got back little more than the seed sown, there was no complaint. This was investment for the future.

There are quite a number of wells in and around our hamlet. Subsurface water can be struck at a depth of a few meters, but in places this is a bit brackish. At first we used to get our daily pailful at a well near the pond. This was sweet and salty and it could never assuage my thirst. I was already experimenting with a still to make distilled water when Lao Man told us about the deep mechanically pumped wells they had. These give fine water, ice cold and pure, pumped up by small electric motors from ninety to a hundred feet down.

The hamlet is exceedingly clean. All garbage is swept daily into the manure pits that every farmyard has, and the latrines are cleaned regularly. This aspect of sanitation is well looked after by the commune, but I often wondered at some of our peasant neighbors drinking unboiled water from the surface wells. I remonstrated about this, but they all swore that they were used to it and it never did them any harm. This I could not help but doubt, and to the end I preached the wisdom of drinking only boiled water, or at least using the deep well water if anyone wanted a fresh, cold drink.

When we arrived in Upper Felicity it was early winter. Not a leaf could be seen on the trees and saplings that surround the hamlet and grow in every yard and along the lanes and byways. Even so they enliven the dun yellow of the loess earth and walls. In spring, summer, and autumn the hamlet is completely embowered in green. Only on the stillest days does the rustle of leaves cease.

To the north and northeast, similar groves of trees on the crests of slightly rising ground mark the sites of West and East Board Bridge. To the south runs a double line of five-year-old poplars on the main road. Thinner lines of poplars criss-cross the landscape along feeder roads. Except for the Taihang Mountains on the west, with their succession of stiffly standing peaks, these trees are all that break the line of the horizon on the vast North China plain under its cloudless blue dome of winter day.

Neighbors' Cottages 📖

By the time I had finished my decorating, our cottage no longer looked like a peasant's home. But then neither did those of the other married cadres who had come to the villages. The only bits of furniture I had which were out of the ordinary in the hamlet were the Peking tallboy and another cupboard of hardwood with dragons carved on some sort of cheap softwood and stuck to its door. Tables, chairs, stools, and bed were cheap mass-produced items, but in arranging them to my taste they became different. The divan was a peasant bed, but I put a kaoliang mat over it with a folk-weave cushion. By the time I had tacked my drawings on the wall the cottage looked just like what it was—that of an artist, a townsman come to live in the countryside for a year or so. The saving grace was that the house was unostentatious. Our peasant neighbors and friends liked it and were quite at home when they visited us.

Lao Man's cottage next door was typical of the peasants' homes around us. It was of three-room size, built exactly like ours, and only its higher foundation made it the main house. The large room held the trestle bed covered with kaoliang matting, the quilts folded and stacked neatly in a corner. Various cooking utensils stood on the unlit stove. (In warm weather, the family cooked in the outside kitchen.) In the place of honor on the wall opposite the door was a life-size portrait of Mao with slogans printed in black on red above it and on either side. Pinned haphazardly around this centerpiece were a dozen or more other pictures of Chairman Mao. One showed him as a young man in Yenan. In another he was reviewing a great demonstration on Tien An Men Square in Peking. Others showed him at conferences, and on holiday, standing on the seashore. In another he was with a group of peasant commune members inspecting a wheat field. He was in shirt-sleeves and wearing a big cartwheel straw hat. There was also a color reproduction of the well-known painting of him as a youth on his way to the Anyuan coal mines to organize the miners.

Below this collection of pictures was the traditional long table, six or seven feet long and about a foot and a half wide. In the old days it would have held a couple of incense urns and the stand for the ancestral tablets. Now it was just a work table with some small tools on it and Ta Sao's sewing and weaving paraphernalia, bobbins and shuttles, and some of the older children's schoolbooks. Two or three ancient chairs and battered stools, a square eating table, a spinning wheel, and straw mats beautifully woven by Ta Sao for sitting on the ground made up the rest of the furnishings. A kaoliang screen and a rough curtain separated this large room from the smaller one. Here were the trestle beds of the children, several large sacks filled with grain, several earthenware jars for storing beans, pickles, and eggs, and two dark-stained old wooden chests for the family clothes.

The more affluent homes of the hamlet were not much different. Lao Man's cottage and ours were some distance from a power line and the co-op had run out of wire, so we still used oil lamps, just a wick put into a bottle of kerosene. Other homes had electric lights. Some had a treadle sewing machine or a radio or bicycle, sometimes all three. Things like flashlights, thermos bottles, clocks, and cigarette lighters were in common use. Twenty years ago this village was inhabited by destitute peasants, clad in rags and with only the barest necessities and sometimes not even that in their homes. Now they were at least adequately housed, clothed, and fed, and saw their way clear to attaining a prosperous life.

Secrets

Only a very few knew of the secret that I kept in my bedroom. This was a large, double-bed, spring mattress.

Before coming down to the countryside, the office had told me to take everything I needed with me. But I was also given the parallel injunction: "Don't be ostentatious." I wondered how this affected the mattress, but I had been sick in bed so much with the flu that I finally decided to take it with me. It came down in the train with us and then disappeared for three days. On the fourth evening there came a knock on the cottage door. Someone pushed his head in and whispered: "Your bed has arrived!" Outside in the darkness I could see several figures struggling to get the bulky thing off a cart. In great haste they hauled it into the cottage, slammed the door shut, and disappeared. The only mattress in Upper Felicity was thus concealed for a year, only to be revealed when we left the hamlet. By that time there was no hiding it. The whole brigade came to see us off.

Mine was not the only secret in the hamlet. Cadres were not allowed to discuss their office affairs with the peasants, or what their actual work or salaries were. Naturally, too, they were not allowed to reveal the events of the Cultural Revolution in their offices, or disclose who had been "pulled down," who had been criticized, or what for. Schooled for many years to observe security regulations, cadres scrupulously observed these injunctions. The peasants, on their part, had been told not to be inquisitive about such things, and they politely refrained from asking possibly embarrassing questions.

By and large, both cadres and peasants kept the secrets they were entrusted with and never let on that they knew secrets they should not have known. I feel positive from a hundred small signs that the peasants had pierced my incognito and knew that I was not an ordinary cadre, but even to this day I cannot be sure.

In West Board Bridge Village one silly cadre, no doubt overwrought, himself blurted out to his host that he had been accused of being a counterrevolutionary, but this was the only such case I heard of in a community numbering several hundred cadres and their families.

Another cadre who should have known better became notorious throughout three villages for striking his old father. This so scandalized peasant opinion that the matter had to be taken up in the commune revolutionary committee itself. This procedure was unusual, and reflected the seriousness with which the matter was regarded. Most of the cadres' problems were dealt with by the cadres themselves. Each group was under its own organized leadership, supervised of course by the revolutionary committee of the office in Peking. The May Seventh Cadre School had its elected revolutionary committee. The West Board Bridge Village group of families had a group leader.

In Upper Felicity we elected Lin to be our leader. That is, we endorsed the recommendation of the revolutionary committee. This was not a rubber-stamp election. After a week or so during which Lin exercised ad hoc leadership we knew him pretty well and thought him fit for the job. If we got dissatisfied with him later on, we could remove him by vote again and elect someone else. In that case the revolutionary committee would have checked over our choice and confirmed it if it seemed satisfactory. Otherwise, they in turn could have made another recommendation. We also elected Tsang and Mrs. Yuan as Lin's assistants. Tsang was responsible for organizing our work, and Mrs. Yuan was put in charge of supplies. She arranged for the May Seventh School to supply us with free spades and sickles. When the co-op shop had some cracked eggs to dispose of, she arranged for them to be sold to the members of the Old, Sick, and Disabled Team. When Mrs. Tsang was unwell, she got her powdered milk. She used to ride miles in all weathers to do things for us. When the coal arrived, since she was one of the strongest of the team, she toiled valiantly on one end of a carrying pole getting it to our homes. She also arranged for the brigade to sell us winter stocks of cabbages, carrots, and turnips.

With our homes, food, and heating taken care of, our group then discussed the important question of study. Every speaker stressed that our main task while in the countryside was to learn from the poor and lower-middle peasants, the firmest allies of the proletariat in the villages. We should learn their good qualities of patriotism and public spirit, industry and thrift, and dedication to the socialist people's communes. In addition to that we decided that we should study four mornings a week for a couple of hours. We had not yet begun to receive the *People's Daily* (*Ren Min Jih Bao*) or the *Red Flag* (*Hongchi*), the Communist Party's daily and weekly organs, so for a few days the whole group used to gather in my cottage to listen to the news and editorials on my transistor radio. Later we would take our stools and gather in Lin's cottage, the most central for all of us, or in summer in Yuan's cottage, which was coolest. After someone gave a précis of home news and someone else a report on international events, we would have a general discussion. Sometimes some special communication on the Cultural Revolution would come down from the Peking office. This would be read out and discussed. Sometimes Party or government statements would be relayed to us by some visiting comrade. Lin arranged for us to hear talks by commune members about their life and work.

The group of thirty families in West Board Bridge Village were similarly organized for work, welfare, and study. In the cadre school discipline was stricter. They were organized into squads, platoons, and companies. They slept in dormitories, got up at daybreak, and studied or worked all day. To toughen themselves up they went on ten-mile marches to the county town to hear lectures there.

Later, after the New Year Festival, the Cultural Revolution heated up again with the campaign to "struggle, criticize, and transform." Then the cadres often gathered from all the surrounding villages at the cadre school, and sometimes the meetings lasted far into the night.

We never told the peasants except in general terms about what went on at our meetings. They never asked us what we were doing as we made our way up the lane with our stools and red-plastic-covered copies of Chairman Mao's *Quotations*. Usually we read a few appropriate quotations out loud together before we started our discussions. They were generally chosen by Lin.

The peasants could, of course, guess a bit about what went on. After a severe criticism meeting some cadres' faces would be grey and gloomy. One day my wife and I went to buy some things at the co-op shop and saw one of the cadres there, looking ashen-faced. When we heard later that the co-op was having a cleaning-up campaign and that someone had been caught embezzling several hundred yuan, we knew who it must be.

This is one of the characteristics of the new Chinese society. Matters of morals and political belief that in the United States might be regarded as matters of conscience that were of no concern to anybody but the individual are there considered to be matters vitally affecting the community to which the individual belongs and therefore matters to be discussed by the community. Belief in individualism, in laissez-faire; disbelief in the mass line of "from the masses, to the masses"; a tendency to rely on "commandism" as a way of getting things done, or in anarchism and spontaneous mass action— all these can legitimately be criticized in a person in open meetings of his small group of peers.

On the other hand, matters like embezzlement of public property, which in another country would be handed over to the police and the courts, are here dealt with inside the group with the group, under the supervision of the higher authorities, acting as prosecutor and defense counsel, judge and jury, and sometimes jailer as well. If the co-op embezzler "came clean" under criticism and showed sincere repentance for his crime, it might well be that he would be allowed to continue in his job, "sentenced" to repay the loss, and that would be the last of the matter. (This, in fact, was what actually happened.) That is why cadres do not discuss private matters outside the office. If he tried to brazen it out (and if he had more criminal charges against him as well) he might be handed over to the people's courts to be dealt with. His study group would decide on this in combination with the co-op managing revolutionary committee. The principle is not to brand or punish wrongdoers but to reform them, "to cure the sickness and save the patient."

Cooking and Vegetables 🌿

*W*e started to do our own cooking as soon as we got the stove going, but we had so many other things to do in setting up house that it was perforce rather rough and ready. We had lots of cabbage—our back wall was piled two feet high with a solid bank of tall Chinese cabbages, sweeter and more succulent than any we ate in Peking. We had a large basketful of delicious carrots and a huge pile of white turnips. Some of the turnips we buried in the yard, marking the spot with four sticks stuck upright in the ground. The carrots, on the advice of Ta Sao, we put in her underground cellar. This was a deep, flask-shaped pit dug in the farmyard and covered with a square of matting and earth. We got meat from the co-op. In the mornings we ate corn porridge with sugar and I drank the rest of my Peking coffee. Later we got an allocation of eggs from the co-op. Then Mrs. Yuan arranged for us to buy a hundred duck eggs from one of our commune brigades that specialized in duck breeding. For lunch and dinner we piled chopped cabbage, carrots, and meat into our largest saucepan and boiled this into soup. When we put potatoes in as well it was Irish stew, and we lived on this for days.

Later our cooking became more sophisticated. I am a tolerable hand, at least I think so, at Western cooking. I can stew or grill, make dishes *en casserole,* salads, omelettes and so on. My wife is a good hand at Shanghai cooking, rather sweet, sometimes with a dash of pepper. Now we learned Northern cooking and made *mantou* (steamed bread), *baotze* (the same with fillings of vegetable, usually fine chopped cabbage, with

meat) and *chiaotze* (small, triangular-shaped, thin-walled pat-
ties thickly filled with savory meat stuffing and boiled). Rus-
sians eat these with vinegar or mustard and call them *pel-
menni*. Sometimes we made the *baotze* with a sweet heart of
black Cuban sugar. Once we had mastered the art of making
dough with yeast, we regaled ourselves with a variety of
dumplings, pancakes, and noodles.

Our peasant neighbors on this northern plain, famous
wheat country, do not like rice and do not like sweet Shanghai

cooking either. They salt their food heavily. They bought ten times as much salt as we did. But they like a bit of pepper as relish.

They eat three times a day and usually, since they are busy folk, do not make much of a to-do about cooking. At most meals they eat a big bowl of cornmeal porridge or wheat noodles or *mantou*, with a side dish of pickles or cabbage, turnips, or other vegetable. This is varied with flatcakes fried with onion or corn pone, hollowed out little pyramids of steamed maize flour, or *baotze* of various kinds. They eat kaoliang meal, but this is regarded as rough food, much as Anhwei peasants call potatoes "famine food." I found kaoliang hard to digest. Sweet potatoes and potatoes are supplementary foods and are sometimes eaten raw. They like to eat cucumber, eggplant, or carrots as we do fruit, at any time and raw, but they also sometimes cook and eat these vegetables as a separate dish at a meal. For a special meal they love to have a feast of *chiaotze* (just *chiaotze*, by the dozen) or *mantou* with dishes of meat, eggs, and vegetables. Very fine tomatoes are grown in the district, but though our Upper Felicity neighbors eat them, they do not themselves raise any.

They like meat, but this is still a dish for a treat, not for everyday eating. They raise no beef or dairy cattle, but occasionally one of their teams kills an ox that is overage, or a household will kill a pig or sheep for some special occasion. Then they will sell what they do not need themselves to other team or brigade members.

Meat, cooked or raw, is sometimes available in the local co-op or in some of the larger neighboring commune shops. But it is not usually available in large quantities. There are no facilities for cold storage. In the county town, however, an hour or two away by bicycle, you can always buy it in the state meat shops if you go there early in the morning. In pre-liberation days the Upper Felicity farmer ate meat only on very special occasions, at betrothals, marriages, death, birthdays, and at the Spring and other festivals. The really poor ate it only once or twice a year. Now, while it is still regarded as special fare, it is no longer thought of as a luxury out of

reach of most peasants' pockets. In the year we lived with
them, Lao Man's family ate meat or fish about once a month.
Fish from the reservoirs or big ponds, and of course eggs also,
form part of their protein diet. Every household has half a
dozen or more chickens. Ta Sao has seven. She gave one each
to little Au Chiu and Hsiao Ching. When their hens laid an
egg (several times a week in season) they either ate it, sold
it to the co-op for saving money, or exchanged it at the co-op
for fruit or sweets, which they promptly ate. Their chicken
was their pocket money or bank account paying a weekly
dividend.

Since casual private buying is not "done" by cadres in the
villages, we could not buy goat's milk. We drank powdered
or condensed milk bought in the co-op shop.

In a word, peasant fare in Upper Felicity was adequate
though frugal. No one compared the situation in this respect
with the old days of yearly, chronic starvation. They compared
this year's food situation with last year's or with some recent,
particularly prosperous or less prosperous year. There was no
untoward anxiety on this score. They had their plans and were
certain that they could carry them out step by step: improving
yields, bringing more land under cultivation, going in for
side occupations, steadily raising their standards of living
and feeding. Like good farmers everywhere else in the country, they were always trying out new things and were always
engaged in some undertaking of capital construction: improving roads and transport, digging new wells or ditches for irrigation or drainage, leveling land to prepare it for mechanized
farming, planting trees.

They have simple but effective ways of making special
foods like noodles or pickles, but are not as keen now on the
pickles that were daily fare before liberation. In spring, summer, and autumn there is a big variety of fresh vegetables to
choose from. In the old days the "spring hunger," when the
winter store of food had all been eaten and the new crops
were not yet in, was a yearly torture. This has long been a
thing of the past. The stores of cabbages, carrots, turnips, and
sweet potatoes now last them throughout the winter and

early spring. But they still make some pickles. I made some myself under Ta Sao's direction. I bought a glazed pottery jar made in the county town. This cost just a couple of mao (twenty cents). I filled it with layers of cabbage washed and cut fine, with liberal sprinklings of salt on each layer, and covered it tight. After a few days this pickle was ready to eat. Sometimes I added chopped turnip or carrot and various spices with a drop of white spirits. This kept well, but did not last long, as we liked it so much.

We made our own noodles either of wheat flour or sweet potato. The latter kind is called *fen tze* and looks like strings of gelatine. Ta Sao lent us a wooden cup with holes in its bottom. We filled this with dough and pressed it through the holes with a wooden ram that fitted closely into the cup. Out the other end came lengths of thin noodles. Pepper is grown and eaten as a relish, but not in the vast amounts that Szech-uan and Hunan peasants like.

We had brought some delicacies from Peking. The peas-ants did not like black tea, and I never saw any of them drink-ing green tea either, a startling difference from the Kwangtung and Chekiang peasants I knew. Coffee they had never sam-pled or even seen before. And it was the same with our butter and malted milk from Shanghai.

When I had finished these I tried for a time to live just like the peasants. I did not miss the butter, cocoa, and choco-late, but I found it hard to digest the heavy meal porridge, and the lack of some stimulant like coffee or strong black tea made me as jumpy as a man trying to give up smoking. While my neighbors ate rice only if they had to, I found that while I liked *mantou,* flatcakes, and noodles, wheat foods they were accustomed to, I, like every southerner, still had a hankering after rice. And of course I missed meat, which I was used to eating practically every day in one form or another.

Within their means the peasants paid attention to their diet. When they did especially heavy work, as in the busy harvest season, their wives saw to it that their men ate more *mantou* and less meal porridge. At such times they relished a bit of beef or pork. Knowing that they should eat more protein, and that these were important export products for the country, they had a plan to raise more pigs, sheep, and chickens. Practically every household was raising at least one pig, and sometimes a few piglets as well. They sold nearly all the eggs from their hens to the supply and marketing co-op. It had to be a very special occasion for them to kill a fowl and eat it. Some households kept a few sheep or goats to give milk to the children. There were no state or co-op facilities for marketing goat's milk, but the goatskins and sheepskins, wool, and the animals themselves were sold to the co-op. A few rabbits were raised, but mostly to please the children.

The hamlet was spending as much as was economically feasible on feeding these animals. All the household scraps went to them and a little grain too as the time for selling or slaughtering them approached. That is why the villagers found it hard to carry out their plan to raise two grown pigs in each household and increase the number of chickens, goats, and sheep. Already not a scrap of food was wasted, and even the one pig that Lao Man raised had a very busy time of it nosing round to fill his vast bulk.

This question of raising pigs in the communes, either individually or collectively, has been much misunderstood. In a relatively poor brigade like Upper Felicity the only way to raise pigs is on an individual basis, mainly using household scraps as pig food. When they can raise two pigs per household, the brigade has reached the level of productivity that will enable it to think of setting up brigade or team piggeries that will feed the pigs regular fodder. That does not mean that the households will not continue to keep pigs. They will feed them household scraps instead of wasting them. Besides, pigs are excellent scavengers and keep the farmyard clean.

Upper Felicity's sheep and goats are raised partly collectively and partly on an individual basis. In the winter they are looked after collectively by one of the older men and are penned and fed in what was the village's ancestral temple. The rest of the year they are looked after by the households that own them. In this way they can be fed on the household scraps that are more plentiful in the milder seasons, and the

children and old people can take them out to graze on odd
patches of grass and the roadside verges. For a small fee the
veterinary clinic of the commune does inoculations and cas-
trations, and treats sick animals. The commune also keeps
stud animals for breeding. It charges a yuan a time for this
service. Artificial insemination is common practice in other
communes, but was not used in Upper Felicity.

Chickens, ducks, sheep, goats, and pigs as well as horses,
oxen, mules, and donkeys can be bought at the fairs held every
week by turns in the larger villages of the county. The sellers
may be communes, their brigades, teams, or, in the case of the
smaller domestic animals, even individual commune members.
It is not in accordance with socialist morality or discipline to
kill a pig or sheep and sell its meat on the open market. But
this is condoned if a peasant through no fault of his own finds
himself in urgent need of cash. It is quite a common occurrence, however, for a commune member to take some of his
litter of piglets, or a pig, sheep, or goat to sell at a fair. A few
old women can often be seen selling off some eggs in this way
instead of disposing of them in the usual way through the
marketing co-op. But this is not a common thing and of course
nobody does it as a regular practice.

There is no "free market" as such. At the fairs the bulk of
the selling and buying is done by the communes, brigades,
and teams. Hides, pig bristles, casings, and eggs are all com-
modities needed for industry and export by the state, and no
private trading is allowed in such items. The small amount of
private trading in meat, eggs, or domestic animals is kept
rigidly within bounds as a very tiny supplement to socialist
trading. As far away as Sinkiang, in China's far western area,
in Ili in the north, and in Kashgar under the shadow of the
Kuen Lun Mountains, I found a similar system in operation.

There are a few commune handicraftsmen who follow the
fairs around. One repairs fountain pens and a few tinkers
repair pots and pans, locks, and so on. Some craftsmen make
hardwood spindles for the housewives' spinning, and others
make shuttles of hardwood and horn. They serve the villages
they pass through on the way from fair to fair. The tinker
blows a horn, the knife-grinder rattles his clapper, the man

with the day-old chicks twirls his little drum with two banging balls attached, and the farm wives come out to do business while a crowd of children watch. They fill a need in the county's economy that has not yet been filled by the supply or handicraftsmen's co-ops.

This is a pragmatic arrangement that for the moment suits the economic situation in the county. It will probably be changed later when the socialist sector, the state shops and service trades, and the marketing and supply co-ops or handicraftsmen's co-ops get around to supplying these needs in a better-organized manner.

The big influx of cadres caused some upsets on the county market. But these were dealt with promptly and were not as serious as one might have expected. They had been foreseen. All cadres were told on arrival that they must live frugally and must not buy eggs, meat, oil, cloth, milk, or grain from the peasants. Small exchanges of gifts of vegetables are allowed, but no more. Purchases in the supply co-op should be modest. When some cadres in charge of supplying their groups started going to the county towns to buy dozens of pounds of eggs (eggs are often sold by the pound), the shops were told not to sell to them. Moral persuasion was also used.

Since no cadre was allowed to disclose his earnings or those of other cadres, this made it easier for all to observe the rule that there should be no lending or borrowing of money between them and the peasants.

These regulations may seem stringent, but were necessary and successful in preventing a great deal of potential upsets.

Raising Capital

Some neighboring commune brigades have large, collectively run piggeries that send regular supplies of pork to the local and national market and bristles, bones, casings, and hides to industry. Others, like the Red Flag Brigade of our own commune, have collective duck farms. These brigades grow the necessary feed as part of their agricultural plan. Our Upper Felicity brigade felt that such large-scale livestock undertakings would overstrain its resources at its present stage of development. As a self-respecting farm it is expected to raise enough cereals (including beans) and vegetables, cotton, and oil seed to satisfy its members' needs completely, pay its grain tax, sell some surplus to the state, and establish locally held reserves as prescribed by the state. In 1969, Upper Felicity was doing that, but only just. Its members thought they would be able to fulfill all these obligations comfortably within a few years. At that stage it might set up a collective piggery. At the moment, as I have said, household scraps were only sufficient to feed a pig and maybe a litter. But a collective piggery was, of course, envisaged. This would not only give brigade members a larger and regular supply of meat and fertilizer but would also help satisfy the state trading organizations' and industry's ever-increasing demands for pork and pig products. It was the fodder problem that limited the number of chickens raised. Ta Sao was very frugal, but seven hens were all she could raise. Even so, the yolks of the eggs her hens laid were not strong.

The larger farm animals like oxen, horses, mules, and donkeys are all owned by the teams and looked after in the collective stables. Each team has its own stable. The animals are admirably kept and are in excellent condition. The old stablemen know their jobs thoroughly and are training youngsters to carry on the work.

About the time of the Spring Festival, a fine pneumatic-tired horse cart was offered for sale by the supply co-op and our Number Three Team decided to buy it. Ready cash was urgently needed. It cost eight hundred yuan. Every household contributed what it could, but still this was not enough. It was decided to sell an overage ox. Alive, it could not be sold profitably either at the fair or to the marketing co-op, so they decided to slaughter it. Lao Man organized the killing and skinning in the shed used for this purpose. Then he and his helpers boiled the meat, gave a share-out to team members as part of their holiday fare, and took the rest to the county town, where they sold it within a few hours. They charged the regular retail price set by the state. The bones, hide, horns, and hooves were sold to the marketing co-op.

Little Pig 🌿

Our Old, Sick, and Disabled (OSD for short) Team decided that it should not only learn from the poor and lower-middle peasants but, as a first priority, propagate Mao Tse-tung's thought. We formed a propaganda squad. The commune contributed whitewash, I contributed a whitewash brush, and someone provided a cracked basin. Together with Lin, as political leader of the team, we chose a number of quotations and slogans and painted them up in two- to four-foot-high characters on various walls in the hamlet. "Serve the people," "Be prepared against war, be prepared against natural disasters, and do everything for the people," "Grasp revolution and promote production," "Long live the Communist Party," and "Long live Chairman Mao" were some of our slogans.

Tacked onto the east end of our cottage is the pigsty. Above it is a wide expanse of wall, and here we wrote: "Be self-reliant!" This is the home of Big and Little Pig. Big Pig is mistress of the farmyard. The hens fly in terror of her. She weighs eighty pounds, is all black, and can scramble over a four-foot wall. She gets all the best kitchen scraps and whatever fodder is going. When there are no crops in the fields, she is allowed to go foraging for herself. She is worth her weight in yuan and will soon be sold.

Little Pig is an unsavory-looking creature. At the best of times she is not the sort of pet you would like to introduce into your living room and kitchen, but she pushes her way in regardless, no matter what state she is in. She is off-white in

color, with ugly pink blotches and sparse, dirty bristles. She
has a black spot on one eyelid so that you never know whether
she is awake or sleeping. This is most disconcerting. She is
always spasmodically twitching her ears or tail from the cold
or her belly from her digestive efforts. We soon found that
she was an indiscriminate eater of unconsidered trifles. One
day, Little Yuan, the Yuans' son, vociferously exposed what
we had already suspected was the unpalatable truth: "She
eats *shit!*"

When she got the chance she also ate our cabbages. Our
turnips and carrots were also to her taste, and she seemed to
have a liking for coal dust too. We would drive her out as
soon as she waddled in, but undeterred by our far-too-gentle
pushes, she would sidle back in again the instant our backs
were turned.

Little Pig is an orphan and desperately seeks mother love
from Big Pig, but the latter is exclusively engrossed in herself
and filling her stomach. She ignores Little Pig and always
drives her away from the trough or anyplace else where there
is something to eat. Ta Sao says that big sows even treat their
own grown-up offspring this way. If cabbage leaves or turnip
tops are thrown into the sty, Little Pig rushes in to snatch a
mouthful before Big Pig can turn on her, then goes off into
a far corner to consume her catch alone and in safety.

When Big Pig lies down to sleep, Little Pig climbs onto
her back for warmth. Big Pig lets her stay there, not for love,
but because that part of her hide at any rate is kept warm in
turn.

There was one time when Little Pig was ostracized completely. That was when her greed led her to fall into the
latrine. Luckily the muck was shallow. Still, she was covered
in it up to her eyes and came out a frightful stinking object.
Ta Sao gave her a wash, but for days the stench clung to her.
We kept her in the sty and, to comfort her, fed her cabbage
leaves and stalks, which she loves.

When she was four or five months old she had her repro-
ductive organs removed. The vet of the commune came one
afternoon and in his matter-of-fact, no-nonsense way put Lit-

tle Pig sideways on the ground. He held her head down with his foot on her neck and while Ching Chun held her hind legs locked on the ground, made an incision just behind the belly, thrust in two fingers, and removed her ovaries. It was all over in a few minutes, with Little Pig keeping up one long continuous squeal. Then he put some salve on her and released her. On the instant her squeal ceased, so the operation could not have hurt her much. She scrambled to her feet and for a moment stood warily in the midst of the circle of children and adults who had gathered to see the operation. Then slowly and still warily she walked away into a quiet corner behind the millstone and lay down near the warm southern wall of our cottage. The vet collected three fen (one cent) and departed on his cycle.

We were sorry to see Little Pig thus deprived of all hope of posterity, and we asked Lao Man about it that evening. "That three fen will save me a lot of trouble," he said. "We only have enough food for those two porkers. There's not enough to feed her while she raises a litter. I'll be needing ready cash soon for a number of things so I'll be fattening Big Pig up for the marketing co-op. Then I'll only feed and fatten Little Pig."

More pigs per household mean more manure, higher yields, more meat, and more money. Every now and then the team collects all the muck from the sty for the team manure pile. Lao Man gets several mao a jin for it.

Big and Little Pig are mainly Ta Sao's responsibility. In spring and summer the children give her a lot of help by cutting "pig-grass" and other wild plants with succulent leaves or stems. The pigs also eat trailers of sweet potato. Since she looks after the seven hens as well, she is in charge of two important sideline additions to the family income. Each egg sold to the marketing co-op is worth four fen. Every day in season the hens lay three or four eggs in the laying nests that Ta Sao has rigged up in old baskets on the high outside window ledges. The family does not eat many eggs themselves, but they are always there in store if they need an extra dish. On the market an egg costs seven fen, but in the off-period around February the price can go up to one mao (ten fen). Since they are such a steady source of income, few chickens are killed unless they have ceased to lay.

Old Ideas Change, New Ideas Grow

Old ideas and superstitious practices in Upper Felicity are going the way of all the "four olds"—out-of-date ideas, culture, customs, and habits. Some, like the idea that prayers cure sickness, have already vanished. Others, such as betrothal and marriage customs, have subtly changed in character to a half-way stage that reflects the present state of social relations and outlooks in the village. The old feudal forms and content of life are being shed, the bourgeois ideas and forms that creep in are being rejected, but the socialist order has not yet fully taken over.

Some customs still retain the harmless exterior forms but have lost the old, superstitious content. It is so with the old Water Festival on March 9 when, tradition has it, the Dragon King rises. No one now believes that the Dragon King or any other king is going to rise in China. The old people pass the legend on only as a curiosity of the past to the youngsters who are mostly ignorant of the significance of the custom and are quite likely (at least the older ones) to treat it as a bit of interesting folklore. Nevertheless, on March 9 everyone thoroughly enjoys the soft pancakes of yellow rice flour that are the traditional food of the day.

On March 8, International Women's Day, we cadres had greeted all women with special warmth to mark this festival of the new woman, triumphantly asserting her liberation and international unity. But this day was not celebrated in the villages with anything like the spirit in the big cities, where women are given a holiday from work and there are rallies, meetings, parties, and posters. Maybe because of the yellow pancakes the Dragon King won out over the women.

The Seasons of the Year 🎋

*I*n marking the passage of time, the new ways are slowly but surely winning out over the old. As in many country places few people are precise about the time. An appointment is made for "tomorrow morning." No one except a rusticating cadre will say "tomorrow morning at ten-thirty." So a meeting starts more or less when enough people have arrived. The same is true of the cinema. But, as in other places, mechanization is bringing clockwork punctuality into everyday life. When our Third Team was digging its latest deep wells there was no approximation about anything. The shifts worked with an accuracy and speed that any oil-rig gang would have been proud of.

In judging the seasons, however, the old calendar is judged tried and true. Lao Man and most of the other peasants paid scant attention to the solar New Year's Day on January 1. Their New Year begins with the lunar New Year that in 1970 fell on February 6 and in 1971 on January 27, and they reckon that the spring begins on February 4, the time of *Li Chun*, the Establishment of Spring. On the other hand, the memory of such formerly important lunar events as the Mid-autumn Festival, when rents were paid and debts collected, has completely died out. But the *Ching Ming* Festival, the Clear and Bright Festival of April 5, which was for centuries the traditional festival of remembrance of the ancestors, is still observed in the hamlet—mostly by the older generation, who still go out and place slips of votive white paper on the grave mounds of their forebears.

I found that most of the villagers measured the progress of the year not as I did, by looking at the calendar to see the date, but according to whether it was near or past one of the times of year that are marked on the Chinese lunar calendar. The time of our arrival in Upper Felicity was always remembered as being a few days after *Hsiao Hsueh*, the time of the

Little Snow (November 23), though I cannot remember if any snow actually fell on that day or not.

Lao Man's ideas of the seasons and times of the year are the traditional Chinese ones of the north of China along the middle reaches of the Yellow River, the cradle of ancient Chinese civilization. These have evolved out of the living experience of the Chinese peasants over centuries of farming in this area.

In the time of the Spring and Autumn Annals—that is, 722–481 B.C. or about twenty-five hundred years ago—the forebears of Lao Man divided the year into spring, summer, autumn, and winter, or the *Ch'un Fen* (Spring Equinox, March 21); *Hsia Chih* (Summer Solstice, June 22); *Ch'iu Fen* (Autumn Equinox, September 23); and *Tung Chih* (Winter Solstice, December 22) of today's calendar. By the time of the Ch'in and Han dynasties (221–207 B.C. and 206 B.C.–A.D. 220), these were supplemented and expanded into the twenty-four seasons or times of the agricultural year that the peasants follow today. Based on the accumulated experience of the working farmers as summarized by astronomers and sages of this part of the Chinese land, these seasonal terms accurately describe terrestrial conditions at twenty-four different positions taken up by the earth in its revolutions around the sun.

Some of these terms describe the length of the day and night or the state of the weather. Some terms denote the beginning of a particular season. *Li Ch'un*, the Establishment or Beginning of Spring, and *Li Hsia*, the Establishment of Summer, are of this kind. In 1970, these fell on February 4 and May 6 respectively. Some terms denote the length of day and night. *Ch'iu Fen*, the Autumn Equinox, is of this kind. It was early noted that at the time of *Hsia Chih*, the Summer Solstice, the day is at its longest (when the sun is farthest from the equator) and that at *Tung Chih*, the Winter Solstice, the day is at its shortest. Some terms describe the degree of warmth or cold; for example, the *Hsiao Shu*, Slight Heat (July 7), or the *Ta Han*, Severe Cold (January 20). Some describe changes of weather; for example, *Yu Shui*, Rainwater (February 19), or *Pai Lu*, White Dew (September

8), which marks the date on which the planting of autumn ripening crops should begin.

The farmers' calendar also includes the nine nine-day periods of cold. Of these the *San Chiu*, Third Nine (beginning January 9), is traditionally the coldest. Then there are the three ten-day periods of hot weather. Of these the *San Fu*, Third Heat (beginning August 8), is traditionally the hottest. The peasants have a vivid colloquial expression for this trying period of still, stiflingly hot days—the "Autumn Tiger." Finally there is the joyously celebrated traditional lunar New Year Festival. In the old days, this festival was marked by a fortnight's holiday. Today it is a three-day holiday of family reunions and feasting and gift-giving, after which the peasants plunge with redoubled energy into preparations for the spring sowing.

The list below shows these times of the year with their names and dates in 1970. These dates are not the same every year. For instance, while the *Tou Fu* (First Heat) is ten days in duration, the *Erh Fu* (Second Heat) varies in duration from ten to twenty days. This depends on when the First Heat starts. In 1971, the Second Heat lasted twenty days. These heats are closely associated with the planting season and also with the best times for the processes of fermentation and distilling, so they are particularly closely considered by the farmers of China in making agricultural plans. Furthermore, of course, since these calendar calculations are traditionally made for the lands on the middle reaches of the Yellow River, farmers in other parts of China have to make the necessary adjustments for their areas north or south of this zone.

Practically every cottage in Upper Felicity had its *Farmers' Calendar*. This thin booklet with a bright picture cover of happy farmers contained in 1969 not only the calendar itself and the seasons of the year but also a variety of other information: current songs, like "The East Is Red," quotations and poems of Chairman Mao, important Party directives, notes on some of the latest agricultural machines and tools being introduced, handy tips for farmers such as how to make a simple container for sprinkling insecticide into maize plants, rules of discipline for the people's militia, and an important article on "Learning from Tachai," the pace-setting Shansi farm brigade.

THE SEASONS OF THE YEAR

The twenty-four solar terms (italicized), the nine nine-day cold weather periods, the three ten-day hot weather periods, and the lunar New Year Festival

No.	Date in 1970 Gregorian Calendar		Chinese Terms	English
1	January	6	*Hsiao Han*	*Little Cold*
2	"	9	San Chiu	Third Nine Days of Cold
3	"	18	Ssu Chiu	Fourth Nine Days of Cold
4	"	20	*Ta Han*	*Severe Cold*
5	"	27	Wu Chiu	Fifth Nine Days of Cold
6	February	4	*Li Ch'un*	*Spring Begins*
7	"	5	Liu Chiu	Sixth Nine Days of Cold
8	"	6	Ch'un Chieh	Spring Festival— Lunar New Year
9	"	14	Chi Chiu	Seventh Nine Days of Cold
10	"	19	*Yu Shui*	*Rainwater*
11	"	23	Pa Chiu	Eighth Nine Days of Cold
12	March	4	Chiu Chiu	Ninth Nine Days of Cold
13	"	6	*Chin Chih*	*Excited Insects (Awakening)*
14	"	21	*Ch'un Fen*	*Spring (Vernal) Equinox*
15	April	5	*Ching Ming*	*Clear and Bright*
16	"	20	*Ku Yu*	*Grain Rains*
17	May	6	*Li Hsia*	*Summer Begins*
18	"	21	*Hsiao Man*	*Grain Fills*
19	June	6	*Mang Ch'un*	*Grain in the Ear, Small Fecundity*

No.	Date in 1970 Gregorian Calendar		Chinese Terms	English
20	July	22	*Hsia Chih*	*Summer Solstice*
21	"	7	*Hsiao Shu*	*Slight Heat*
22	"	19	Tou Fu	First Heat
23	"	23	*Ta Shu*	*Great Heat*
24	"	29	Erh Fu	Second Heat
25	August	8	*Li Ch'iu*	*Autumn Begins*
26	"	8	San Fu	Third Heat (Autumn Tiger)
27	"	23	*Chu Shu*	*Heat Continues*
28	September	8	*Pai Lu*	*White Dews*
29	"	23	*Ch'iu Fen*	*Autumn Equinox*
30	October	9	*Han Lu*	*Cold Dew*
31	"	24	*Shuang Chiang*	*Hoarfrost Descends*
32	November	8	*Li Tung*	*Winter Begins*
33	"	23	*Hsiao Hsueh*	*Little Snow*
34	December	7	*Ta Hsueh*	*Heavy Snow*
35	"	22	*Tung Chih*	*Winter Solstice*
36	"	22	I Chiu	First Nine Days of Cold
37	"	31	Erh Chiu	Second Nine Days of Cold

The Commune Center 🌿

*T*raversing the fifty yards or so of tree nurseries west of our hamlet, we crossed a road, went down a sharp declivity, and climbed the steep bank on the other side. From this height we could look over a large part of the village that was the administrative center of Great Felicity Commune. We then saw that we stood on the sizable remains of the tamped earth wall that had once surrounded the village. The wall must originally have been about twenty feet high, tapering from a wide base to a width of three feet at the top. We had crossed the old moat, now partly overgrown with grass and planted with saplings. Wall and moat were visible reminders of the old feudal and warlord days, when such villages had garrisons to protect them from bandits or marauding troops of rival war-lords. The southern part of the wall had been torn down. Only the gatehouse and postern stood there, isolated build-ings by the bridge over the moat, one now a stable and the other a shop. Those murderous, troublous times were less than twenty-five years away.

On the west and north, wall and moat were weather-worn but more or less intact except where new roads ran through or over them. Here on the east, the wall enclosed the commune's middle school and a primary school. These gave a full, free, ten-year education to children of the commune. From where we stood we could see some of them pouring out of the back gate with spades and other tools to do some farmwork. We could hear the shouts of others cheering their sides at a basketball game.

Almost directly below us was the supply and marketing co-op with its bright blue shutters and window frames. This had three departments. One sold all manner of dry goods: the usual household necessities, soap, toothbrushes, flashlight batteries, towels, handkerchiefs, prints, knitted goods. The second sold foodstuffs: fruit, vegetables, biscuits, sweets, canned goods, soy sauce, and other condiments. The third, in an adjoining building, was packed with farm tools and necessities: rope, hoes, rakes, mats, carrying poles, baskets, jars, buckets, ironmongery, harness, cycle accessories. It had a lot of electrical goods like wire, insulators, and switches. Since power lines had reached the neighborhood, the peasants were putting electric lights into their homes and mechanizing wells, mills, gins, and other machines. In all three depart-ments we could see how well the co-op salesmen knew their customers' needs. The co-op's third department bought the peasants' pigs and sheep, eggs, hides, bones, and herbs, and brooms and other handicraft products for the state.

There were many trees inside the old wall's perimeter, but I would not have liked to live there. It was too much like a run-down town. I preferred our hamlet with its big pond and free fresh breezes outside the walls.

Pestle and Bell

*N*ear the roadway, halfway down our hamlet's main lane, is a large hollow stone. The cavity is more than a foot deep with a nine-inch mouth. The walls are five inches thick. Inside the stone is a pestle with a two-foot wooden handle and a heavy, rounded stone head. It looks like some Stone Age man's weapon. This is the Third Team's community mortar and pestle. Here housewives pound and crush rough rock salt or a pound or two of maize when they have run out of flour and have no time to go to the brigade's mill with its electric milling machine.

Hanging by chains on the locust tree that shades the mortar is an ancient bell, so worn that the hieroglyphs on it are quite indecipherable. This is rung to summon the team members to work or to a meeting, in case of fire or other emergency. Rung at dawn before cockcrow, it rouses the hamlet to work. It rings again at nine telling the peasants to finish breakfast and go do the midmorning tasks. Fieldworkers return home for lunch at noon. In winter the bell is rung for the afternoon shift at two-thirty. In summer it is too exhausting to work in the scorching noontime sun and the midday break is extended to after three. Then, for the light lasts until eight or later, the peasants work on into the cool of the evening.

Vegetable Supplies 🌿

*T*hroughout the rest of the winter we ate our cabbages (excellent keepers), still fresh and green, and turnips, carrots, and onions. The only time we had any difficulties with vegetables was in the early spring when we ran out of cabbages and carrots before the new spring vegetables came in. For a time we got by with the help of neighbors who knew better than we how to keep cabbages and carrots. But for several days we depended almost solely on our turnips. The ones we had kept in our cottage were getting limp. The ones we had buried in the yard were sprouting. We dug these up and, instructed by Ta Sao, cut them up into thin slices and laid them out to dry on the roof. After a few days we put them in a bag and hung it from a nail in the wall. When we needed some we took out a handful, boiled them lightly, and then washed them clean in cold water. Then we could boil or fry them with soy sauce and they were very tasty. But of course one gets tired of turnips twice a day!

By the end of March we were getting *tcho tsai* (a sort of chive) and spinach, then, in April, lettuce and spring onions. After that the vegetables came in with a rush.

The first of the spring vegetables was unusual. Ta Sao has a large locust tree growing in her yard, and as soon as the blossoms appeared, looking like white laburnum, she plucked great clusters of them along with the topmost, succulent new leaves. She boiled all these up together and pressed them into tasty balls. When these balls are cut up and fried in pork fat or vegetable oil and served with soybean sauce, *weijin* (a condiment made of monosodium glutamate), and salt to taste, they are delicious. There are many locust trees in the hamlet. Most of the oldest date from the time of the Japanese invasion when the invaders brought in seeds to grow in "their new land." That May everyone was enjoying this early spring delicacy.

It was astonishing to see the old ladies of the village clambering up the locust trees and wielding their long pruning knives.

Our main source of vegetables was the regular distribution of products from our team's vegetable plots. Since we worked in the team we too got a share. We were quite ashamed how little work we could do, so, although the team leaders and peasants protested vehemently, we insisted that we pay the team for our share. In this way we got spring onions and Spanish onions (here called foreign onions), *tcho tsai*, lettuce, spinach, eggplant, cucumber, *nan gua* (pumpkin), peas, beans, sweet potato, corn, and various herbs for cooking.

A commune peddler occasionally came through the hamlet pushing a cart or riding a bicycle fitted with panniers filled with the surplus vegetables of one of the teams. These peddlers also sold fruit in season, and chicks. The melons were fine eighteen- and twenty-pounders, better than those of Paoting. The apples, plums, apricots, and dates also were very good. But the pears, peaches, and grapes were only so-so. Although the peasants liked the local cotton melons (looking like pawpaw) I could never get used to their cottony texture.

In the early spring a few days might go by after a distribution of vegetables. Then we looked at our shelf and sighed: "Dried turnips again!" But soon a neighbor would come in with nice fresh lettuce or some spinach and we were glad of the change. Sometimes we suffered an embarrassment of riches. The team would send us radishes and several neighbors would think of us and bring us more than we could hold. It was no good saying "No, thanks!" Their generosity would not take no for an answer, so for two days it would be radishes for lunch and supper and breakfast too. Soon we learned what to do. We in turn took a little present to friends in another team, who had cucumber but no radishes in their distribution and were glad to make a fresh salad. Usually, however, the villagers never went to the trouble of making vegetable salads with dressing. They ate their cucumber or radish and even eggplant raw with just a dash of salt or sauce.

If we were really low on vegetables I could always get on my bicycle and within a radius of fifteen to forty li find half a dozen places where I could buy. These were communes that grew special crops or the two nearby county towns that had permanent markets and state vegetable shops. Here one was always sure of getting the usual vegetables in season. The tomatoes especially are splendid in this area.

Midwinter Days 🔆

*I*n December, all through the time of *Ta Hsueh,* Heavy Snow (when in fact no snow fell at all), and the first two Nine-day Periods of Cold beginning with December 22, we enjoyed the cold, dry weather. It was delightfully bracing, only beginning to grow uncomfortably cold out of doors in late midwinter, that is, around mid-January when the Third and Fourth Nine-days of Cold came upon us with the truly severe *Ta Han,* Severe Cold, of January 20. And even then it was only really uncomfortable when the wind blew. By that time the bone-dry loess roads were powdered to a fine dust three or four inches deep. Underfoot it was like a soft pad. The slightest wind whirled it up. A sizable breeze created miniature tornadoes that danced across the courtyards. A big wind sent the dust swirling skywards in dense clouds.

In late January a slight but steady north wind blew. It was so cold that the ink in my fountain pen froze out of doors and I had to use a pencil for sketching. At this time, Yuan-tsung, my wife, was still so solicitous of my health—I was always subject to colds and coughs in Peking—that she wanted me to put on my hat even when I only wanted to look through the door.

But when the wind dropped, the weather was mild again and it was a pleasure to put on warm clothes and bask for a bit in the sunshine outside our cottage. At night the dark sky was studded with stars and the moonlight made the ground look as if it were covered with a thin film of snow.

Li Ch'un, Spring Begins, came on February 4. The large pond that spreads its irregular bays and inlets to the east of our cottage is a never-ending source of joy. In the predawn grey light of winter it is a misty, inscrutable mirror, inert and still, giving an exact mirror image of each tree and bush on its banks. Against the luminous dawn from the east that silhouettes the trees, everything, even the yellow loess, is grey-black like a photographic plate. When the pond freezes solid in deep winter, it is a dull sheet of steel. Then one morning, soon after the north-flying wedges of birds heralded the spring, I opened the cottage door to see a diadem of glittering diamonds set in the black velvet of its southern edge. I walked to the bank. The ice still held under the eastern bank, but thin now. The surface of the rest of the pond was a dancing crowd of sparkling wavelets, clear, bright ripples of approaching spring. In the shallows, the thin transparent ice covered a small subwater world of waving tendrils of waterweeds and pebbles.

In late winter, field work was at a minimum and Ching Chun, once school was finished, hadn't much to do. So he asked me to teach him to ride a bicycle. I took him one afternoon to the threshing floor and first taught him how to fall off without hurting either himself or the cycle. This took an hour or so. Then I let him try to ride. He didn't make it that day, but the next, confident that he could not hurt himself or do any serious damage if he fell, he was soon riding in circles and learning to mount and dismount without the aid of a handy millstone.

His father came to help with the learning and his little brother and sister hopped around in ecstasy. In the distance, standing at the door of the cottage, I could see Ta Sao looking on. At first I thought all this was simply family interest in Ching Chun's progress. It was only after he had taken the cycle out for the fourth time, by himself, that I learned the real reason for his and the family's interest in cycling. Of course, it was partly because they thought it was a useful accomplishment; someday they would buy a bicycle and use it for shopping in the county town. But the main reason, Ta

Sao confided to me, was that Ching Chun in a few years would be bringing home his wife. They all wanted him to bring his bride home in the "modern way"—on the back of a bicycle.

Betrothal and Marriage 🦋

*I*n the spring, the fancies of all the eligible young people in Upper Felicity turned to thoughts of . . . well, not exactly love, but betrothal and marriage. They were quite sure that if they did their part of the arrangements properly, the love and mutual respect that should characterize a good family would surely come. The idea of romantic love followed by personal courtship and marriage never crossed their minds except as something that happened in operas.

Yuan-tsung and I never risked telling Lao Man or Ta Sao how we had got married in the city way: how I had seen her in the company of a mutual friend, got myself introduced, courted her for months, proposed to her, and married her. It would certainly have seemed bizarre, if not shocking. But we were city folk, a bit strange, so they took at face value our simple statement that ours was "a free-choice marriage in the modern way" and left it at that. They accepted the information a bit wonderingly—perhaps in the way I reacted to the information that somewhere in the Himalayas there was a strange custom of a family of brothers all marrying one wife, and thought: "Well, that's mighty interesting but it won't happen to me."

Once my wife did confide in the newly married, bright-eyed beauty who lived next door. She was fascinated by the story. When Yuan-tsung asked her if anything like that ever happened in Upper Felicity, she was silent for a moment, not wanting to appear rude, but candor triumphed and she said that if a girl acted like that, "people would think she was either mad or a loose woman."

Lao Man and Ta Sao had been married in the old style. Thirty years earlier they had been chosen for each other by their parents and had never seen each other until the wedding was over. Their parents had chosen well. The Mans had raised a fine family; there was deep regard and affection between them. What more could be wished? But now the people's law would only recognize and register "free-choice marriages," so their son Ching Chun would be married in the new way. In Upper Felicity this means that the tentative choice of a partner for son or daughter and the initial arrangements for betrothal and marriage are made by the parents. Then the two prospective partners meet each other. If they agree, the betrothal takes place to be followed almost certainly by the wedding. There have been local cases of the prospective bride breaking the engagement. There was even one notorious case, not in our hamlet, where a girl had broken two engagements. But no one could recall an instance where a young man had backed out of his commitment. This would have been so scandalous that it would have been difficult to find a wife for him afterwards. The girl in the case mentioned is exceptionally good-looking, a beauty in fact, and her family background very "respectable." But there was much shaking of heads over her and her family. Apparently they had jilted the previous fiancés in favor of a more advantageous match, taking advantage of the fact that in this district there are more men than women.

Because of the delicate nature of such marriage arrangements, the services of a go-between are nearly always required. And there is another peculiar circumstance: In these Honan hamlets many families have the same surname. Thus most families in Upper Felicity are named Man and so presumably are related, therefore marriages cannot be contracted between them. That means that spouses have to be found in other hamlets and how is one to know who there will make a suitable spouse? Short of parents themselves going out to make

inquiries, they must use the services of a go-between to learn
of possible spouses for their children. The go-betweens thus
obviate a lot of possible embarrassments. They may be male
or female, but are usually in middle age or older. Sometimes
they are asked by a family to act in this capacity, or they may
take it upon themselves to initiate arrangements for a suitable
match. They do not get anything out of it but the excitement
and satisfaction and, of course, a very active presence at the
meals and entertainments attending such transactions and
ceremonies. But in a small village these are not small considerations. Who does not like to play Cupid?

There were mysterious comings and goings around Lao
Man and Ta Sao's cottage, and when the visitors came the
children had been sent out to play, an unusual phenomenon.
But finally Lao Man couldn't keep the secret any longer.
He wished to discuss these things with someone who was
experienced in life but would not gossip. One proposal concerned a young woman from a former rich peasant family.
She was an able housewife and fieldworker and good-looking
as well. But should a red-flag poor peasant get allied in marriage with a former rich peasant family? It wasn't only the
two young people who had to be taken into account. Then
there was a highly recommended young girl from a poor-
peasant family, also a good housewife and worker, but of her
three younger brothers and sisters two were feeble-minded.
Was it wise to take a chance here? How about the children-
to-be?

After a few days Lao Man brightened up. The frown of
thought disappeared from his forehead. This time the match
seemed very suitable. The girl was an able young daughter
of a poor-peasant family, and she and Ching Chun had known
each other at school. Ching Chun said he was willing. And
the go-betweens were encouraged to carry their discussions
further. The next day they came in the evening after work
and Ta Sao prepared a fine dinner for them with *mantou,*
eggs, cabbage, and pickles. One was a young man of around
thirty, the other a veteran of over sixty. After dinner they
packed the children off to bed and began to discuss what

dowry Lao Man should give the bride. Afterwards Lao Man wore that worried frown again. It was not so much the sum but the fact that as an activist in the commune he didn't like this dowry business at all. It seemed feudalistic—and it was. Though the dowry was actually no more than a few small presents, these gifts were clearly a remnant of the feudal "bride's price." Like the wining and dining of the go-betweens, this custom should have died out as it had in other parts of China. The new society definitely frowned on it.

The go-betweens came to dine with Lao Man three times before the whole thing fell through. Lao Man did not like to admit it; in fact he never did admit it to us. But Ta Sao was very forthright and matter of fact. She told us that the young girl had turned down the idea, and that now Ching Chun said, "Anyway, I don't like her!"

For a time, there was no more talk of these matters in our family. But marriages were being discussed in several other cottages.

In the southern part of the hamlet was a widow with five children. The eldest, a boy, had already got married and was working in a factory in the county town. The second of four daughters was also married and had left home. The two youngest were still at school, but the eldest daughter, a fine-looking girl and a teacher in the commune's middle school, was eminently marriageable.

Now, we heard, the widow had been approached by a family in a village some distance away. They proposed a marriage between the only son of the family and the widow's eldest daughter. It was said that go-betweens had already come to them with proposals for an alliance with another family, but that they were willing to break off these negotiations if the widow gave them a favorable reply. After due consideration, she did. Serious discussions then began between the two families through the intermediary of the go-betweens. They went on for some time and, I gathered, only concluded when the young man himself returned home from the northeast where he was working on a state livestock farm. His family was well off. The father was a worker in a factory commune and the boy got a good wage. The two of them combined could send the mother and the rest of the children, who remained in the ancestral village, some fifty yuan a month. As is very common in the villages, the family wanted a local girl for the son's bride, and he had come home on a long vacation to settle this important matter.

The young teacher was regarded as a very desirable match. She was well educated and also well versed in all housekeeping skills. Good-looking and of an independent character, she had no misgivings about going out into the Big World. She and the young man had several talks together, and it seems that she put him through a stiff examination. He didn't pass it with flying colors. Finally he pleaded that his primary-school education could not match her middle-school education, but that he would learn and study hard.

It was unusual for two young people to meet in this way several times, but this lack of shyness in them was probably due to the fact that the young man had got used to the freer ways of a sizable state organization and the young woman was exceptionally advanced in her ideas. Their agreement clinched the matter. The dowry was duly sent. It was more than generous. It included four lengths of silk to make up her trousseau. When the young teacher went with her sister to visit her future in-laws, they were considerably impressed with the family house. This was a new one, two stories high and all of brick.

The marriage was celebrated soon after, because the bridegroom had to return to work. It was a simple affair in keeping with the times. The Communist Party had enjoined everyone to eschew extravagance. Only family members, the go-betweens, and a few very close friends were present. Registration of the marriage with the commune authorities was followed by a lunch with meat and vegetables, steamed bread, a little wine for toasts, and cigarettes and sweets. A few days later the couple left for their new home in the northeast.

Some days later when I was discussing the marriage with the widow I asked her if she would go and see the new house of the bridegroom's family. It was just twenty li (ten kilometers) away. She threw up her hands in a gesture of surprise and exclaimed: "I'm not so bold!" It turned out that in all her fifty-odd years she had never left the environs of Upper Felicity even to see the county town, thirty li away. But her daughter was setting out on a journey of one thousand miles! I mention this because unless one realizes how heavy was the weight of old tradition that had to be overcome by the commune's new social order, it is hard to understand many of its difficulties or comprehend the scope of its achievements.

For several weeks the question of marriage was in the air. Besides Lao Man's at least four families in the hamlet were discussing marriage plans with other families. For a peasant family this is an important question. As soon as a boy or girl approaches marriageable age the parents and go-betweens get busy. Propriety and modesty require that until the moment when it is agreed by all that they should meet under proper chaperonage and have the final say, the prospective bride and groom should keep well in the background.

One young wife told us: "A girl who made friends with boys with an eye to marriage would be considered too bold." We gathered that if a young man found that he could approach and make friends with a girl rather easily he would be very chary of marrying her himself or advising any of his friends to do so. She would be considered too "easy" or even "loose" in her relations with men. Of course, young men and women work together in the small work teams and groups, but propriety demands that an adult be in charge of the team or group. Anyway, the girls chaperone themselves. In rest periods they will sit slightly apart, and the boys would not be so forward as to intrude on them. The sons or daughters of families that are close neighbors will, of course, mingle together in the family groups, eating together with the rest and chatting together of an evening, but this is always in the family group, never tête-à-tête.

We heard of one marriage in which the bride was just eighteen and the bridegroom just over nineteen at the time of marriage. With no little surprise we heard that because of

the youth of the couple, the commune had refused to sanc-
tion or register the marriage, but the couple had got married
anyway and now had a bouncing baby boy of twelve months.
The bride, Mei-ying, was the beautiful girl next door. Her
thick braids of jet black hair, cherry-red lips, and brilliant
complexion made her one of the most attractive girls in the
hamlet. On the strength of this we had jumped to the con-
clusion that it must surely have been a love-match. However
we found out later that it had in fact been arranged mainly
by the mother of the boy. She was getting on in years; he
was an only son and she was anxious to have a grandson.
When we met her later it was clear whence came the strong
will that had rebuffed the criticism of even the commune
committee. No mere man would have dared to do what this
matriarch had done! Technically the young couple was "living in sin," but the whole hamlet complacently accepted them
as married. The old matriarch had ordained them so.

Lao Man often dropped in after dinner for a smoke and a
chat. Tonight he said seriously: "I can't stay long this evening.
Someone is coming to discuss a proposal for a bride for Ching
Chun."

He didn't use the old term of "go-between," as this has a
rather bad odor in these days of free-choice marriage, but that
was really what he meant.

He continued: "I'm not anxious for the lad to get married.
He's only eighteen and still in middle school. But I must be
polite. I'll listen to what they say but not give a firm answer
yet. Anyway, they can be betrothed now and wait a few years
to marry." He went back to his cottage soon after and the discussions lasted some two hours.

Ta Sao next day told us confidentially that they were in
fact seriously considering the match. I was sure they were not
treating the matter with anything but the deepest circumspec-
tion. It was very unlike the rather flighty way I had seen some
marriages contracted in the city. According to Ta Sao the
most important consideration, apart from such obvious factors
as age, health, family background and good political outlook,
was that the bride should be a hardworking, diligent, and
thrifty housewife. Looks, liveliness, vivacity, exceptional tal-

ents, such as the ability to sing or act, were very much sec-
ondary considerations with her. From others I gathered that
what the average mother in the hamlet looked for in her
future son-in-law was the ability to be a good commune member, husband, and head of a family—qualities that must be
based on diligence in work, honesty of purpose, steadiness,
the ability to get along with people.

Neither Lao Man nor Ta Sao ever divulged the names or
exact details of the matches they rejected. But once Lao Man,
after lighting his evening cigarette and smoking reflectively
for a time, said very deliberately, "I'm not keen on this new
proposal for Ching Chun. He's too young to marry." We
agreed with him readily. We also thought eighteen was too
young for betrothal. Ching Chun's uncle thought as we did.
And anyway it was against the advice of the People's Government, which was now strongly advising later marriages to
keep population growth down. Young men were being advised
not to marry until their late twenties, and girls were being
advised to wait until they were at least out of their teens.
But it seemed to us that Lao Man was also swayed by other
considerations.

Next day, when Lao Man dropped in, we took the opportunity of asking him what had been the final result of the
discussions.

After a moment's hesitation he said: "Everything has been
called off." And then added: "Ching Chun is not willing. He
says he'll never marry that girl. So that's that! Anyway, he's
too young."

Just then Ta Sao came in and Lao Man was called away.

"So, it's over again," we said, with a tone of commiseration.

But Ta Sao is very straightforward and utterly without
false pride. "What did Lao Man say?" she asked quizzically.
And when we told her, she laughed. "It's true that Ching
Chun said he'll never marry that girl, but it didn't all happen
quite that way! The girl is going to marry someone else."

"But Ching Chun?"

"When she wouldn't agree, Ching Chun said she was
stupid anyway!"

Ta Sao was quite complacent about it all. Lao Man was

really keen on this betrothal but did not want to "lose face" by a refusal, so he hedged and always pretended he was not really interested.

Ta Sao said that she also thought her son was too young to marry, but it was not too soon to be looking out for a good wife for him. Really good wives were not all that plentiful, so it was best to start looking early and take one's time. If they found one right off, so much the better. If their search was fruitless for the time being, there was no harm done.

Later on Lao Man admitted that he had really been keen on the match. The proposed bride was a member of the same commune and lived just a few li away. She was of poor peasant origin, a nice-looking girl, able about the house and with a full primary-school education. Ching Chun and she were acquainted, or at least had seen each other at school. Lao Man thought that she would have made a good daughter-in-law and that such a marriage would have been a happy step that would have pleased Ta Sao. Ta Sao was older than he and would be glad of a daughter-in-law's help and a future grandson or granddaughter. When these things came to pass when one was in middle age, it was a great satisfaction. He agreed with Ta Sao that Ching Chun was too young to marry, but it was also his opinion that it was quite time to start thinking about the marriage although it might not take place for a year or more.

What Lao Man had told us earlier about the need for a go-between was true. I could see that for myself now. In this way the matter had been handled in strictest confidence and through third parties, so when negotiations had broken down no one had lost face, except deep down in the secret heart where vain hopes are buried.

This was the time that I realized I had solved another small mystery. Soon after I arrived Lao Man had been greatly interested in the price of sewing machines, transistor radios, electric lights, and bicycles. At the time I wondered why. These were all useful things and other households in the hamlet had some or all of them. But now I could see that for a family entering on talks of marriage, these were things that were something special that go-betweens could talk about to the prospective bride's parents.

Lao Man came in one evening and jovially discussed buying something with some of his savings. There were some nice-looking clocks in the co-op that week, but he rejected the idea of purchasing one because nobody was that punctual. Finally he decided on a transistor radio. He let the cat out of the bag when he added: "It's useful . . . and noisy. Everyone will know we have one." All this clearly had to do with Ching Chun getting married.

"So Ching Chun is cycling!" we heard in the hamlet. Old ladies and public-spirited persons who liked match-making took note. A cycle, sewing machine, or radio are I suppose the nearest things to status symbols that Upper Felicity has. How hard the old Adam dies!

The various negotiations went on over a period of weeks. It was past the Spring Festival before several visits from the go-betweens carried matters in one proposed match to the stage where Lao Man could admit, "It's nearly settled." The girl was of poor-peasant origin and was suitable in every other way. Ching Chun said they had also known each other at school though they were in different classes. He had agreed to the match. There had been a hitch at the beginning, but this had been untangled. Lao Man had heard that the girl's father had once been brought before the People's Court in regard to some affair that might have involved punishment at the hands of the court. Although the case against him had been dropped, an explanation was called for and after a bit of hemming and hawing on the part of the go-betweens it was given. Far from putting a bad light on the father, it made him something of a hero. It turned out that it was really his younger brother who had been involved. Had the matter turned out badly he might have been jailed and this would have affected his chances in the matter of marriage. The older brother, already married, offered to stand trial and take the blame, if there was any, in place of the younger man. This involved a little innocent deception of the court but all who knew of it praised him instead of blaming him. All ended happily, however; the accused was let off with a caution. The divulging of this secret removed the last obstacle to the proposed match.

Since the two young people were only nineteen and eighteen, it was agreed that they should wait at least a couple of years before actually getting married. They might even have to wait three years because the commune might not agree to register their marriage.

Then quite a bit of discussion took place between the go-betweens concerning the amount and type of presents that should be given to the girl. I know the gifts included cloth and towels, scented soap, and other household articles. The total sum spent was not more, I suppose, than Lao Man would have spent on bridal presents of his own accord, but he quite justifiably disliked this concession to the old ways.

This part of the discussions having ended to the mutual satisfaction of the two families and the honor of the go-betweens, the day was set when the bride-to-be would come to visit the Mans and formally meet her future bridegroom. Then eggs were hoarded and arrangements made to procure meat for the feast. Wine and cigarettes were bought and there was a great borrowing of bowls and chopsticks, stools and cups.

Lao Man went to the county town to fetch the meat and buy the presents. Big Pig had recently been sold, so there was ready money. On the day appointed Ching Chun put on a new suit, but disappeared before the bridal party came. I think he went to sit with his uncle at the stables. From the moment of the visitors' arrival until after lunch no male member of the Man family was to be seen. Even I, as a male inhabitant of the house, kept away, and the two babies were sent out to play. Lao Man went to work in the fields as usual and Ta Hsiang, nearly as excited as the bride, buried herself in the kitchen helping her mother.

Chaperoned by a girl cousin and her uncle and aunt on her father's side, the girl arrived an hour or so before noon. On the Man family's side Ta Sao did the honors, but since she was busy up to the last moment preparing the meal her place in the house was taken by the grandmother of the family relatives next door. This matriarch presided over a family of three generations. Truly an auspicious personage! Her duties were mainly to welcome the guests and introduce the stream of female visitors who came to the house to "see the betrothed," and offer her congratulations. No men came, not even old men, but the women and girls were there in force. It was a testing ordeal for the girl. My wife told me she stood to receive their greetings, very shy and embarrassed but hiding her emotions decorously under an impassive face and replying in low monosyllables. The neighbors said that she made a very good impression on them as a modest, polite, straightforward working girl.

At lunchtime Ta Sao and Ching Chun's aunt served all the women in the main cottage. The men ate next door at the aunt's cottage. It was a big party: seventeen people in all. It was only after the meal that the whole Man family joined the guests in the cottage. This was the first time that Ching Chun had a chance to see his future bride and chat with her. Apparently they hit it off and in sign of this arranged to go to the county town next day to get their photo taken together and do some shopping. This trip was now traditional for the newly betrothed couples. It was part of the new marriage customs that were growing up in Upper Felicity.

The next day they traveled into town by bus. The two to three hours they took to walk back gave them ample time to talk over this and that. They took the traditional photo, showing the two of them standing shoulder to shoulder and looking very straight and seriously at the camera. Then they went to the department store and bought two jackets for her and a headscarf and two pounds of sponge cakes for her mother, who wasn't well. Ching Chun came that late afternoon to borrow my cycle to ride her home. Shy still, his newly betrothed preferred to wait for him at the bus stop on the main road.

While the general opinion in the hamlet was that the match was a good one, there were critics—there always are critics—who commented that the arrangements for the betrothal, including the presents, were "too extravagant." I reckoned that Lao Man had spent about seventy to eighty yuan all told. This was just about what he would get from the sale of Big Pig. And I wondered, if this was extravagance what of that other marriage we had heard of lately? This bride had got several lengths of silk costing goodness knows what. She had broken off another engagement to enter into this more advantageous marriage. We had heard that she was going right away to set up house for her husband in the city, but here she was two weeks after the marriage, still at home and wearing a new silk jacket, the only one to wear such finery on workdays!

A couple of weeks after the betrothal Ching Chun went to visit his in-laws-to-be, taking some eggs for his ailing mother-in-law, as he already called her. But for weeks after that he seemed to forget his prospective bride completely. It didn't seem proper to me, but when I asked Ta Sao when he would go visiting again, she said: "He can't go too often. It wouldn't look proper!"

As I said, there was a shortage of girls in the Upper Felicity area. Our next-door neighbors, the Man children's aunt and uncle, had a daughter. She was over twenty and we were told that every spring for the last four years the matchmakers had come in a stream to the house. But her parents were in no hurry to get her wed. She was an only child and when she left the home they would be lonely, until little Au Chiu grew up and, as they had arranged, would live with his bride in their courtyard. She was also in no hurry to wed and take on new and many responsibilities. So they had decided to wait awhile, at least a year or so. They couldn't put it off more than that. At twenty-five a girl is already considered a bit of an old maid and it is more difficult to find her a suitable husband. Till then anyway they felt they could still be unhurried, so they enjoyed the luxury of being very choosy.

The old-style professional matchmaker is no more. No doubt her unsavory stage image had a lot to do with her demise. The amateur matchmakers or go-betweens of today in general perform their duties in a responsible way. They still perform an essential service for the community at this period. The only criticism I heard about them concerned their inordinate appetites at feasts. Though most are by common consent regarded as sincerely desirous to serve, there are naturally some black sheep and some curious contretemps. There was the much-discussed case of the half-blind son of one neighbor. This young man is in his mid-thirties and has not yet been paired off. One day there appeared a man from, so he said, Li Village, who proposed an advantageous marriage with a young widow. He consumed a fine dinner of eggs and steamed bread made of the best white flour, and innumerable cigarettes, and then it emerged that there was really no widow and no match. But such cases are few and far between.

The great majority of marriages arranged in the new way turn out well. This is due in no small measure to the highly moral nature of the peasants and the steadiness of feeling and loyalty to the family that is early inculcated into the young people. Divorce is thought of as the last and uttermost resort in solving marital tangles. In case of a really serious husband and wife row the usual safety valve is for the wife to pack up and go back to the parental home. I heard of only one divorce in our hamlet in recent years, and those with whom I chatted could only remember one in the near neighborhood. This case was not of an exceptional nature in these days of rapid social change and greater mobility of populations. A go-ahead young peasant lad had a middle-school education and had been selected for medical training. At the hospital he met a nurse; they became friendly and then fell in love. In the meantime he had been growing apart from his young wife back in the village. She had not developed culturally as fast as he had, and when they met they found they had less and less in common. In this dilemma he had asked for a divorce, but she had refused to agree to it. In view of her refusal the court, of course, wouldn't grant his application for a divorce. In an attempt to mend matters, the hospital had in the meantime posted his nurse friend to another place. When the young fellow went back home, his wife, her feelings outraged, had refused to receive him back and had herself demanded a divorce, which, since he had already expressed his wish to divorce her, she got.

A married couple without children can obtain a divorce if they both desire it by simply going to the registrar of marriages and divorces and making a declaration of their wish. If children are involved, then a more serious attempt will be made to prevent a divorce and it will be refused if one party objects to it. This involves a hearing before a People's Court. If it is granted both parties must contribute to the care of the children. The parent who earns more will contribute more.

Modern marriages in the cities today are genuinely free-choice marriages. The young people, particularly in the universities and factories and big state organizations, have ample chance to choose their own life partners and usually do so with the advice of their parents and friends. The degree of freedom they enjoy in this respect is much greater than exists in Upper Felicity and its environs. Many make use of that greater freedom far less wisely than the parents and young people of Upper Felicity make of the more restricted freedom their community has imposed on itself. But that is not to say that Upper Felicity's ways in this matter are best. In social development, in the advance toward socialist social conditions, Upper Felicity still lags behind. Segregation of the sexes there both among the youth and adults is still too great. It is in part an inheritance from feudal conditions and feudal outlooks of the past, and in part linked with the strict and somewhat straitlaced ideas of the village leadership in matters of sex. The current way of arranging and solemnizing marriages is a reflection of social conditions at the present time. It is a compromise between the old way of wholly arranged marriages, in which the two persons most concerned were confronted on their wedding night with a *fait accompli,* and the modern, city way of wholly free-choice marriage. This is clearly a transitional state of affairs. Modifications will take place gradually. This is not a matter in which government or social organizations can unilaterally prescribe rigid rules and regulations. The Party and government prudently guide development of a new outlook on marriage. They have set a legal minimum age of eighteen for marriage for both men and women. They have also established the processes for registration of marriages and conditions for divorce. Through the communes and education of public opinion they discourage too early marriages as a measure of birth control. But beyond such steps they wisely allow the community itself to feel out the way it shall go. Party and government naturally take action if abuses arise. One instance of this was at the District Conference of Activists in the Study of Mao Tse-tung Thought.

Here one speaker brought up a case in which a very "desirable" young woman had found engagement gifts good business. She had exploited the natural reticence of the families with whom she had broken faith, and it was now revealed that she had broken no fewer than three engagements and was now in her fourth matrimonial adventure. This would evidently be her last, because to be publicly criticized at such a conference was a heavy disgrace indeed.

The more politically awake peasants like our Lao Man want to follow government advice on later marriages, but the old ideas die hard. Old matriarchs know that country women in early middle age often stopped conceiving. So they look forward to early grandsons and granddaughters. They do not realize that barrenness was due mainly to hard conditions of life in the past and that the improved conditions of life in the new society should lead to more fertile marriages.

How long will these present marriage customs last? Not many more years I think. Young girls like the schoolteacher or the vigorous vice-commander of the militia troop will not long remain content with their parents doing most of the choosing. They will want to take a bigger part themselves in such crucial decision-making. And men like our Lao Man will back them up.

Marriage customs differ greatly from end to end of China. In 1957, for instance, I found that marriages in the Kazakh-inhabited areas of Sinkiang were still subject to complicated family, clan, and tribal customs quite different from those of other nationalities in China. But here too, as a result of the People's Government's urging, the trend was toward increasingly "free choice."

Fleeing Flood and Drought ✖

Upper Felicity, despite its name, lies in a depression in the northern part of the central China plain. In the old days this was an unmitigated misfortune. When heavy rains fell here or to the north or northwest, the Taihang mountain streams poured down onto the plain and filled the nearby Wei River, which overflowed its banks and flooded out over the lowlands, seeking an outlet to the sea. The Upper Felicity basin was a sump directly in the path of these floods. Its lowlands soon got waterlogged. With continued rain the water would rise until it covered the fields and reached the higher ground where the peasants' cottages cluster.

The great danger, however, came when the Yellow River broke its banks and poured north seeking a channel to the sea. Upper Felicity lay in the path of the flood.

The old warlord and Kuomintang governments had no coordinated water conservancy system or weather service, so there was no advance warning of the nature or extent of the danger. The first warning would be the waters themselves advancing on the fields and hamlets. Rumors would be rife. There was no way of knowing whether the flood would be big or small, whether you should stick it out or flee for your life. Who knew whether the rain would cease soon or continue for a month or what was happening a thousand li up the Yellow River? Some said one thing; some said another. Some went off; some decided to hang on a bit longer.

Rain fell in solid sheets. Paths and lanes became quagmires of sticky loess that bogged down even the strongest of mules

or horse teams. Roads, such as they were, disappeared except
for stretches on the higher ground. Should you take your
shoulder pole and baskets, pack the babies into them, load
your wife with what food you had, and try to get away?
Should you leave the cottage with its few hard-won scraps of
furniture and cooking utensils, your tools and crops, and probably find them wrecked or stolen when you returned—*if* you
returned? And where would you go? Perhaps relatives in the
next province four or five hundred li away were in the same
or a worse plight than yourself. But if you stayed, what then?
The water might quickly subside, and you might be lucky.
But it might go on rising—come in at the door. Then you
would have to stack your things on the bed or the table and
splash around your room in mud.

It might go higher, lapping up your legs as you piled things
higher out of its reach. When there was danger of you and
your family being marooned and drowned under the rafters,
you had to think of getting out and onto the roof. But at any
moment then the walls of dried mud might collapse and throw
you and your family and all you had saved into seven feet of
swirling, murky water. And how to subsist on a roof with a
hungry brown flood all around you? And how to subsist in
the flood-devastated hamlet afterwards? You faced questions
and decisions that involved death or life.

Flood and drought were everpresent hazards of life in old
Upper Felicity. Apart from rain and snow, the peasants depended for water on surface wells. Water can be found in
many places ten to twenty feet down. In normal weather
there was no difficulty. Winter usually brings the hamlet rain
or snow between November and March. In summer the annual monsoon brings rain in July and August. These water
the crops adequately and keep surface wells filled. But sometimes summer rains are scanty, and no snow or rain falls in
winter. A drought of nine or ten months in the old days left
the surface wells dry and the Wei River, thirty meters deep
at flood time, became a dry gully. The stunted winter wheat
dried up and disappeared in a brown desert of cracked loess.
The spring crops, watered with the last of the well water,

sprouted and then withered. The leaves on the trees shriveled and turned black. The annual spring famine after the winter stores were eaten merged into a summer starvation that reduced humans and animals to walking skeletons of dried skin and bone. Without stamina to resist such hardships, the children and old folk died first, and the able-bodied grew steadily weaker and more debilitated. Then, just as in times of flood, there were the same agonizing questions and fateful decisions. Flee or stay? Sow a crop and chance it that the rain would come in time to nourish it? Or chance it on the road, eating up your seed grain and then go begging? And where to go? Precise information was hard to get. Rumor was rife. Flee north or south? Perhaps if you went north where you had friends and relatives you would find the same parched fields, and hordes of starving peasants like yourself. South, and away from your own kith and kin, you might find yourself in worse state than before.

One night Lao Man told us about the big flood of 1941 and the drought that followed in 1942. He was ten years old at the time. His mother had died and he and his father lived alone in the cottage we were sitting in now. That year there was heavy local rain, but worse, both the Yellow and Wei rivers broke their banks. Before the Man family knew what was happening, a brown mass of liquid mud was filling the sunken road in the hamlet. While they anxiously debated what to do, the mud rose relentlessly and poured into the cottage. They postponed leaving until the last minute. By midday the water was knee-high and rising fast. If they delayed much longer they would have to swim to make higher ground, and none of them could swim. Outside they heard a crash and splash above the noise of the rain. The shack next door had collapsed as its adobe walls, sodden with water, melted away. One by one the poorer hovels disappeared under the water. Pots, pans, furniture, clothes, and other possessions that had been laboriously dragged onto the roofs fell into the muddy current and were carried away. A panic-stricken mother clutched a baby in one hand and vainly stretched the other to rescue something from the floating wreckage. Standing

crops of kaoliang and corn finally bowed their heads to the
water and sank out of sight.

One by one, families fled. With the crops gone there was
nothing left to stay for. There was very little in the Mans'
cottage, anyway. Their few ragged clothes were stored among
the rafters; some tools and pots had been buried. Father and
son took what they could carry on a long trek and left. From
the door of the cottage to the high ground owned by the landlord, the flood engulfed everything. The moat around the
dilapidated wall of the nearby town was filled to the brim.
Gaps in the wall had been hastily filled, and for the moment
the inhabitants were safe and dry. But many of the houses
were already below water level. At any moment a breach
might be made and the waters would pour in. To the south
all was under water except the road along the ridge. By making a long detour they might hope to reach the high ground
of the Taihang foothills and thence make their laborious way
to Shansi and distant relatives near Taiyuan, the capital of
that province.

It took them the best part of three days to cover the distance
to higher ground. By then their clothes were drenched and
caked with mud. The little food they carried was sodden.
There was not a dry place on which to rest their tired bodies.
The roads were filled with homeless people. Luckily the Mans
had tough constitutions or they would never have survived.
After some time they met others from Upper Felicity making
the same trek to what they hoped would be salvation. Some
were burdened in their flight with babes in arms or aged
grandparents. Old women inched along on bound feet. Some
grannies, knowing that they would never make it back alive
anyway and would hamper their children in the desperate
struggle for life, had simply refused to move from their cottages. They were given what food was left, took their seats
on some high place, and waited stoically for the end.

Sometimes quite a large group would plod on together,
helping each other as best they could. In some more prosperous district the men might be able to get odd jobs or cut and
sell firewood, and they would rest there for a while. The poor

helped the poor. In some villages untouched by calamity the peasants took pity on the refugees and gave them food. Sometimes the Mans ate the bitter food of grudging charity. When the area they passed through was poor, they split up into smaller groups and took different parallel paths to a rendezvous farther on.

Some families, like the Mans, were traveling back along the road they or their grandparents had traveled not many years before. At that time they had been fleeing from famine in Shansi. When they came to the place where Upper Felicity now stands they had found it a deserted wasteland, a partly waterlogged marsh on the edge of an alkaline flat. The local people did not want to farm this natural flood basin, and the Shansi refugees were glad to rent land there at what in their desperation seemed like cheap rents. This was how the Mans came to live in Upper Felicity and to have relatives in Shansi. They never corresponded with these relatives. They were all illiterate. But Shansi was the only place where they knew they had relatives and the only place they could look to for help in times of need.

When they reached their destination the Mans failed to locate their relatives. They plodded on to Taiyuan. For a time in this big city they managed to subsist on scraps from the tables of the wealthy and the refuse of the markets and food shops. But they were farmers, not beggars. They turned their footsteps home again. They traveled south down the valley of the Fen River, seeking along the road for some place where they could take up squatters' rights, raise a crop, and live for a time. But all possible holdings had long since been taken. The only free land was high up on the waterless shoulders of hills or in barren gullies. Even if you carved out a holding for yourself there, you could be sure that some landlord would appear and demand rent—50 to 70 per cent of your hard-won harvest. The Shansi landlords were screwing rents up to the limit. Finally there was nothing left to do but to return to Upper Felicity, as their forebears had optimistically named the place where they, in their day, had found refuge.

It was two years before the Man family regained their cottage. They found it gutted by marauding Kuomintang soldiery. Yet they felt themselves lucky. Other families had returned to find level ground where their homes had been. Sixteen of the forty refugee families simply disappeared. They never returned and were never heard of again. Perhaps they had found some place elsewhere to settle. Perhaps they had all perished from the hardships of the road. Few of the families that went came back intact. Members got separated and lost, others succumbed to hardship, starvation, or disease. Over a hundred inhabitants of Upper Felicity failed to return. Some were children whom their parents had been forced to sell or give to better-off families because otherwise they could not be fed. Adoption or even slavery was better than death. In those two years over two-thirds of the Upper Felicity peasants had been forced to flee.

"Those were bitter days!" exclaimed Lao Man.

Just before Lao Man told me all this I had been reading an American magazine in which a writer mourned the fact that the "Communists were breaking up the family." When I told this to Lao Man, he laughed in disbelief. "It was the old times that broke the family up," he observed. "Now for the first time we feel really secure as a family."

In the old days nearly 90 per cent of Upper Felicity households were landless or land-poor peasants living a hand-to-mouth existence, or so-called lower-middle peasants living just a cut above subsistence level. Only the landlord had weathered the flood. His courtyard of solid brick houses stood on high ground, and when all other houses were in or under water his stood high and dry. His granary was filled with grain enough to withstand the siege of flood or drought. Ready money assured him of other foods. The peasants came to him begging for loans or to sell their tools or other valuables to him at any price. He coined money out of the people's misery. When there was a cake to eat, he got the biggest share of it. But the increasing pauperization of the peasants was making the cake smaller and smaller.

The flood of 1941 was followed by a plague of locusts. The winged mass obscured the sunlight and left the fields a leafless desert. While the area was still reeling from these twin disasters, there had come drought and famine, and banditry by demoralized marauding troops of the Kuomintang. And all this was in the midst of the war against the invading Japanese armies. In those two years of 1941 and 1942, three million people died in the province, according to a rough calculation from reports to the Kuomintang government by a few magistrates and missionary sources. No true estimate of the total dead, still less of the homeless, sick, and disabled, is possible. No one in authority in the corrupt Kuomintang administration who knew the facts cared two straws about the death of peasants.

The horde of undisciplined troops that flooded through the area like another natural calamity was yet another of the effects of Kuomintang misrule and miscalculation. More afraid of the Chinese masses than of the Japanese imperialist invaders, the Kuomintang under Chiang Kai-shek had plotted and schemed with the warlord Yen Hsi-shan, who ruled Shansi Province, to undermine and erase the guerrilla area north of the Yellow River. The people of this area were fighting and pinning down large numbers of Japanese soldiers and, by threatening from the flanks the Japanese lines of communication, were preventing the invaders from advancing farther west and south down the Peking-Hankow Railway and into the Central China Plain. Finally these plots came to fruition. While the Japanese attacked from north and east, the Kuomintang and Yen Hsi-shan began attacking from south and west and from within. Guerrilla leaders were caught and killed, progressive intellectuals were rounded up, good local government leaders elected by the people were denounced as Communists and beheaded. Terror stalked the villages and towns. The guerrilla forces were compelled to withdraw. Some went back into the Taihang Mountains. Some joined up with the Communist-led Eighth Route Army and guerrillas farther north.

But having taken over this strategic area and crushed the whole democratic basis of people's war by which it had been held so far against the Japanese, the new Kuomintang administration was powerless to hold the area when the Japanese attacked. Its troops had antagonized the people and had no friends among them. Grown slothful and undisciplined, they were useless on the battlefield against the regimented might of the Japanese invader. During the spring of 1941 many strategic points were given up without even a pretense at resistance. The Japanese fanned out over the whole area and across the Yellow River.

The troops of the Kuomintang general Sung Tung-shuen, who were supposed to be defending this war zone, had for months past been engaged not in fighting the enemy but in smuggling goods from Japanese-occupied areas to be sold at a fat profit in so-called Free China. Now, when the invaders advanced into the Central China Plain and over the Yellow River, these smuggler troops simply folded up. Those that did not succeed in making a getaway south and west simply took to the open country on either side of the enemy advance. From there they might have harassed the Japanese lines of communication, but that was not their way. They lived off the country, terrorizing and robbing the peasants and press-ganging conscripts in the name of the Kuomintang government—to help them carry away what they had looted.

Lao Man is forty, not tall, but strongly built. Work-hardened, his forearms are solid sinew and muscle, with hands hard and bony and palms callused from years of handling hoe and shovel. His head is close shaved and this, with the deep wrinkles on his sunburned face, makes him look older than he is. He moves slowly, but steadily and tirelessly. Wherever there is work to be done you will find him. If a work chantey is needed it will be he who leads it. He is indomitably cheerful. At work or at leisure he usually wears a smile, and he laughs often. But his mouth was tight closed as he paused in his story and let his mind hover over the past.

No More Fear of Flood or Drought 🌿

*L*ao Man soon brushed the bitter memories away and smiled again.

"Things got better after liberation," he continued. "There were big changes. It would take too long to tell you all about it. There was land reform. We all got land. Then we formed mutual-aid teams. Then co-ops. We worked hard and were doing well and then—kalump!" And he brought both fists down with a thwack! on the table. "There was a flood in 1961 almost as bad as that other. It covered the crops again and reached into this very room. It was so high here." And he drew a line on the stove six inches from the floor.

"But this time it was different. The People's Government told us not to run away because the rain would soon cease. And it did. But anyway we had to leave our home, although by then we had built it higher than it was. We all collected on the ground around the landlord's old house—it had been taken from him in the land reform—and on the high ground on the main road. But we were completely cut off there. We were all wondering what we would do for food when we heard the sound of an airplane. Sure enough, it flew right over us and then came back again flying ever so low, just skimming the tops of the trees. And out of it came sacks of cooked food! Good fresh steamed *mantou* they were, with pickles. Some of the sacks burst, but that was a small matter. Not one of them was lost in the water.

"There happened to be a small unit of P.L.A. men in the big village over there. They were all local youngsters just going off for training. They didn't need an order. They threw themselves against the flood as if it were the enemy. They worked till they couldn't move for tiredness. The only thing they thought of those days was how to help save our things.

"That's the way the People's Liberation Army saved us!"

Lao Man paused, filled his pipe again and tried to remember some more.

"Later, boats came from the county town bringing supplies. They also helped us save our property. We were well looked after until we could go back home. A lot of our things were washed away that time too and there was heavy damage to crops. But the People's Government gave us relief grain and helped us start up again. By that time we had our commune. It was stronger than the co-op. It shared out what it had justly. Share and share alike. Still, that was a bad upset. Just when we thought everything was going fine, too!" he added ruefully.

"Aren't you afraid it will happen again?" I asked.

"Not a chance of that," declared Lao Man confidently.

The young worker from down the lane who had dropped in for a chat broke in: "We don't fear flood and we don't fear drought! That 1961 flood was the last."

"How can you be so confident?"

Seeing that Lao Man, his senior by age, remained silent, the young man, a local lad who worked in the commune's tractor repair workshop, went on: "We've built three big reservoirs. They can store or release tens of millions of cubic meters of water. We've deepened and widened and straightened the Wei. We have a network of drainage and irrigation canals and channels that can carry off or bring in water quickly. From source to mouth the work of harnessing the Yellow River is going ahead. That settles the danger of flood.

"Here on the spot our Third Brigade has four deep mechanized wells and owns half of another. This year we are going to dig and equip another two. That will give us ample water, rain or no rain, to irrigate our crops. The wells and the reservoirs settle the danger of drought.

"And we'll have plenty of fish too. The reservoirs are stocked with fish and now that we have the mechanized wells we'll restock our big pond."

Lao Man nodded his head as each item was ticked off. He admired the logical, scientific mind of the young worker. He himself, as we knew from previous conversations, could have described every reservoir and the tale of each well he had worked on, but it would have come out bit by bit and you would have had to envisage the overall set-up for yourself.

"I worked on one of those reservoirs myself," he volunteered as if to confirm the young worker's words. "And I helped dig every well!"

"Did you get all that work done since liberation?" I asked.

"Yes! All of it! And most of it was done after 1960. That was after we had organized the communes. The mutual aid teams and co-ops could not have done it. Even one commune could never have organized such a big plan of work covering such a huge area. All the communes of the counties concerned with the project got together. They sent hundreds of thousands of men and women to dig and build."

"I was away from home for several months," put in Lao Man. "I took my own tools. The commune put up tents, shelters, and kitchens and gave us food. We got work-points for our work just as if we had been farming here at home. The People's Government helped us with the cement work and sluice gates and things like that. And of course, the surveyors and engineers. But mostly we used local methods and materials: earth, stone, wood, and our hand tools. There wasn't much big machinery. A lot of people came from the towns to help in shifts: cadres and students, doctors and nurses. The P.L.A. helped too. It loaned us some trucks and things like that, but mostly it was carrying pole and basket, pick and shovel, hammer and muscle——"

"Once the big job was done," added the young worker, "the communes, brigades, and teams took over most of the job of maintenance and carried on with the smaller, local work like digging channels and ditches, improving the banks of the Wei, installing pumping stations and so on. And, of course, digging wells."

"But I thought you said the wells here dried up during a drought," I said. "How does mechanizing them help?"

"It's the surface wells that dry up," explained Lao Man. "The mechanized wells are different. They are deep wells."

The young worker elucidated.

"Thirty to forty meters down there is an underground lake

of water here. The commune and People's Government geologists discovered that. We dig down to that. We have a quick method. We can do it in a week or so. Then we line the bore with prefabricated brick-and-cement well sections, put a pipe down, and use an electrically operated pump to pump up the water. Power lines were brought here about seven years ago. There is so much water down there that we couldn't drain it out even if we tried with all our pumps going full blast. Now we can get 'rain' with a flick of a switch. And have it on any field we want, too!"

For centuries past the Upper Felicity folk in their lowland basin had been perpetually harried either by flood or drought. Regularly every ten years or so they had been thrown back into an abyss of complete destitution. Listening to Lao Man's story I had been wondering at first how they were intending to carry their ill-situated hamlet forward to the high productivity and prosperity that one associates with socialism. After living for a while in Upper Felicity I realized that there is no easy magic of "aid" or "science" that they can invoke. When all is said and done they have to be, and are, their own magic, their own providence.

Former Landlords and Rich Peasants ✣

The landlord of the hamlet, who once lived in the group of brick buildings on the high ground southwest of the pond, had not been the worst of landlords by any standard. But the system of feudal land ownership he stood for had kept the peasant masses poor and exploited for centuries. Any discussion of him developed into an "accusation meeting." He had lorded it over the hamlet, exploited hired labor, engaged in usury, and was high-handed. When others were hunted as conscripts, he and his got off scot free. It was the same with Kuomintang levies and taxes or forced labor.

When I say "exploited hired labor" this has to be understood as it is understood in China today. Any man who hires another to work for him is exploiting labor: that is, seeing to it that he gets more than he is paying for. That is why every capitalist is by definition an exploiter of labor. If he did not

get more than he is paying for, it stands to reason that he would be losing money, or at the very least breaking even but certainly not making a profit which must come as "surplus value" from the labor of others. Landlord Man regularly employed hired hands to do his farm work for him, so he was by definition an exploiter of labor.

The younger and more politically aware people in Upper Felicity accepted this reasoning without question. But some of the older people still could not follow this Marxist analysis. Some of them had even been taken in by the phrase put out by Landlord Man and his hangers-on at the time of the land reform: "We are all of one family, all Man!" It was true that he was a Man and four-fifths of the hamlet were Man by name, but belonging to the Man clan had had little effect on his attitude when money was involved. Mans were as cruelly exploited by him as other families. This spurious appeal to clan feeling had blunted the edge of their understanding of the class distinction between them and him. That was why they had been overlenient in their treatment of him during the land reform of 1952.

At that time when the accounts were totted up it had been agreed by all that Landlord Man had received far more in rent and gifts and interest and free labor than he was entitled to, and he was ordered to return the surplus to the needy, the landless poor, and hired laborers of Upper Felicity. All debts and interest owing to him were canceled. His land and tools were requisitioned, but he had been left with three mu of land for himself and as much again for his wife. This was the same share as the landless peasants got and was strictly in accordance with the land reform regulations. He had also received a share of tools like the others. Some of his houses and furniture had been requisitioned and handed over to the destitute. But he had been allowed to retain his old home on the mound and its furniture. This was discussed during the Cultural Revolution of 1966 and judged to be wrong. That year he was told to move out into a smaller cottage, and he was relieved of the last of his ill-gotten gains. The big house was reserved for public use as a brigade office and meeting room.

While the mutual-aid teams and co-ops were being formed he was not allowed to participate. He farmed his land by himself. When the commune was formed he had had no say in its arrangements, but his land was incorporated into the commune, and he was provided for by receiving work-points for his work the same as full commune members. He himself was still not a full member even in 1969. He could not attend production and other meetings where substantive questions were discussed and, of course, could not vote or stand for election to any post. Apart from this political neutralization, he was not doing too badly. A son, working in a North China city, sent him a small allowance each month. And even he was learning that the old social system had given him only relative well-being. He had been like a cock on his dunghill of an estate. Warlord misrule and the mass poverty and anger of the peasants around him were a constant threat to him too. In the new society he had initially lost out, but the general order and security and increasing well-being would eventually (if he were law-abiding and still more if he actively collaborated and integrated with the new society) enhance the well-being of himself and his family too.

The exercise of dictatorship over the landlords and rich peasants by the people's power was not a matter of vindictiveness or vengeance. It was essentially a measure to prevent them harming or hindering the new society and to remold and liberate them too.

Up in the commune center there were several other landlords. Most of them were treated in the same way. But one of them refused even to reconcile himself to the new society. As a result, even after all these years, he was still working under supervision by his neighbors. They saw to it that he did not get up to any big mischief. It seems incredible, but such was the hatred some of these old "bourbons" nursed against the people's state that they sometimes took a chance to do acts of big or little sabotage even ten or twenty years after the Liberation. They had set fire to ricks, broken embankments to flood fields, stolen grain, encouraged drinking and gambling. They saw their chance when the excitement of big mass campaigns like the socialist education movement or the

Cultural Revolution rose to a height. During the Cultural Revolution some of these diehards had been found preserving old land deeds, Kuomintang flags and citations, and arms against the day of revenge. Actually, one of the worst reactionaries in the commune was not a landlord but a former rich peasant.

In Upper Felicity, the three former rich peasants had been gradually assimilated after a period of probation. I knew only one personally. He was a mild-looking old fellow who had been assigned to the vegetable-plot team. He was an educated farmer and before the land reform had become a schoolteacher. But his old outlook could not help coming through in his teaching. Finally he had been advised to retire and had come back to the hamlet. Here, because he clearly tried his best to be socially useful and get rid of his reactionary ideas, he had been allowed to join the commune as a member, as had the other two former rich peasants. He received nine work-points a day (Lao Man got ten) and sat in on all ordinary meetings, but was not allowed to vote or be elected to any leading post. He had his cottage in the north end of the hamlet and two sons and grandchildren, so he was pretty comfortably off and living as happily as the situation allowed. In the course of time the last disabilities of his rich-peasant status would be taken off him, if he continued to be well-behaved.

Each case involving the former exploiting classes was treated on its individual merits. Landlords who it was generally felt had completely discarded their past had had all the rights of commune members given to them. The only disabilities they still suffered were no voting rights and no right to be elected as cadres. But not long before there was a landlord son who had plotted to "settle accounts" with a poor peasant cadre. This fellow, a generally bad character, had been charged before the People's Court and locked up. On the other hand, landlord sons and daughters who have dissociated themselves from their own class can be found all over China occupying various positions even among the highest in government and party organizations. What is demanded is that they draw a strict line of repudiation between themselves and their past and former connections.

There is naturally a difference between the way society

looks at the son of a poor peasant or worker and that of a land-lord or capitalist, but what finally determines society's atti-tude is what the man in question has made of himself and his life, what stand he takes. From him who had more, more is expected.

The question of the landlords' children is a complex one, however. Many brilliant and dedicated leaders of the Chinese Communist Party and the Revolution are sons and daughters of landlords, but much depends on the particular area and place in which they are. Here in Upper Felicity and environs, the younger sons and daughters of landlords who were too young to leave home and go as teachers or cadres before or immediately after liberation (a time of great mobility of the population) certainly found themselves socially disadvantaged. These youngsters usually live with their parents, and this alone sets them apart. When working in the fields you can see no difference between them and the other young people they are with. They chat, joke, laugh with everyone normally, but their friends naturally do not like to visit them at home. It is difficult for them to get married. The girls, who are usu-ally better read than the average girl and have mastered more housewifely skills, find it easier, because they go off to their husbands' homes. But the young men will bring their wives to households that are to some extent taboo. Girls of the poor and lower-middle peasantry and even rich peasant families do not relish that. It is a nagging problem that only time and socialist education will solve.

Bringing Up the Children 🐝

When not studying, Lao Man's oldest son takes part in farmwork as a full ten-work-point adult. He got his name, Ching Chun (Celebrate Spring), because Lao Man and Ta Sao lost their firstborn and were overjoyed when he was born.

Usually, however, Ta Sao calls him Nao Dan. This strange name, meaning Addled Egg, was given him because of the death of the eldest son. It is a hangover from the old superstition that such a disparaging nickname will "fool the Fates," and save his life. I don't really think Ta Sao believed this. She used the name much as people in the West sometimes say, "Touch wood." But I do know that she spoiled Nao Dan when he was young. And she knew this too. Now in her maturer age and wisdom as a mother of four children, she was making up for this with greater strictness to the youngsters. There was no spoiling of them. The older girl, Ta Hsiang, is a model young housewife at fourteen. She can spin and weave and knit, cook and sew, look after the poultry and the house. She goes to school and can read and write and do sums. She has a little snub nose and a wide mouth, a well-shaped head, and a pomegranate complexion, and is boundlessly cheerful. Like her mother, she was always around when we needed help with the fire or a bucket of water. Like her mother, she ruled the two younger children with a firm hand and a pair of lungs that could summon them in a moment from the farthest confines of the hamlet.

One day while she was busy spinning in the courtyard, Lao Man stood with us at the cottage door. We sincerely praised her industry both in the house and at school. With the parental disparagement he thought proper, Lao Man said: "She's plain-looking. She needs an education."

Au Chiu is Ta Hsiang's small male counterpart. When he is not lost in his games or asleep, he is ready to try his hand at every sort of farmwork. He is seven, stocky and tough. He works hard at his studies, doing his sums, $2 \times 2 = 4$, $5 - 3 = 2$, in the dust of the courtyard, on the doorposts, and on lovely pieces of drawing paper which he slyly appropriated from the pile in my room until I found him out.

He takes his studies seriously. After the first week he came home reciting the new quotations from Chairman Mao that he had learned at school that day: "The theoretical basis guiding our thinking is Marxism-Leninism." "Be resolute, fear no sacrifice, and surmount every difficulty to win victory."

Until he went to school his inseparable companion was Hsiao Ching. At five, she is too young as yet to know what sort of a person she will turn out to be but clearly will be pretty, intelligent, and self-willed. One day I heard Ta Hsiang upbraiding her for some fault. Hsiao Ching was standing well out of arms' reach making a series of horrific and provocative faces that finally put her sister out of all patience. Of course, it ended with a couple of shrewdly administered smacks and howls from the culprit. But she was making faces again two days later.

Au Chiu and Hsiao Ching both have their farm chores to do. Au Chiu sweeps the yard and is always planting trees. Ta Sao regularly sends them both out with baskets and small sickles to gather firewood and cut pig-grass or other fodder for the pig. When there is suitable farmwork the team gives them jobs and work-points just like any other commune member. They went out gleaning after the wheat harvest and got paid by the weight of ears they brought in. They didn't really make a big contribution to the work, but it was excellent training for their future life as commune members. Au Chiu earned two and a half work-points in one day.

Ta Sao is determined that her boys will be good workers and heads of families and that her girls will be assets to any home they may enter on marriage. She uses her tongue mostly to educate them, holding her palms in reserve. Her language is often surprisingly strong, "cussing," as Mark Twain would call it. On occasion, when Au Chiu is found hitting a neighbor's boy or raiding the larder, she gives him a few hearty smacks. This, of course, would cause very adverse comment in town. There parents are constantly admonished: "You mustn't beat children!" But in the countryside this new way of bringing up children is not so strictly or universally enforced. Of course, public opinion would no longer stand for the sort of beating that used to be normal in the old days. But nobody, except some of the town cadres coming to work for a spell in the village, remarked on Ta Sao's smacks. In the winter, when Au Chiu wore his thickly padded clothes, smacks or whippings had little effect other than to hurt his dignity. And he had such an ebullient nature that in summer ten minutes after getting a thwacking on his bare behind he would again be his usual cheerful self.

Our Old, Sick, and Disabled Team 🌿

On arriving in Upper Felicity, all of us cadres who were old, sick, or disabled asked the Third Brigade to arrange for us to do some productive manual labor according to our capacities. The brigade leaders willingly agreed. Usually they sent some veteran along with us when we went to work. Sometimes when we were assigned jobs that needed real muscle they would send a youngster to help us. This was so on our first job: planting trees along the roads and around the ponds and in the tree nursery west of the hamlet.

As I have said, once an ordinary road has been made and surfaced by the state, the communes along it take over its upkeep. The communes, of course, make and maintain lateral roads and lanes as needed for their own use over their own land. These roads were simple affairs: just bare stretches of leveled loess ditched on both sides. Our job was to care for all stretches of main and lateral roads running through our land. These were already bordered on both sides by a row of poplars about five seasons old. Now we added another pair of rows of willows inside these to make four rows, with trees spaced about a meter and a half apart. In some cases we planted poplar saplings a year or two old or willow slips about a meter high. Poplars are hardy and willow slips will take easily in good soil. Besides digging holes for the saplings and earthing them in, we also repaired the ditches and filled in deep ruts or potholes and pruned the older trees. When we had finished with our roads we turned to the ponds and any empty spaces left around the hamlet. We dug in slips of willow around the ponds where they could get plenty of water.

After the Spring Festival we went collecting the nuts of the *lien* trees and the pods of the locust trees. We knocked them down with long poles. Later we dug up and broke the clods on the empty plots of the nurseries, leveled them, and raised embankments round them for irrigation. Then we planted them thickly with seeds or slips and flooded them. In addition to poplars, locusts, and willows we planted date, tung oil, *chung,* and *lien* trees, and later watered them all.

Practically all of our hundreds of new trees grew up. They are all hardy, swift-growing types. Poplar slips planted in March had taken root by mid-April and were putting out leaves and branches. We were very proud of this effort till we went on a trip to visit communes to the north of Felicity. It was then that we realized why our hamlet was considered "a bit below average." Here we saw the results of ten or more years of systematic tree planting. Looking north or east from Upper Felicity you could see a flat horizon but thinly lined with trees. In the districts not fifty li away to the north and south too there was not a single flat horizon. On every side the skyline was serrated with lines of trees sometimes six rows deep or great groves and stands of thick-trunked trees. And the crops seemed rich in proportion. This was an object lesson in the significance of the work we were doing for our commune. Improvement of the soil of Felicity was an essential part of the operation to increase yields, and one way to do this was to plant trees, to get more organic compost from leaves, to loam up the sticky loess, and to form windbreaks to prevent topsoil erosion. In addition to this the trees would provide fruit, shade, and timber for house-building, furniture, and firewood—a constant problem in our area where war, poverty, and general governmental mismanagement under the feudal regimes of the past had denuded the land of its natural covering of green.

The poplars, dates, and locusts are most highly prized locally. Poplars grow fast. Thickly planted, they make good windbreaks and shade trees along the roads. Their trunks are used for building and their twigs for firewood and for wattle roofing. It is a pleasure to walk along a fine poplar avenue.

The dates ripen in August and are one of the few fruits that grow well in Felicity's poor soil. Every farmer tries to cultivate a big shade- and fruit-giving date in his courtyard.

The locust tree is prized for its good, strong building timber. It is also used for furniture-making. After the plum, it is the first of the trees to blossom in spring. It is a gay time in early May when the rich clusters of white blossoms come out, and the pruning knives go into action. The *lien* tree, with its tall, smooth, straight trunk, is also used for building and furniture.

The willows make a lovely frame for the ponds and provide material for basket-making. They grow fast and so do the *chung* trees, which are not as highly regarded as the other locally grown trees, but have the advantage in swift growth. The nuts of the tung tree give a valuable commercial oil when crushed. Its timber is also good for building.

We also planted mulberry trees. If these take well the brigade will think about setting up silkworm cultivation as a regular sideline.

Work was a test for us cadres. I believe that all of us came down to the village determined to do some work, but some were just as determined not to do more than they could. First reactions came when Lin, in a burst of misplaced zeal, gave us a platitudinous pep talk with pointed emphasis on carrying out the policy of the Party, serving the people, learning from the poor and lower-middle peasants, and so on and on. This put our backs up, but I took it as I take all such exhortations to do good. I objected to Lin's tone, but I fully concurred with what he said. The next day I labored for two hours solid, dragging myself home to bed. Next day I ached all over, had frantic fantasies that I was getting ill, and failed to show up for more work. The day after I turned out again and, having decided that an hour and a half was quite enough for me, did this stint and simply puttered around till Lin gave the knocking-off signal. Lin himself worked steadily, doing his best to set a good example, but we felt he was showing off self-consciously. Old Ling, the artist, buried himself in the job. Tan coddled himself shamelessly and his wife covered up for him by showing enormous commiseration. The Yuans were competent and showed off just as shamelessly. Old Tang showed his usual incompetence with his hands. The Tsangs were their usual sincere selves. They toiled away until we all insisted that Mrs. Tsang simply stop working and go off home.

It was clearly a mistake to have us working as a separate team. We all sensed this and at our study session next day unanimously voiced the wish to integrate more with the peasants by working with them. Lin was instructed to take this up with the brigade leaders. They agreed, and from then on we worked mainly with the teams in which we lived. The peasants showed great consideration for us. No one fed us platitudes. They prevented us from overworking, while we on our part felt eager to work as best and as much as we could. From then on work became a happier and richer part of our lives in the village.

One of Lin's main tasks was building and maintaining good, comradely relations within our team and between it and the peasants. He succeeded, but not without difficulty. One thing that helped was that the peasants recognized the old farmer in him in spite of his city ways.

Not long after we arrived, I am ashamed to say, the OSD Team was rent by internecine strife. One wife accused another of depositing unnamable objects in the latrine to the dismay of the local housewives and the horror of the night-soil collector (a man). There was attack and counterattack. Both protagonists came to Lin with their conflicting complaints. The case threatened to draw in the farmers' wives. There were tears and recriminations. Lin, pulled in opposite directions, enlisted the aid of the most reliable people on the spot, the Tsangs, whose integrity and impartiality were universally acknowledged. They investigated, the truth was established, and the aggressor and talebearer put in her place. The real and unwitting culprit was admonished to be more careful. Peace in the team was restored.

Sometimes I asked myself if we were really getting remolded. Tempers and nerves had certainly relaxed here in the village after the alarums and often tense struggles during the Cultural Revolution in the city. We were all far healthier than we had been and we gained a new understanding and respect for the peasants, but had our way of life and outlook really been remolded? I think to some extent, yes. One would have to be blind indeed and thick-skinned in the extreme not to be benefited by the peasants' friendship and example.

One day in the summer several of us went out to prune a cotton field with Lao Man. He paused on the edge of the field to consider the situation. Without waiting, as know-it-all as ever, Old Tang plunged in and begun to "prune." Lao Man watched him in some surprise for a moment. Then, seeing how the plants were being mangled, he said good-naturedly: "Hold on a moment, Comrade Tang! See, this is the way you must do it."

Tang was editor of an important magazine, a scholar, a traveled intellectual. Lao Man could not read, was a small work-group leader. Tang straightened up, taken aback. It was clear that he was thinking: "I must learn from the poor and lower-middle peasants." He looked on silently as Lao Man showed him how to prune. Without a word he went down on his haunches again and began to prune, properly this time.

Would he remember this lesson when he went back to his editing? I think he would—for some time at least.

Spinning, Weaving, Making Clothes

*W*hen the cotton crop is picked in late autumn, each commune household gets a share of cotton from its team. In 1970 this was something over four hundred grams per person. This they spin into thread, bleach, dye, and weave into cloth, which is enough for most of their needs. All of this is done in the home, except for the ginning, which is done in the brigade's millhouse on the electrical ginning machine. This is a tough old hand-me-down, one of those discarded from the county textile mill when it was converted into a large, up-to-date plant with modern machines and sold its old machines for a small price to the local communes.

The farm wives make black homespun for their men and themselves for winter wear and white for the summer, and colored plain, striped, or checked cloth for the children and young women. When the dyeing and weaving are going on there is much talk of colors and patterns. In the spring the fashion was all pin stripes. In the autumn it was all checks. Older men and women wear sober colors outside, but the housewives let themselves go on linings even for the old men. A staid black jacket will sometimes sport a bright emerald-green lining. After the suits and jackets are made, the scraps and any old rags are washed clean and used to make cloth soles for shoes. The uppers are of tough black homespun. The soles are made by soaking the scraps of cloth with wheat paste and then spreading them flat in a double layer on a board to dry in the sun. When dry, they are glued together and are as hard as cardboard. Five or six layers of these are then put one on top of the other and cut to the shape of the sole. Their edges are bound with white tape and they are sewn together with strong hemp thread to form a sole about half a centi-

meter or more thick. Even with heavy country wear, such a sole will last several months. Making cloth shoes is a constant chore of the housewives. They go at it leisurely while having a chat, attending a meeting or lecture, or just sunning themselves beside their cottage doors.

Ta Sao was busy day and night for several weeks before the Spring Festival making cloth, suits, and new shoes for every single member of the family of six. Ta Hsiang helped her with the spinning and weaving, and Lao Man helped her with the dyeing. She used the spinning wheel I have drawn. It was rather rough but worked all right. As the other sketches show, she and the other housewives had their own simple cottage methods for combing, drawing, and blending the threads. The weaving frame was just like the heavy looms I was familiar with from Käthe Kollwitz's famous etchings of *The Weavers' Strike* in old Germany. It wove lengths of cloth about thirty inches wide. There were several of them in the

hamlet owned in common by a few families or privately owned but ungrudgingly lent out to neighbors. When the cloth was woven, Ta Sao dampened it and then "ironed" it by laying it flat section by section on the battling stone and then pounding it with the battling sticks. The stone was placed under the locust tree just outside our bedroom window. She and

Ta Hsiang would sit on opposite sides of it, each armed with these sticks like policemen's truncheons, and beat away in cheerful rhythm as their ancestral housewives must have done for centuries past and, as I learned later, housewives along the Mississippi used to do in Mark Twain's day.

Ta Sao bought commercial dyes and hemp thread from the co-op. For Ta Hsiang and the babies she sometimes bought a bit of gaily patterned cotton print. Very, very occasionally she bought a headscarf for herself or a singlet for her older boy. But with her skilled fingers she could have been completely independent of the commercial market so far as clothes and shoes were concerned.

How Lao Man Went Cooperative 🥀

While we ate together one evening with Lao Man in the cottage, we learned how his father and mother had wandered down here as famine refugees from Shansi. They had built up a farm of seven or so mu, but the soil here was so poor that at the time of liberation Lao Man had hired himself out as a laborer to the local landlord to bring in a bit of extra money. Hard as they toiled, they could never make ends meet.

At the time of land reform the family had been classified as poor peasants and had received fifteen mu of land. By then Lao Man was married. His mother had died some time before, so there were three grown-ups in the family and two babies. Their landholding had given them just about enough to live on, but very little extra. Soon after land reform they had pooled their land with that of his uncle and his wife, both able-bodied workers, and in good times had cropped over two hundred jin a mu. With four adult workers that gave them a respectable income of over four hundred jin per head. But with the coming of more children this dropped even in good times to something around three hundred jin per head. They found that after an initial spurt following the land reform it was not possible to go on raising yields in pace with the increasing number of mouths to feed. Just about this time, seeking a way ahead and following the Party's advice, they formed a mutual-aid team with nineteen other families. This lasted until 1954. Soon after this Lao Man's father died and this increased their difficulties. In the spring of the next year they joined the advanced co-op that had been formed in the village on the basis of an existing elementary co-op. Their mutual-aid team thus skipped the stage of the elementary co-op and became part of the Third Production Team of the advanced co-op.

In 1959 the advanced co-op of Upper Felicity joined up with many surrounding co-ops to form the big Great Felicity People's Commune of twenty-eight thousand members. Lao Man's co-op became the Third Production Team of the commune's Third Production Brigade. The Mans thus became part of a socioeconomic unit of no inconsiderable size. It was not unusual for up to eight thousand people to attend a big general meeting of commune members.

We soon found that Lao Man was strong on facts but weak on analysis. When it came to action he was right there up in front; in a discussion he would usually sit back and offer his opinion only when called on. The evening he told us about the formation of the commune he was relaxing after a hard day's work. He looked bulky and warm in his black home-spun, smiling contentedly as he savored his pipe, with his clean-shaven head glistening in the light of our hurricane lamp. But when I asked him a question that had been on my mind for some time, he just looked at the ceiling for a long time as if seeking the answer there in the shadows.

He had his little red-covered book of Chairman Mao quotations in his breast pocket so that the top edge of it showed like a red flag on his breast. This was in the nature of a badge —he could not read but always carried it there. He would take it out at meetings like the rest when slogans were shouted and wave it in his right hand like a small flag. He knew a

number of quotations by heart but despaired of being a theo-
retician. My question was this: "You say that compared to
other farms, Upper Felicity is a bit below middling, economically speaking. But you have had a commune for the past ten
years and I can see that your brigade works hard—why haven't
you done better? And what do you plan to do about it?"

This really was the sixty-four-dollar question, and Lao Man
looked stumped.

Fortunately he had a bright young commune member next
to him who was quite ready to take over the story. Hsiao Ren
lived just down the lane and had been sent by the Third Brigade to work in the commune's tractor repair workshop. From
here he had been sent out on various outside jobs to county
factories and other communes and as a result had a much
broader outlook on things than most in the hamlet. He had
picked up the Peking common speech from northern colleagues in the workshop and many workers' ways also. He
smoked a short-stemmed pipe and lit it with a cigarette lighter.
He wore overalls and a cadres' uniform jacket of blue instead
of the farmers' black homespun. He rode a bicycle and kept
the cold out with a thick knitted scarf wound round his neck
in city style.

Now he spoke with the proletarian's firm control of logic.
"The commune gives you the conditions for solving problems
that couldn't be solved in the co-ops, but the members and
their leadership have to know how to use those conditions.
Our brigade members worked hard, but they didn't always
work hard in the right way. After they joined the commune
they joined in capital construction that was really basic to
progress here. They helped build three big reservoirs and improve the channel of the Wei River. That lessened the menace of big floods in Upper Felicity. Without that work we
couldn't have got ahead at all. But that was only the basis of
progress. Many other things have to be done. We have to dig
enough deep wells to remove the menace of drought and raise
yields. We have to dig channels and ditches to drain off local
floodwaters; plant trees to make windbreaks and level and
improve the soil; open up more land on the salt flats, and a

lot else. Much of that was started and some of it done, but not enough by any means. That was the trouble. Members worked enthusiastically on the collective fields, but they did not see or plan far enough ahead. They had their eyes too much on the present and there was too much self-interest in their hearts."

This seemed to me a contradiction. "How could they have too much self-interest when they worked the collective fields hard?"

"They planted crops that would give a quick cash return. This ate up the soil so that it got worse instead of better. That was shortsighted. They didn't think of continuing to invest more means and labor power in long-term, radical measures to improve the soil and so increase overall yields. They didn't fall completely for Liu Shao-chi's ideas about expanding individual plots, but they dug the first deep well near the home vegetable plots and put in most of the best natural fertilizer here. They got more vegetables for their tables, but when those were eaten—what then? They increased production, but not as fundamentally and as much as if they had fully exploited the advantages of cooperation. Then you must remember that 1959 to 1961 were the three years of natural calamities. Those difficulties set us back. We also did not use our manpower properly. This led to waste of effort and grumbling in the teams. Then came Liu Shao-chi's *San Zi Yi Bao*. Among other things he advocated an increase in the size of plots for private use and bigger and more free markets and the fixing of output quotas on the basis of individual households rather than on the teams. We did not fall for that line.

"It is a good thing that the leadership here was staunch in following the socialist road. We did make some mistakes but in general we stood firm, so the effects here were not as bad as in some other places. Still, the Liu line had some bad effect by fostering the selfish tendencies I spoke of. It is these things that held us back and that's why we are 'below average.'"

"How about now?" I asked.

The young worker thought for a moment and then summed

up: "I think we are getting rid of all those wrong ideas and ways of doing things. Since the Cultural Revolution began we understand better that all along we have been in the midst of a struggle between two ways of doing things, the revolutionary way and the revisionist way, the socialist way and the capitalist way. So now we are putting more efforts into basic construction. We are digging more deep wells and doing other work so that now we really don't fear either drought or flood. You'll see that we are deep-digging our fields, planting more trees, and much else. Later we will tackle our alkaline land and reclaim that. That will give a big boost to output. But at the same time we don't neglect the members' everyday welfare. Our advance is better balanced now. I think most of us want to take the socialist road, and not only that, we are firmly on that road now."

Lao Man agreed with this verdict. Some time later we returned to this discussion. By then I knew more about the hamlet and could understand better what the young worker said and did not say. Upper Felicity was getting rid of those wrong ideas, but it had not yet done so completely, and so the peasants as a whole were not putting all they had into the job. This was a problem that would not be solved overnight. That is what Mao Tse-tung meant when he exhorted: "Put proletarian politics first" or, in other words, put socialist ways of thinking and doing in command of everything you do.

Upper Felicity Crops and Animals

Upper Felicity Third Brigade, or, as they usually call it in the hamlets, the "Big Brigade," to distinguish it from its three production teams, has 480 men, women, and children and sixteen hundred mu of land. Not all of this is usable even now. There is a large stretch to the southeast bordering on the alkaline flat. Here the salts form a white crust on the surface of the earth and only coarse grasses and weeds can grow, sometimes not even these.

The Big Brigade has seventy-five cadres. None of them are full-time officeworkers; all do farmwork. With its three teams it has one horsecart with pneumatic tires, several ordinary carts, half a dozen horses, more mules and donkeys, and two score oxen. It has a milling machine, a ginning machine, and an oil press, all run by electricity. Its four deep wells all have electrically operated pumps. It shares a fifth electric pump and well with the commune's Second Brigade. Its members also raise sheep, goats, pigs, and chickens. Nearly every household has a half-dozen chickens or so. Most have at least one pig. Some have a few goats and sheep. Most of the eggs are sold to the state through the marketing co-op. One lonely duck had the run of the big pond. This was the sole survivor of a large flock. The pond ran dry a few years ago before they had the deep wells. The fish in them all died and the ducks had no swimming pool. Now that the cadres have the deep wells, they are able to keep the pond full all the year round and are planning to get fresh fry to restock it.

Their main crops are winter wheat (harvested in early summer) followed with maize, kaoliang, barley, and black beans. They pay the agricultural tax in kind with these crops. They also raise cotton (a short staple variety) and red flower as subsidiary crops either wholly or partly for their own use or for sale to the state. In June the girls come in with baskets full of brilliant red and orange petals that are laid out in thick carpets to dry on the threshing floors. Out of the petals an herb medicine is prepared that is used by traditional doctors to treat various "women's troubles." The best red flower comes from Tibet, but the Upper Felicity variety is also good and fetches four yuan a jin. The red flower fruit gives a fine oil and the stem a kind of hemp. A small amount of tung oil is also produced.

The vegetables and fruit, mainly dates, that they produce are almost exclusively for their own use. Their cabbages, the long, sweet North China variety, are better than those grown

around Peking. The round European sort that they also grow later in the year is good too but has a slightly bitter taste. What food they do not raise themselves can be supplemented by purchases from peddlers sent out by other communes or brigades of their own commune, or from the co-op shop, which gets its supplies under the national distribution system.

Except for spinning and weaving, their cottage industries do not play a major role in the brigade's commercial economy, but do play a big part in making their own household self-sufficient. They make their own brooms, straw mats, and baskets of straw or willow twigs. What they do not need for themselves they sell to the marketing co-op or at the fair. Kaoliang stalks are used largely for firing and making screens and mats. There is still a shortage of wood, so not much carpentering is done. The brigade has its own smithy and can turn out hinges, nails, staples, horseshoes, and various home tools like pokers, tongs, and simple farm implements.

Upper Felicity Brigade can feed, clothe, and house itself and make all its own simple tools. It earns enough more to maintain a "barefoot" doctor (paramedic) and veterinary paramedic, send all its children to school, and have regular film shows and other entertainments. It has its mechanized mill and ginning machine and cadres who can set up electric power lines, do cement construction, run a tractor, and maintain machines. It has a militia defense force, and it is creating cadres of competent, educated officials and other experts. Increased yields through mechanization and electrification and chemicalization with proper attention to environment and ecology will put it on top of its problems. It is raising itself out of the past and building its socialist way of life.

Deep-Digging

*A*s part of their plan to double grain yields in the next couple of years the Upper Felicity peasants in 1970 were beginning to *fan ti*—turn over their soil to a depth of two feet. This is a new method of raising yields employed with success in the pacesetting Tachai Brigade in northern Shansi, which has raised yields from seventy-five pounds of grain per acre before liberation to eight hundred pounds per acre now.

The attention of farmers throughout China was attracted to Tachai when Chairman Mao, after a study of this brigade, exhorted all farms to "Learn from Tachai!" Every day for a month in January and February, before and after the Spring Festival, the teams went out with red flags flying and armed with three-pronged mattocks and spades. It was hard work and the men came back covered with sweat despite the cold. First went a line of the strongest men and women. Wielding their mattocks with mighty swishes, they dug a foot deep into the loess, leaving broad swatches of broken topsoil behind them. Next came a line of older men, who piled the big clods in parallel ridges. Girls or women with spades then shoveled the loose earth out of the trenches so formed and piled it on top of the ridges of clods. Another line of strong mattock-wielders then dug down another foot into the cleared trenches and the spade team shoveled all the loose earth into the next trench, first shoveling in the clod walls and then putting the earth from the bottom of the second trench into the top of the first trench, and then from the third into the second, and so on. In this way a whole field was turned to a depth of two feet. Since there was little rain or snow that winter, water was then run into the field from a deep mechanized well. This deep-digging, with a top dressing of manure, gave the new crops a flying start.

I went out once or twice with our Third Team but was no good with the heavy mattock. I contented myself with making sod walls or shoveling. Each small group of mattock-wielders and shovelers had a red flag. As we worked we stuck our red banners into the ground to show how far we had advanced. When the First and Second teams also came out to deep-dig, the dark figures of the men, the bright jackets of the women and their headscarves, and the lines of red banners streaming in the wind made a brave show. We all felt that Upper Felicity was really getting down to it. By the end of January the great plain around us was dotted with field teams turning up the soil.

At the same time, a big effort went into planting trees. Our OSD Team was strongly reinforced and more and more lines of trees appeared along the roads and lanes, along the banks of the canals and ditches and in marshy hollows, around the ponds and houses and even in the latrines, where they gave shade in summer or a handy hold to those who needed it.

Work was also going ahead on the thirty thousand mu of saline soil to the south. Two feet down is good soil. You can raise a few crops if you turn this deep soil onto the top but the salt soon oozes up again and the crops die. There is therefore no quick solution to utilizing these thirty thousand mu. The only permanent solution, it seems, is to dig a system of drainage, then bring plenty of water in and leach out the salt, plant trees and grass and green manure to enrich the soil cheaply, and then add on chemical fertilizer suited to the crop you want to raise. This is a time- and manpower-consuming task that the commune has not yet tackled in real earnest. But a considerable amount of work has gone into the preliminaries. Several major canals have been dug across the area. Double lines of trees criss-cross it in several directions and all along the roads that run over it. Several youth teams from various brigades are reclaiming small areas of it to get experience and test out theories in practice. They have all learned from the bitter experience of a group of cadres from a city institution. These had brought down tractors, deep-plowed, poured in fertilizer, and reaped two good crops at an uneconomic rate before the third crop failed due to a recurrence of salination.

Greetings and a Watch

*L*ao Chen! Where are you going?"
"Lao Chen! Have you eaten?"
"Lao Chen! So you're fetching water?"

Thus the peasants greet you. These are greetings, not really serious questions or statements of fact. They can be answered with the equally traditional, "Yes. I've eaten!" or simply, "Aye, aye!" Or, if you like, you can ask the question or make the appropriate comment first. They do not have the modern Peking custom of saying, "*Tsao!*" (early, meaning "good morning!"). When I did this the children quickly mimicked me and my even more Western, "*Ni hao ma?*" (How are you?).

The locals have a throaty, rather indistinct way of speaking. They move their lips little and seem to speak more from the backs of their throats. In the children, this gives an effect of twittering or warbling, cute to listen to even if it's hard to understand. In the grown-ups, particularly the women, it results in a peculiar, deep intonation that is sometimes rather harsh. But this is made up for by the lilting sounds they add to their speech. If you ask Ta Hsiang for something she doesn't have, she will smile and cry, "*Mei-yo la!*" The "*la*" has no literal meaning. They also pronounce many words differently, and Peking people initially have some difficulty understanding the local dialect.

It is an unusual fact that in Upper Felicity the children don't as a rule use the word "papa," and many don't say "mama." We were much puzzled by this at first till we realized that "mama" had been transformed in the liquid local dialect into *"mei."* Once we asked a little fellow whose father we knew well, "Where is your papa?" and he answered to our astonishment, "I haven't got a papa!" It was only later that we found out that they call their father *ta yeh.* The difficulty in understanding was that *mei-mei* is the Peking term for "younger sister" and *ta yeh* is the term used by a nephew in speaking to or about his father's elder brother. Here they don't say after dinner, *"Chih bao-la!"* (I've eaten enough), but *"Chih baa-la!"* or more usually, *"Her baa-la!"* (I've drunk my fill), as most days they drink millet porridge rather than eat steamed bread or rice. In fact, they don't like rice very much. When Ta Hsiang was unwell, my wife took over a bowl of rice gruel, almost a must in a southern Chinese sickroom, but Ta Hsiang only sipped a little of it out of politeness. When they do heavy work they like to eat *mantou* or *wawatou.*

After a bit I became the hamlet's walking timekeeper. I always wore my watch, and with its silvered band it was conspicuous on my wrist. The children, even the toddlers who did not know what time was, invariably greeted me with "Lao Chen! What's the time?" And soon the adults too took up this special greeting for me suitable for any time of day.

My wife and I didn't like the slightly sweet, saline water in the surface well nearest to us. We preferred the water in the well at the end of the hamlet's only lane or the lovely water from the deep mechanized well farther on, just outside the hamlet in the vegetable plot. When this well was working the water poured out of the pump sparkling, fresh and clean at all times and ice cold even on the hottest day of summer. Every day we took our carrying pole with the pail slung at the middle and walked up the lane. Sometimes only the children and grannies would be sitting in the cottage yards or by the public mortar crushing salt or corn meal; sometimes it would be between nine and ten o'clock when everyone would be eating breakfast by the cottage doors. Before we set out I would look at the time and be ready to answer the volley of greetings as we went up the lane: "Lao Chen! What's the time?"

Few of the villagers yet had wristwatches or clocks. They depended on the radio to tell them the time, or the bell that was rung to call them to work. Team leaders had watches, but most people just looked up at the sun when they wanted to know more or less what the time was—unless they saw me coming.

Before getting down to the countryside all of us cadres had been enjoined to observe a common discipline and not disclose or give any indication what our salaries or earnings were. Although our monthly earnings were modest by any Western standard, the highest, 250 yuan (around U.S. $125), were still quite considerable judged by Chinese village standards, so it was thought best to keep these facts confidential. However, quite a number of the younger peasants read English, had been to Peking during the Cultural Revolution, or had worked in other places. These could guess knowledgeably what we really earned.

"That's a nice watch," one said to me.

"Uh, uh," I replied, and thinking to forestall further explanations added, "I got it cheap. Just over a hundred yuan." This Swiss timepiece had in fact cost me 250 yuan.

The young man took my arm and scrutinized the watch face quizzically. "That's really cheap for twenty-one jewels!" he said.

We all burst out laughing.

Spring

A TIME OF GERMINATION

Spring Festival Preparations 🌸

*P*reparations for the Spring Festival began several weeks in advance. They heralded the busy days of spring. Ta Sao, like all her neighbors, was already busy in December, spinning, dyeing, and weaving cloth for new clothes for everyone in the family. By January, a month before the festival, the cloth was already taking shape as jackets and trousers. Ta Hsiang's busy fingers were knitting new socks for the children.

Soon after *Ta Han,* the time of Severe Cold (January 20), Lao Man came home one day smiling broadly and breathing bursts of steamy breath. Ching Chun followed him carrying a two-tiered iron cauldron for making steamed bread. "It will never be idle," he laughed. And it never was. If Ta Sao wasn't using it, a neighbor was. If ever a pot steamed forth joy, that pot did.

Up in the team, brigade, and commune offices the cadres were busy finalizing 1971 production plans. The teams, the basic production units, had considered the quotas assigned them and discussed whether they were feasible or not or even whether they could be increased. The decisions made by the team members had then gone up to the brigade and so on up to the commune, county, and province. When all the results had gone up to the central planning organs in Peking, the final plans and quotas would go down again to the production units for implementation. In this way the whole vast area of rural China was this spring again working to a master plan, democratically discussed and agreed on.

A Story of the Past 🦋

Sometimes of an evening a few of Lao Man's friends would join him in our cottage for a smoke and a chat. They smoked either cigarettes or their own long pipes with tiny bowls that held only enough fine-grained tobacco for a dozen puffs. I smoked my little stub pipe with coarse-cut tobacco from the south. They tried this out but didn't like it. Our chats were quite informal, but one night I asked Hsi-Kun, a grizzled old chap who was one of the leaders of the Second Team, to tell more about himself. The others fell silent, smoking, and gave him the floor.

"There were over sixty families in this hamlet before liberation, and whether they were poor or lower-middle peasants, they were all poor. Only a few families could keep their heads above water, and only the landlord and a couple of other rich peasants could sleep nights in peace. Apart from these few the whole hamlet owned only eight oxen. When flood, drought, or famine came it would send most of us fleeing with everything we could carry. Many never got back. Those were bad days. Bitter! Homes were ruined. Families broken up. Once in such a time of calamity, an old woman died and not eight men could be found to carry her coffin to the grave.

"Taxes were heavy. If you didn't pay your tax, those reactionaries would take away your windows, one by one, and sell the timber; then your door, and even the roof beams so that the roof fell down. If you borrowed grain to pay the tax, it was like hanging stones around the neck of a drowning man to save him. You had to pay back five tou for every one you borrowed.

"If you hadn't paid the tax and the authorities heard you had a little food laid by, they came and seized it. We were never able to pay the tax in full or keep up with the interest payments on our debts, and we were always being persecuted for the one thing or the other. Once my father tried to run away from it all, but they caught him before he had got very far. They brought him back, tied him up, and strung him up all night from a beam in the headquarters of the *pao chia* [headman of the village].

"One night my brother ran away with all his family. They got away all right, but we never heard of them again. They must have perished. Those of us who stayed were no better off. My father died. My mother had died when I was only a year old. My aunt looked after me, but she died of hunger when she was seventy years old. I was the only one left and we were so poor that I didn't have a coffin to bury her in. I feel very sad that I couldn't look after her better after all she did for me. I was tending cattle for the landlord when I was thirteen. At fourteen I had to look after myself. When the Japanese invaded China in 1937 I was twenty years old. There was a big flood that year and I fled to Shansi, with a lot of the other villagers. For the next seven years I worked as a laborer for one landlord after another. I worked for anyone who would give me food to eat. I didn't even ask for wages. And still I was constantly humiliated by them. They treated me like dirt, worse than their cattle. If I could get a bowl of porridge to eat twice a day I felt I was lucky. But often I wasn't able to get even this for my work. Sometimes in winter I was just thrown out of doors when there was no more work to do.

"Sometimes the reactionary government [he meant the Kuomintang government or whatever warlord happened to be ruling the area] sent people to conscript soldiers. I was caught twice by these press gangs. The first time I was just in the middle of helping a family celebrate the marriage of the young master. The press gang just came into the kitchen, tied me up, and took me away. After a few days they grew a bit careless and I managed to escape from them and get back to the village. They were too lazy to come back and recapture me.

"The second time I was coming back to the farm from the fields after working for a landlord. I didn't know that some men I saw coming up the road were a press gang and I walked right into their arms! 'You're coming with us!' they yelled. They wouldn't even let me go home to turn in my hoe. It was only after several days that I managed to escape from them. I hid myself by day and moved only at night. I felt like a hunted animal. Every time I heard a dog bark in the dark I was scared stiff: I thought, they are after me. But I finally reached my aunt's home.

"For a few days I thought everything would be all right, that they wouldn't bother to come after me. But one day I saw a troop of soldiers in their green uniforms coming to the cottage. I ran round the back of the cottage and hid in the fields. They ransacked the cottage, and since they couldn't find me they took my cousin instead. He was the main breadwinner in the family and when I returned and heard the news I didn't know what to do. My aunt and uncle could only sit and cry. We didn't know what to do. If I turned myself in they might hold the two of us and we would all be worse off than before. My cousin's wife cried all day. I was scared too because I knew how they treated deserters. They beat them insensible, then poured water on them to revive them and beat them again. And I had run away from them twice already! Still, I was a bachelor and no one depended on me, while three people, including his wife, depended on my cousin. So I gave myself up. Luckily, once they had caught me, they let my cousin go.

"This time I didn't dare run away for fear of what they might do to my cousin. I was in the army a year. I never did fight any Japanese and by then the Liberation War had started. I didn't know what it was all about at that time, but when our regiment came up against the P.L.A. our whole company went over to their side. We didn't want to fight any-

way, and why should we fight people like ourselves? That
was how I was liberated and able to get back home.

"Things soon began to change. We landless laborers all got
land in the land reform. Then the Party showed us how to
start mutual-aid teams and cooperatives . . . well, you can see
yourself how well we live now. Now we are all liberated.
Youngsters today can hardly understand what we mean when
we talk of starvation in the old times. Everyone in Upper Felicity will eat meat this Spring Festival. Everyone will have
new clothes. When I recall the old days, how can I not follow
the Party?"

He looked straight at me with his candid eyes. I studied his
sun-browned face, deep-lined with the sufferings of the past.
He ended by asking a question that was in itself its own
answer: "Who has the power now?"

Another evening we were chatting about this and that and
the conversation came around to landlords.

"What was the old chap here like?" I asked.

Hsi Man-tou, a very old man who to this day wore a grey
towel bound round his head instead of a cap, said, "Well, I
worked for him for many years. I can't say he was very bad.
He paid me my wages, although he never helped me get rich!"

"He didn't beat people himself, that's true," put in Lao
Man, "but that doesn't make him good!" He couldn't let
muddle-headed Hsi Man-tou do propaganda for the landlord,
but he didn't want him to lose face in front of strangers.

"I didn't say he was good," Hsi Man-tou said. "I worked
for many landlords and they didn't look like those fellows you
sometimes see in movies!"

The young worker from next door put a word in. "You've
got to look behind what they looked like and see what they
were really like! He's working quietly enough now, but do
you think he wouldn't like to go back to the old times if he
got the chance? Then you wouldn't have the commune and
you wouldn't be sitting so comfortably smoking your pipe with
Lao Chen!"

Man Chia-chen, another old veteran with a towel turban
and a round, deeply lined face (he was just over fifty but

looked ten years older), said, "The landlords, the *pao chia* head, and the soldiers ran things. They all went together." He pointed his pipe stem at Hsi. "You had a bit of land, so they didn't press you so hard. But I had nothing but my hands and the old shack I lived in. I worked for Man Wen-hua [the landlord]. He paid me wages like everyone else, but they were never enough. I never had enough to pay the tax or even enough to eat. When those scoundrels came for the tax they were just like the landlord's running dogs in *The White-haired Girl.** They'd say, 'Have you anything to pay with? No? Then you come with us.' *Ta ma ti!* And you'd have to go and clean their barracks for them! What did we eat at the Spring Festival? Just a bit of porridge. And we'd be so scared that we'd be found out. 'What? Eating porridge and you won't pay the tax!' *Ta ma ti!* And they'd take the porridge out of your mouth! When you grew old then, what could you do? Hunt for dung on the roads and lanes and try to sell it, or just go out to beg! When the floods came whole families went away and just disappeared. You never knew what became of them. Did Man Wen-hua ever care? Would he ever take a cent less for his wheat even though he knew you were starving?"

Hsi Man-tou was stumped for the moment, but remembering another argument he had heard, said stubbornly: "It wasn't the *rent* that held us back. It was the poor soil, the floods, and the drought."

Man Chia-chen threw his arms up in consternation. "That's just the point. As long as Landlord Man and his like ran things we could never tackle those problems. Now that we run things ourselves, there's no flood or drought. We've got our commune reservoirs and our wells. Yields are going up. In the old days things were getting so bad all round that even the landlords were getting poorer. There was less of everything. Less for them to squeeze. Now they've lost their land. But even they will be better off as the whole country gets richer."

---

* A famous opera and ballet. Persecuted by a landlord and his bullies, a peasant girl is driven into the mountains and her hair turns white.

Hsi Man-tou was reduced to silence. Man Chia-chen had got quite heated and his face shone with sweat, although the weather was cold.

The Brigade Secretary 🌿

*I*n some communes the teams still retain a great deal of autonomy, and the brigade is simply a clearinghouse and co-ordinating center. In other communes the brigades are already the basic accounting units and direct most of the activities of the teams. Upper Felicity was at a midway stage where more and more decisions were being taken at the brigade level, although the teams remained the basic accounting units.

The brigade had a collective leadership. Final decisions and routine management were handled by a relatively small group of the brigade's team revolutionary committee. This comprised the chairman, who was also the Party secretary, the three team leaders, the militia leader, and one or two veterans, all elected by the brigade's general meeting of members. They issued the announcements about who would be in charge of this or that work; when the new wells would be dug; what manpower should be allocated to rebuilding so-and-so's cottage; what acreage should be sowed to this or that crop. Some of these matters were left to the leadership group to discuss and de-cide on. If it was an important question that affected every-one in the brigade, such as a sowing plan, it was discussed by all brigade members. Sometimes the small leading group would debate a proposal put up by a rank-and-file brigade member or by a whole team. Sometimes they would take the initiative in putting forward their own proposals. When Party or government directives or instructions were sent down, they would be the first to discuss them and propagandize them in the teams so that the whole brigade could go into action like one man to execute them.

These leaders were mostly in their thirties and forties. Our Lao Man and other veteran brigade members, like all the other activists, took part in the brigade or team discussions. They were an invaluable source of farming experience that was readily used. But they seemed to me now to be not a leading force but a supplementary force of key importance. One or two could read and write, like the bookkeeper of the brigade, a fine old cadre of over fifty (the father of the young worker), but most of them were still illiterate, like our Lao Man, and so as leaders labored under a great disability. The brigade, however, made good use of their abilities as consultants or team leaders or small production group leaders of the practical work in the fields and workshops and on the threshing floors.

It was they who called the teams out to work and sang the work songs at the house-building or well-digging, who whipped up enthusiasm among the women to leave their kitchens and take to the fields when the sowing and harvesting were at their height. They could badger or cajole, reprimand or joke in the village way that their standing as "old heads" (*lao tou-tze*) gave them the right to. No decisions were made without first getting their opinions. And to really carry out decisions their willing concurrence was essential. This was another part of the collective leadership.

Yet a third part was made up of the young men and a few of the young women. These were all graduates of the commune primary and middle school, literate youngsters with a view of things less trammeled by the conservatism of the past. They were sometimes apt to urge rash, bold action that had to be restrained by maturer counsels, but their drive and enthusiasm and love of the new was also an essential part of the collective leadership. You would always find such youngsters wherever anything new was afoot, on the experimental plot or where new machines or methods were being tried out.

Once these three elements were united in backing a proposal, it would certainly carry the day against conservatism or cautious doubt and carry the middle-of-the-roaders forward. If one or the other of these elements hung back or opposed, the chairman and Party group could be fairly certain that something was wrong with what was proposed.

The Party secretary and brigade leader was a man of nearly forty, but he looked much younger. Small, wiry but not strongly built, steady but by no means pushing, he had been elected by unanimous vote of the brigade. He hadn't sought the job, we knew. It had been more or less thrust upon him.

In this way the Upper Felicity Brigade exemplified the leadership principles developed in the Cultural Revolution— that the leading group should be representative and have revolutionary authority, that it should be tripartite and be composed of the old cadres, the representatives of the rank and file, and of the militia or P.L.A. and also of the veteran old toilers, the middle-aged, and the young.

There was an easygoing streak in Upper Felicity. This I had seen in old Hsi Man-tou's attitude toward the landlords, and while that attitude was now only a remnant, at one time it had dominated thinking in the hamlet, particularly among the older heads. This was fertile ground for the revisionist thinking that during the Cultural Revolution was exposed as the "Liu Shao-chi line." As everywhere else, it had held Upper Felicity back politically, economically, and socially.

The land reform had been carried through, the landlords' and rich peasants' surplus lands had been confiscated and distributed among the landless poor and lower-middle peasants. They had been roused up to "speak out bitterness" and expose the landlords and landlord oppression in general, but this mass movement had been reined in by this streak of laissez-faire. Where did it come from? One source was feudal clan feeling. Practically the whole of Upper Felicity—80 per cent of the households, as I have said—bore the name of Man. In one way or another, they were related to each other and even to the landlord, and these family ties based on the clan had lower-middle peasants and "family ties" hadn't made any struggle. This despite the fact that more than half of these Mans were poor peasants and most of the rest were only blunted the edge of their militancy in waging the class difference to Landlord Man when he wanted to exploit his

relatives. The result was that while the land had been confiscated, the landlord families in the area managed to keep
too much of the rest of their property, such as clothes, houses,
furniture, and quite a bit of money. The result of that, in
turn, was that these reactionary, backward-looking elements
retained some economic power that they used subtly to undermine the subsequent co-op movement.

The adults of those days who had been in the van of the
land-reform movement and post-land-reform village affairs
were the "old heads" of today. At that time some of them
were inclined to look to the rich and upper-middle peasants,
as successful farmers, in getting guidance on village and farm
affairs. A drink, a feast, and some of the smooth talk at which
these people were adept soon got the inexperienced cadres
into a sticky mess that they found difficult to get out of.
Soon they were drinking and playing the finger game regularly with these people who had no understanding of, no interest or faith in, cooperation. They believed, in fact, in the
very opposite—the "every-man-for-himself," capitalist, laissez-
faire outlook, which if allowed to develop unchecked would
have led inevitably to the polarization of the peasants into rich
and poor, the dominance of the rich, and the development of
capitalism in the countryside. These people thought that if
there had to be cooperation, then it should be cooperation only
as a means of self-interest. Such "cooperation" between poor
and rich peasants was not something that you could immediately detect unless you were well acquainted with hamlet
conditions. The rich peasants lived in the midst of all the
others. They dressed the same, worked alongside them in the
fields, and sat at the doors of their cottages at mealtimes along
with all the others. Their influence was as all-pervading as it
was insidious.

It could not entirely hold back the hamlet from the forward
movement of cooperation that was sweeping the country.
It could not stop the formation of mutual-aid teams and
elementary cooperatives, but it could and did brake these
movements and give activities in them detrimental twists of
conservatism.

It was only when the hamlet was well into the co-op stage of development that this situation began to be exposed. When experienced Party cadres from the county came to check up on Upper Felicity's development, they quickly spotted this trouble and it was brought into the open. The "old heads" who had been guilty of blurring class lines and following the line of the class enemy were criticized, shown the error of their ways, and helped to make a thorough self-criticism. But still this exposure and criticism did not go deep enough. Though the new leadership avoided personal entanglements with the landlord and rich peasant elements, they were not yet sufficiently awake to the danger of ideological entanglement.

This circumstance affected the outlook of the present Party secretary and chairman of Upper Felicity's Big Production Brigade. One day he told me about it. Other brigade members were present, but he was telling them nothing new. They had all gone over the matter in much greater detail when summing up the work of the brigade recently and doing self-criticism in the socialist education movement, with particular reference to the "struggle between the two classes, the two roads and the two lines," between the proletariat and the bourgeoisie, between the socialist road and the capitalist road and the revolutionary line and the reactionary line.

"I should have known better and been more vigilant," he admitted. "After all, I am a poor peasant and suffered like all the rest in the old society. Our family was forced to flee regularly either to Shansi or Kiangsu when there was drought or flood. The first time I can remember fleeing was in 1938 when I was seven years old. That time my father carried me in a basket at one end of his carrying pole when I got too tired to walk. We went all the way to Hsuchow [in Shantung], working when we could and begging when we had to. Five years later we fled again. Our cottage was under water when we left. This time we went to Shansi and I remember cutting firewood on the mountainsides to sell for a living. My father was a fine farmworker but even with my help we couldn't make enough to live on.

"This was the time of the Japanese War. Traveling was

dangerous. But we were desperate. We tried to make it to the village where my cousin lived. Neither the Eighth Route Army [the Communist-led forces] nor the Japanese controlled this district entirely. We didn't know it then, but this was just the time the Japanese were trying to conquer the district and, with their 'kill all, burn all, loot all' policy, wipe out the guerrillas. In the confusion we got separated from my father, and my mother and I were rounded up by the Japanese. They didn't beat me like they beat up or killed older boys, but they made us watch while they burned down a village and shot the men they caught. It was only after we got home that we were reunited with my father. Luckily he too had escaped and managed to reach home.

"When we came back here I worked as a shepherd for a landlord, but three years later another flood came and off we went again. Neither the landlords nor the rich peasants we had worked for did a thing to help us in that calamity.

"Then came the Liberation and land reform. We got land and I married and children were born. At last we could settle down and life grew better. Unfortunately my father died before he had time to enjoy the new life. In 1958, the first communes were formed. Soon our co-op too joined with others to form the Great Felicity People's Commune. Upper Felicity became the Third Production Brigade of the commune. A lot of basic construction was going on at that time, and I and many others went from here to help build a big reservoir. When that was finished in 1959, I joined a group opening up an iron-ore mine. After that I went on to work in the agricultural bureau in the county town. It was then that I began to think of returning home.

"At that time Liu Shao-chi's line of *San Zi Yi Bao** had influenced this area. In the commune here the private plots

* Meaning "Three Freedoms and One Guarantee," signifying an increase in the area of plots for private use, encouragement of the free markets, increase in the number of small enterprises which would have the sole responsibility for their own profits and losses, and taking the individual farm households and not the production teams as the basis in fixing output quotas.

were quite large, too large. Some peasants were concentrating
on these rather than on expanding and developing the collective fields and economy. This was putting short-sighted, short-
term interests ahead of long-term interests, putting selfish
interests ahead of collective interests. But I didn't see things
in that light then. I didn't realize that it was part of the struggle between the two roads, between capitalism and socialism.
All I could think of was that if I went back to our farm I
could cultivate our private plot, even open up some extra land,
grow and sell turnips and make more money than if I worked
as a cadre in the county town. I kept pestering the leadership
to let me come back home, and at length they let me go.

"I was a Party member, but I was so badly influenced by
Liu Shao-chi's poison that when I got back home I no longer
wanted to be a cadre. I spent a lot of time cultivating our
family's private plot and opening up some wasteland that I
could use for myself. I went out to work in the collective
fields, but really it seemed as if this was my sideline and not
the other way round.

"These reactionary ideas in my head made me slide back
step by step until I was even doing things because of belief
in superstitious practices of the old society. As I said, my
father died. A sore had broken out on his body and three days
later he was dead. We were still mourning his death and had
not yet buried him* when my mother also got a sore on her

* In accordance with old custom, the corpse might lie in its coffin out
in the fields, covered with bricks and earth in a temporary interment,
until a propitious date was forecast for permanent burial. The position
of the grave would also be determined by the dictates of *feng-shui*
(wind and water divination). It is for this reason that graves were
placed so apparently haphazardly all over the fields in old China, and
created an enormous hindrance to modern methods of mechanized agriculture. Gradually the fields are being cleared of these burial mounds
as the peasants are persuaded to remove the graves of their ancestors.
This is done at public expense and, of course, with the complete voluntary agreement of those concerned. The dead are now cremated where
facilities exist or they are buried in sequestered spots. If they are buried
in places likely to be used for farming, they are buried deep, so that
the graves will not be disturbed.

body. Actually, as we found out later, my father had died of cancer and my mother's sore had nothing to do with this, but under the influence of the old people's gossip I got to believe that it was ill luck dogging us and that the only way to change it was to change the *feng-shui* of the cottage.

"I had a bit of ready money in my pocket by that time. I had already made money from my private plot and had got severance pay from my job in the county town. So I pulled down the old cottage and rebuilt it better than it was before, on higher ground, and changed its outlook from east to south.

"All this time I thought I was not doing so badly. I even became a cadre again. There was a movement to think over the bitter days of the past and serve the people, and although the meetings we held then didn't wake me up thoroughly, they woke me up enough to see that by neglecting everything but my own private interests I was far from being a good Party member. Under that influence I agreed to become a cadre again. You see I was literate and knew a bit about organizing, and our hamlet needed as many cadres as it could get. The old heads were finding it difficult to keep pace with new things. Then a few years ago the socialist education movement started."

The Party secretary then told us about the incidents of this movement in Upper Felicity. At the start things went normally enough. He said: "I was criticized for believing in superstitious practices. All that business of changing the house site was exposed. At first, although I knew I had been in error, I found it hard to take the criticism. But bit by bit I came to realize how wrong I really was. We Communists must be scientifically minded. We must look on sickness and death as natural phenomena. Unless we rid ourselves of superstition, our minds are shackled. Superstition means that instead of depending on our own efforts, we stupidly depend on outside forces, on ghosts, to do things for us. I realized what a bad ideological example I had set the people.

"Then the brigade members went on to criticize my new house and the amount of money I had spent on it—or, as they said, 'wasted' on it. Well, one could argue about that. But perhaps they were right. But then under the urging of a work team sent down from a higher party level, the question of my economic cleanness was raised and people began to question whether all the money I had spent was honestly come by. I felt that this was really going too far. [It was. It was a result of the Liu Shao-chi line in the county leadership.] I had perhaps not been public-spirited and I had not been a good Party member, I had not always put the public good before my own interests; that I realized, but I had done nothing illegal in making that money I used for my house. I got angry and I did not want to work as a cadre any more. I handed in my resignation and walked off to the county town. The brigade members and the Mao Tse-tung Thought Propaganda Team of Poor Peasants in our commune phoned me, but I would not answer."

By this time the Cultural Revolution phase of the socialist education movement had begun. Liu Shao-chi's Draft Ten Points had come under fire; the 23-Article Document prepared by Mao Tse-tung had been issued and clarified matters. It made it clear that fair criticism was in order, but the unfair denigration of a poor-peasant cadre was not to be tolerated. (See page 354.)

Upper Felicity rallied round its Party members, who might have made some mistakes but were essentially loyal to the Party policy of cooperation and wanted to serve the people. The Party secretary said: "Wen-yuen, our militia leader and my brother too, came to find me in the county town. They told me that the brigade members had reelected me brigade chairman and the comrades still wanted me to be Party secretary. This moved me much. As they talked I realized that what they had said about my mistakes was for my own good and not out of enmity . . . that only the class enemy, the landlord and rich peasants and some rascals, hated me. I realized better my duty as a Communist: I must go on making revolution all my life and must not be afraid of making myself a target of the Revolution. Again I remembered the past. I came back to the hamlet. I looked at the eight rooms I had for myself and my five children to live in, and I thought again of all my old mother had suffered in the old society just to bring us two boys up, just to keep us alive. All this new happiness came to us because the Party had led us to liberation and cooperation. Even then Mother did not want me to be a cadre. "Why do you have to take a job that only brings you criticism?" she asked me. She cried. But I reminded her too of the old life and the new, and I won her round. I told the masses at a meeting that from then on I would work hard, serve the people, and make revolution till the end of my days.

"During the Cultural Revolution we discussed all these matters, particularly Liu Shao-chi's bad activities, and we came to understand many things that we had not understood in the past. We realized that although we had in general gone in the right direction, we had not followed a firm revolutionary line at the time of the land reform and for all the years after. So we reviewed everything from the revolutionary point of view of the poor and lower-middle peasants and working-class policy. We rejected Liu Shao-chi's teaching that the class struggle had died out after the land reform. We saw that though the landlords and rich peasants had been overthrown these people and the capitalists still exerted a bad influence on us. That is why it was decided by the members to confiscate all the things we should have confiscated before from the landlords and clean up our way of thinking. This time we did it thoroughly. We confiscated their surplus furniture and valuables but left them all the essentials like tools, cooking things, and clothes. But we took away their beds. People said that before liberation the poor peasants didn't have beds, so the landlords for a time should also learn what it was to live that way. There was no Party directive about that. That was our own idea.

"We learned more about these people. We criticized one poor peasant. This young chap was very friendly with a landlord's son with whom he used to go to school, and he tried to defend this pal in every way although he in turn always backed up his landlord father. It was in trying to reeducate these two that we found out that they and another man, a former *pao chia* village head, were members of a reactionary underground group called the Central China Party. It was a revelation to everybody that we had three such people here in our own Big Brigade. They had a slogan: 'When the gentlemen want to take revenge, ten years is not too long to wait!' They had sworn to settle accounts with me personally.

"We cadres also had to 'make ourselves the target of revolution.' We criticized ourselves. But it was only when the masses began to criticize us that we really had our eyes opened to ourselves and understood how and why we had made mistakes in the past and fallen for Liu Shao-chi's wrong teachings."

Learning from the experience of the old leadership group and their own experience too, as seen under the scrutiny of the Cultural Revolution, the present leading cadres of the revolutionary committees of the three teams and the brigade are a young, energetic, and devoted group. They enjoy the trust of the brigade members because they have been sifted and tested. In another two or three years they will be up for election again. I don't think there will be many rejects. They are all well-known by their brigade colleagues, as they live and work with them every day, and the results of their leadership are there for all to see.

The top commune cadres, the commune revolutionary committee members, are also the local government and are all elected. Some are appointed by the county administration, though confirmed in their positions by the vote of the masses. The Party therefore puts particular stress on urging them to go down among the masses and regularly do productive work with them in the brigades and teams. Not only does this steel them and keep them "ordinary workers," but it enables them to know their constituents and their constituents to know them. If the masses are dissatisfied with them, they are subject to recall.

Spring Festival 🕊

*F*or several weeks before the three-day Spring Festival the propaganda workers of the commune were urging us to cele-brate it in revolutionary style. All agreed that its good features should be retained, but any features linked with feudal super-stition, bad customs, and habits, such as wastefulness, drunk-enness, gambling, and laziness, must be resolutely rejected.

The day before the festival we attended a number of meet-ings held to guide our conduct. In the morning we went to see an exhibition on class struggle in the district. Ling and four other *hsia fang* cadres who were artists had worked with local propaganda cadres to arrange it. They set it up in the mansion confiscated from the biggest and worst landlord in the village. This was a group of three two-storied grey brick buildings in the very center of the commune village. They were now much dilapidated, having served a variety of func-tions under various temporary users. Most recently they had been the offices and dormitories of one of the big brigades. But they could never have been very comfortable. They were built in the traditional u-shaped arrangement with the main rooms facing south at the base of the u. All the rooms were narrow with small windows that let in little light although they were glassed. The courtyard too was narrow, and narrow steep steps led from the outside to the upper rooms.

Stout, high walls, enclosing and joining the buildings of the compound and its own well, turned it into a small fortress. It was a grim relic of feudal warlord days, days of ruthless ex-ploitation and oppression of the people, days of banditry and peasant insurrection.

The upper floors now housed the exhibition. Neatly framed with split kaoliang stalks, pictures in color showed life in the old days in Great Felicity: landlord brutality, floods, drought, refugees, press-ganging, then scenes of the Japanese War and the Liberation struggle. One large final section described the plans of the commune and celebrated the deeds of its outstanding rank-and-file members. Among these was a volunteer in the struggle to aid Korea and oppose U.S. imperialism. He was our close neighbor. Another was one of the young girls who had proved herself a real model worker in the fields.

The artists had made an attempt, not too successful, to create two tableaux of clay-modeled figures, painted and dressed in real clothes. One represented a poor peasant family fleeing from famine and the other a landlord supervising the beating of a poor peasant for nonpayment of rent or some other "crime."

A group of cadres from our nearby May Seventh Cadre School were going through the exhibition just ahead of us. They would hold a meeting after seeing it. A representative of the commune leadership told them that a poor peasant had been invited to tell them firsthand what he had suffered at the hands of the landlord and that the landlord himself—recalcitrant even to this day—would be brought to the meeting so that they could see for themselves who the oppressor was.

After seeing the exhibition we returned to our hamlet to find another meeting going on. The whole Big Brigade, men, women, and children, was gathered in the office courtyard. Standing by a table on which a portrait of Chairman Mao had been placed, one of the team leaders was giving a talk on Spring Festivals in the old days. He was followed by the Party secretary, who exhorted everyone to celebrate this Spring Festival in real revolutionary style. His main theme was that we should all reject uncompromisingly everything linked with feudal superstition. This was particularly apt, because everyone present knew how he had himself been influenced by old superstition in the matter of *feng-shui* and the location of his cottage, and how he had painfully overcome this. He ended up with a list of "don'ts": "Don't give wasteful feasts and presents. Don't drink or play cards or mah-jongg [once the most notorious gambling game in China and the ruin of many families]. Don't let off firecrackers or fireworks late at night. Don't laze around and go visiting after the third day of the

three-day holiday, but get back promptly to work. Don't visit the ancestral graves to pray and offer sacrifices even of paper tokens or incense and don't let the children kowtow to the elders."

He put particular stress on the last. He warned that parents who made their children kowtow would have to be criticized by their teams, while children who kowtowed would be criticized later at school. He also warned that the brigade's militiamen would be on patrol and would haul in anyone letting off fireworks late at night. The class enemy was not sleeping and might take advantage of the festivities to create trouble.

I wondered at first why the ban on kowtowing was so strong. This old custom had long passed away in Peking and the big cities, of course, and in all the villages I had ever been in after the advanced co-ops and communes had been formed. Children no longer knelt before grandparents and other elders and bowed till their foreheads touched the ground. Peking children and parents now felt this to be utterly outlandish and unworthy of human self-respect, but here in Upper Felicity, I was told, despite propaganda against it, there were families in which this ancient custom had been practiced only last year. The ban was made so strong this year because it was generally felt that this was completely incompatible with the new spirit after three years of the Great Proletarian Cultural Revolution that aimed to destroy the out-of-date ideas, culture, customs, and habits of the exploiting classes. The kowtow was a sign of submission. It had been exploited by the class enemy to reestablish the authority of undesirable elders over the younger generation. That is why it had to be eliminated.

As to the other prohibitions, no one was inclined to waste money on feasts or elaborate presents. I never saw a set of mah-jongg or heard of drunkenness in the hamlet. There was little lazing around after the holiday.

The admonishment against offerings at the ancestral graves was not so strictly enforced. After the festival I passed many grave mounds surmounted with little bits of white paper held down with a stone. It was clear that they had recently been visited, and this was done openly by the older people in the hamlet. Some came to borrow the white tissue paper I used to cover my drawings. The youngsters, saying nothing to hurt the feelings of their elders, only in some cases gently admonishing them to be more modern, simply let this old custom die by default.

But some days after the festival there was a short, sharp meeting held in front of the brigade office. Three young chaps and an older man had been caught in another brigade gambling for stakes with dominoes. Round their necks were hung strings of imitation paper money—gold paper folded into the form of the ancient money called "gold shoes"—and they looked thoroughly crestfallen and ashamed of themselves. A squad of commune militiamen were taking them around the commune, and their transgressions were recited in each brigade. It was a lesson they would not soon forget, and it would not be lost on other flighty spirits tempted to indulge in this ancient evil of the villages.

On the eve of the festival, every house in the hamlet was cleaned up. Many put up new portraits of Chairman Mao and new New Year pictures (nien hwa), and all pasted new red slogans on and around their doors. I was one of a group of cadres that went to all the households with menfolk in the People's Liberation Army or who had fought in the war to aid Korea repel the invading U.S. forces led by MacArthur. We brought them festival greetings and Chairman Mao badges and portraits and pasted up new red slogans on their doors: two long strips on either doorpost and one over the lintel. Some of these read: "Long live the Chinese Communist Party!" "Long live Chairman Mao!" and "Long live the People's Commune!" Some carried the current popular slogans, quotations from Chairman Mao: "Be self-reliant" and "Serve the people"; "Concern yourself with state affairs; carry the Great Proletarian Revolution through to the end!" On the two door panels we pasted larger rectangular pieces of red paper with longer quotations from Chairman Mao printed on them: "The basic task in political work is constantly to imbue the peasant masses with socialist ideology and to criticize the tendency towards capitalism." Or one short slogan in larger letters, like "Never forget the class struggle!"

I remembered how many years ago in Yenan, thirty-two years ago to be exact, and at the height of the Japanese invasion, I had gone around with a similar team to "Comfort the Families of Heroes." Yenan was then the headquarters of the Communist Party. That team had been composed of youngsters and was more elaborate. One group expressed greetings, another group sang "comfort songs," a third group vigorously swept out the cottage yards and fetched in water, while a young writer undertook to write the families' greetings to their men at the front. There was no need for such services now. The courtyards were all extremely clean, due to many years of the mass sanitation campaign, water gushed out of mechanized wells, and every cottage had literate inmates. And after a tentative rehearsal, we decided to spare the heroes' families the singing voices of our Old, Sick, and Disabled Team!

On the first day of the festival everyone in the hamlet ate *chiaotze*. Until late the previous night we had heard the tap, tap, tap of the choppers cutting up the meat and vegetables. Upper Felicity ate *chiaotze* at every festival. After the meal there was general visiting. Our cottage was rarely empty. It was open house, and the children swarmed in to see my drawings and be treated to sweets. Their elders came to offer greetings and could usually be prevailed upon to stay for a smoke and a chat.

In the afternoon a performance was put on at the big threshing floor near the tractor repair workshop. Hundreds of members came in from all over the commune. A temporary stage had been built, and the commune's concert troupe gave a performance of songs, dances, and sketches. Many of the songs were quotations from Chairman Mao's works set to music. Practically everybody blossomed out in new clothes. Some wore new things from top to toe, especially the children. Nearly everyone wore a badge with the Chairman's portrait on it and the children sported large red plastic rosettes. The little girls had rouged faces, a round smudge of cochineal on each cheek and four dots placed in a square on their foreheads. The older girls were a pretty sight in bright-colored hair ribbons. Many dropped in to see us on their way to the show. It was quite in order to offer cigarettes to the men and sweets to the women and children, but that was as far as hospitality should go. In Peking we would have served wine.

The second day of the festival was family visiting day. The married women took their children to see their maternal grandmothers. Sometimes their menfolk accompanied them. Quite a number of family parties went out from our hamlet. Often the mother sat with the wee ones in a handcart pulled by the father or the older boys. Ren Ming-fan, a pretty young mother who lived four courtyards away from us, was excited to be able to introduce her husband, a railway worker who lived in the provincial capital and had got Spring Festival leave to pay a visit home. This was a time when, as for ages past, every Chinese household tried to renew the ties of family.

Many other young men working elsewhere came home for the festival. Not a few came from hundreds of miles away. They all brought gifts for the folks at home and made the festival full of gaiety with interesting talk of other places. Most had a holiday leave of a week or a fortnight, and some who had saved up their leave were able to stay longer.

On this second day of the festival several activists were already back at work in the fields, and on the third day they were joined by more enthusiasts and the boys and girls from the school.

Only a few of the older people went to tend their ancestral graves. Though held down at first by the stones or clods of earth they placed on them, the squares of white votive paper they had put on the grave mounds were soon torn away by the wind, or fading, became an indistinguishable part of the brown-yellow earth around them.

Big Pig Goes to Market 🐖

*A*fter the Spring Festival, while Little Pig was allowed to roam at will, Big Pig found herself confined to her sty. She grunted and squealed with displeasure. But there were compensations. She was sumptuously fed and waxed fat. This went on for a month till the day came for her last journey to the supply and marketing co-op. She put up quite a fight. When Ching Chun came up to her cunningly slowly, she seemed to sense something was up, wriggled desperately out of his grip, and escaped. Loyally followed by Little Pig, she made for the tree nursery by the pond. Here she was cornered again by Ching Chun but, with a desperate rush, clambered over a four-foot wall with amazing agility and was off again. Ching Chun headed her off and, fool that she was, she bolted back to the sty, where she stood at bay, grunting and glaring sullenly from the shadows of her den.

Ching Chun called up reinforcements. While he guarded the walls of the sty, two heavyweight schoolmates approached Big Pig front and rear. As she circled round, one of them grasped her tail and while she vainly pawed the ground and struggled to get free, the other took hold of her long ears and twisted her to the ground. Ching Chun swiftly tied her legs with rope. Ignominiously suspended upside down, she was weighed. She tipped the rod at over 100 jin. Then she was bundled into a handcart. Even then she struggled to her feet to jump out. This time she was tied down and finally lay still. Lao Man received eighty yuan for her. Discussing the sale later, I asked Lao Man how much he would have realized if he had sold the meat on the market or to his neighbors (as he could very well have done without breaking any regulations) and the rest to the marketing co-op. He figured it out roughly and said: "Perhaps ten or more yuan. But I'd rather sell her all to the state. That helps the country better and the cadres and workers in the city. It's glorious—and," he added with a chuckle, "I don't get criticized!"

By the time Big Pig was being wheeled away, Little Pig had lost interest in the proceedings and was munching carrot tops in a corner of the yard. She would enjoy a quieter life for the next seven months at least. She no longer needed Big Pig even for a warm mattress. The sun shone brightly every day, and she could stretch out at her ease under the sunny south wall. Big Pig had been most unkind to her, leaving her only the worst scraps of food. Out of Big Pig's shadow, Ta Sao said, Little Pig would quickly fatten up and grow.

"I suppose Big Pig treated her like that because she was not her own child," I surmised. But Ta Sao said, "No. Big Pig would have treated her like that anyway. A sow will suckle her young just so long and no longer. After that she gets quite heartless. My sister had a sow that suckled her litter well. Then the little ones were sold. One happened to go to a near neighbor and after a few days he thought that it would be a good idea if the sow suckled the young one a bit longer, as it seemed to be ailing. But the sow refused to have anything to do with it. And not only that, when it tried to suck, she bit the poor thing till it bled."

It was exactly as Ta Sao said. Little Pig increased in size visibly day by day. She had all the slops and scraps to herself now and quickly took on Big Pig's old ways. When carrot tops or skin were thrown down in the yard she gave a glare and a grunt and frightened off the hens. She rooted in the compost and the woodpile, and you would find her foraging far afield in other people's yards. One day I found her rooting hard in the yard. Though I stood over her to see what she was after, she took no notice except to redouble her efforts. Ta Sao saw me looking down into the hole and hurried out with a cry: "Little Pig's at the carrots!" We drove Little Pig away, overturned the wheelbarrow over the place where our carrots were buried, and put a prickly branch of thorn on top of that. That taught Little Pig not to nose around our carrots. These were doubly precious then because we had eaten all our cabbages, and the only vegetables we had at the moment were onions, garlic, and dried turnips. *Bo tsai* (spinach), the first spring vegetable, was still hard to come by and would not be in good supply for another three weeks.

From that moment Little Pig was Little Pig no longer, but Big Pig.

Work-Points and Allocations 🌿

On inquiry I found that the income of members of the Great Felicity Commune varied considerably from family to family, depending on a variety of circumstances.

First, the economic standing of the various brigades and teams in the commune differed. Secondly, some families received all their income from within the commune, while others had members or relatives working in factories, offices, or other organizations in other parts of the land. The latter were usually better off than the former. Finally, of course, it is impossible to assess their standard of living solely in terms of money income. Too many other variable factors have to be taken into account—the food allowances they receive, medical care, and other commune services. In the case of an old couple this might include the rebuilding of their home at no cost to themselves. A mother-to-be receives free prenatal treatment and fifty days' paid leave to be taken as she wishes before or after childbirth.

Furthermore, what is described below can only be taken as a basis for orientation in assessing how China's five hundred million peasants live. Economically speaking, Upper Felicity is a subaverage community. I know of communities that are much better off, and I have heard of communities that are somewhat worse off. From what I have told of the life of various families as I saw them you will see that all had at least a sufficiency and more. They had good clothing, adequate housing, and enough to eat, schooling for their children and

cultural amusements and leisure. They were assured of care
in old age or disablement and decent burial after death. For
this they worked hard under their own leaders and their own
voluntarily established standards of discipline, and they were
putting in work that would certainly steadily improve their
livelihood year by year. The specter of devastation from flood
or drought had been banished. The time had long since passed
when such calamities could throw them back to bare subsistence level every few years. In the event of any lesser
calamity they were assured of the help and support of their
own big commune with its tens of thousands of members and
the whole people's state behind that.

For those who could remember the old days, this was a
miraculous change indeed, truly a transition into a real upper
felicity!

With the production team as the basic accounting unit,
each person in the commune receives a basic allocation of
food. Calculated in cereal grain, this includes beans as well.
The amount of this allocation is arrived at in the following
way:

Out of the gross output of the team the grain tax (tax in
kind) is paid to the state. The amount of this tax is set; therefore it varies from year to year as a percentage of any team's
gross output. As output increases, the percentage paid as tax
decreases. Nationwide it is probably between 3 and 7 per
cent now. In Felicity it was around 5 per cent in 1969. In
1972 it dropped to around 3 per cent. The state receives most
of its revenue now from its state industrial, agricultural, and
commercial enterprises.

Giving due weight to the claims of the individual, collective
(team), and state interests, the net output of the production
team after tax is divided after democratic discussion into four
unequal parts. One part, 20 per cent, is set aside as the reserve
fund. This includes the collective grain reserve set aside
against "calamity, flood, drought, or war," the fund for investment, seed grain, operating expenses, and, finally, welfare,
which was 1 per cent of output in 1969 and gave members
care when sick or too old to work, and burial expenses.

The remaining part is for distribution among team members. Unless they insist otherwise, this (according to Party advice) should not be less than 50 per cent of the total. Part of this (around 20 per cent of output) is sold to the state at the state-set price and the proceeds in cash go to the members who sell it.

The distribution fund is divided in Upper Felicity into two fairly equal parts. (In other teams it may be divided 40:60 or 60:40 or in other proportions, depending on the results of discussion.) The first half is then divided by the total number of people in the team, and this gives the amount of cereal grain allocation for each person in the team.

A person on the average needs at least thirty jin of grain a month to live on (a man doing heavy work may eat half as much again) or more; that is, every soul in the team should have at least 360 jin of cereal a year. No team can be doing really well unless it can provide its members with this basic ration. In Upper Felicity's Third Brigade it was 380 jin in 1970. If it suffers some calamity like flood, a team can appeal

to the brigade or commune for help, but in response to the slogan "Be self-reliant!" it will do its utmost to rely on itself. If the amount available for allocation as the basic food ration falls short of the total needed, the team will sell less to the state or decrease the reserve fund.

The other part of the distribution fund is used for the payment of work-points earned by team members.

Not every commune uses the same method of assigning work-points. In Upper Felicity, every able-bodied adult member is rated at ten work-points a day. But depending on the work you do and how you do it, you may get more or fewer. For instance, when Lao Man was doing strenuous transport work, hauling coal from the county town, he was credited with twelve work-points a day. There was some discussion in the Third Team that a man doing duty as threshing-floor leader, a very responsible job during the harvest, should rate twelve points a day. But the team leaders still evaluated this job at ten points. This caused a bit of grumbling. Had the grumbling been more vocal and received greater support "from the masses," the rank-and-file, the extra work-points would undoubtedly have been given.

When I visited the brigade's mill I asked the two young girls in charge what they got for their work. They said, "Seven points a day." Their duties are light. They are under cover rain or shine. Their main work is to keep things tidy and merely flick a switch to start and stop the electrically operated mills and ginning machine, and do ordinary maintenance work. Repairs and major maintenance are done by a technician. One day I met two youngsters of perhaps thirteen or fourteen on the road returning from hoeing the maize. They were still at school and worked only in vacations or when it was deemed more important for production that they work rather than study. They got five work-points a day. At the height of the wheat harvest our Au Chiu and little Hsiao Ching went out gleaning and on the basis of the weight of ears they brought in were credited with two work-points that day.

A full-grown, able-bodied male member of the team can

earn over three thousand work-points a year, ten or more points for each day worked. For every day or half-day he does not work he naturally forfeits his work-points. And a man who is found to be systematically slacking on the job can, of course, also be fined by having his work-point rating reduced to nine or eight. There are rarely such cases, however. Perhaps that remnant "laissez-faire" attitude in the brigade explains why. Perhaps it is because everyone is equally conscientious, but I would find that hard to believe. Holidays, sickness, time off to do household jobs like mending a wall or a roof account for lost work-points. Extra work assigned by the team (above a member's norm) will bring in extra work-points.

Most women, girls, and young boys do not rank as fully able-bodied manpower, so the most any of them are rated is seven and a half work-points a day. This is not discrimination. It is based on the actual amount of farmwork they do and the need for muscle. A few Amazons, however, like the woman head of the team militia, do rate ten points a day. A woman teacher, of course, rates the same wage as a man doing that job.

There is no special difficulty in getting women to do field

work. They have done it traditionally in the area. (In some southern areas I have visited it was considered "unlucky" in the old days for women to work in the fields.) But the older women are very busy doing household work. I never saw Ta Sao with idle hands. From early morning till late at night she was busy working for her family: cooking, cleaning, mending, sewing, tending the chickens or the pig. But when needed she dropped everything and went out to the fields.

The value of the work-points is determined by dividing the total amount of output set aside for work-points by the total number of work-points earned by members. The value of the work-point therefore varies from year to year depending on the output of the team. (In 1971 a work-point was worth more than 7 mao in the Second Team.)

In addition to the allocation of grain (a half share for a baby or toddler) each person in the team gets allocations of vegetable oil, corncobs and maize and kaoliang stalks for firewood, and cotton. These are in amounts that are enough for daily needs if economically used. In 1971 they got something over a jin of cotton per head. Upper Felicity, following the Party directive to "take grain as the key link," was concentrating on growing grain and so only planted enough cotton for its members' personal use. They calculated what was "enough" on the basis of a normal yield from a certain number of mu. If the planned yield was exceeded, then there was more cotton to go around. Members could do what they liked with their allocation of cotton. Most housewives spun and wove it into cloth for their families' clothing. What was left over could be sold either to the co-op or to neighbors. Bachelor households bought their homespun.

The collective work of their team is therefore the basic source of income of the commune members. Their share of that product is determined by their individual or household efforts, but the basic livelihood of every commune member, young or old, able-bodied or disabled, is guaranteed.

The average commune member has other, additional sources of regular income. Practically every household, as I have already described, raises chickens. Shortage of feed grain limits the number that can be kept. Our Ta Sao with her family of six and seven chicks was average. Most of our neighbors kept at least half a dozen. I do not think anybody kept a dozen. Sales of eggs to the marketing co-op was a regular part of household income. Each egg brought in four or five fen. Some old ladies sold their eggs at the fairs, where they could get better prices—depending on the season up to ten or more fen per egg. But this private selling was frowned upon. The commune leadership and advanced public opinion looked on it as putting self before the public good.

Practically every household also raised some domestic animals. Nearly all raised a pig or two, sheep and goats, rabbits or geese. Sales brought in ready cash during the year. Nearly every household, particularly those with children, cut and stored fodder grass, which could always be sold to the team or brigade or commune for the collectively owned cattle. The contents of the compost pits, sties, and hen coops were regularly collected by the teams and also brought in extra income. If you pulled down your house or your outside kitchen to build a new one, the old earth walls impregnated with chemicals could also be sold as fertilizer. When our neighbor's ancient cottage was rebuilt, sale of the old earth in it defrayed the cost of rebuilding.

The ratio between food allocation and work-points funds varied depending on the level of political or social consciousness of the teams and their members. The more advanced teams allocated more for food allowances and welfare, and once these were adequate, sold more grain to the state. Other teams felt that an increase in the value of the work-point was needed to raise productivity and therefore living standards. All agreed that it was necessary to raise and maintain the value of the work-point, but there was considerable discussion about what that level should be. The work-point was something that went to the individual, in the nature of a material incentive. What was a reasonable rate for the work-point, what rate was "ultra-leftist," and what rate verged on revisionism? This was a matter that had to be carefully considered by the leadership and rank-and-file in a team.

In Upper Felicity this system of fixed work-points with flexible application had been instituted in the days of the elementary co-ops and had been carried over into the commune. Other communes I heard of had the system of work-points fixed to the job, and not to the man. In these cases each job had its work-point tag fixed by common agreement, and anyone who did that job would get that number of work-points. Of course, if he did it badly or took too long doing it he would get less work-points for the day. This was a difficult system to operate, but teams that had used it for a long time got quite skilled at applying it. Upper Felicity had tried it out once but found that it caused too much discussion and waste of time arguing the merits of a particular job and the way it had been done. Like the system used in Upper Felicity, this system led to an average able-bodied commune member earning around ten work-points a day, but those communes that used it felt that it provided more incentive to faster and better work.

Not far from Felicity I found a brigade whose members were rated at nineteen work-points a day. When I ask why the rate was not twenty, they said because Chairman Mao had advised "leaving a bit of leeway" in planning.

A tinker came round regularly to our hamlet to mend pots and pans and make keys or repair locks. He carried his tinker's tools on a handcart: saws, hammers, files, drills, and a small blacksmith's bellows and furnace. I once asked him how he came to be doing this job. I could not believe that he was an "element of private capitalist enterprise," and I was right. He was a commune member in good standing, but he was not particularly good at fieldwork and had always done tinkering. So as before, he and other such handymen traveled from hamlet to hamlet plying their trades, but they paid their teams five mao a day as the equivalent of the work-points that they would have earned theoretically each day if they had done regular farmwork.

Though they use electricity, tractors, and other machines, the level of technology in the Upper Felicity teams cannot be said to be high compared with what has been achieved in other areas in China, not to mention that on the world's most technically advanced farms. Nevertheless, the social relations of production are socialist in these commune production teams and the distribution of output is based on the socialist principle of "to each according to his work." But just as the people's commune has elements of communist ownership-by-the-whole-people, so distribution—in allocations to all members, quite apart from work-points—insofar as it is inspired by communist principle and ideals, to some extent goes further than socialist principle demands. People, for instance, get food and fuel according to need, not only according to what they earn.

A small part of output—the grain tax—goes to the people's state, that is, to all the people, and thus in part indirectly comes back to Upper Felicity. The money that is received for grain sold to the state goes back directly to the team to be used by its members in one form or another. The remainder that is put to reserves, used as running expenses, or distributed as food, cotton, or oil or fuel allocations, or welfare or work-points, also goes to the collective. That is, well over 90 per cent of the output of the team goes back directly to improve the livelihood of members.

What then is the income of an Upper Felicity farmer?

He receives something around four hundred jin a year in cereals, which with vegetables and potatoes gives him a sufficiency of food. With various allocations and free services (health, education), income from eggs, pigs, and sidelines of various sorts, he gets enough and more to provide him adequately with clothes, housing, and other necessities. But he has just a bit in addition for savings and buying such luxuries as a bicycle, radio, sewing machine, thermos bottle, flashlight, and so on. Depending on the team's general economic condition, his own household situation, and such extraneous factors as relatives working outside the commune, a member may be a bit better or worse off than the average. But in normal times, or in ill health or suffering natural calamities, he is backed up by the team, the brigade, and the commune and state, and enjoys rock-firm basic social security. This is no small thing in the world today, and he knows that it is the commune, socialism, that provides him with this.

Upper Felicity has achieved this on the basis of yields for grain that are below those set for the area by the National Program for Agricultural Development. According to that program it should have been raising four hundred jin per mu. Actually it was raising less. Only in 1970 did it reach the National Program yield. Its 1970 and later advances will put it well on the way to being called a prosperous brigade, or, as its Party secretary would put it, "firmly consolidating its socialist positions."

As a comparison, an average member of an average team in the pacesetter commune of Yangtan, in Shansi Province, in 1965 was already receiving 400 jin in cereals plus 130 yuan in cash per capita together with all the usual commune services and allocations of cotton, oil and fuel, medical service, education, and entertainment. The average team in the richer communes of the southern provinces, which crop two or three times a year, are even better off. That puts Upper Felicity incomes somewhat behind that of an average industrial worker.

Tractor Repair Shop 🌾

*T*he production teams of the commune run a number of collective undertakings. Our three production teams in Upper Felicity each had its own collective stable. Our Second Team had one horse, three mules, seventeen oxen, and several donkeys, together with handcarts and clumsy wooden-wheeled, iron-tired carts which were being phased out. Our Third Team was more affluent—it had three horses and a foal, five mules, more than a dozen oxen, and some donkeys. While we were with them they bought that brand-new horsecart with pneumatic tires for eight hundred yuan. Part of the funds for this came out of the collective purse and part was made up by borrowing from team members. Lao Man lent eighty yuan. This was part of some money sent to the family on the occasion of Ching Chun's betrothal by an uncle working in a coal mine in Northeast China.

The three teams, jointly as the Third Production Brigade, also ran a number of collective undertakings. First there was the small millhouse with two mills, a ginning machine, the three electric motors, and three permanent workers. Then there was the blacksmith shop. This worked as and when needed, usually with a staff of three young men. They made horseshoes, bolts, brackets, hinges, and pokers and repaired all kinds of farm ironware and tools. In the winter all the brigade members' sheep and goats were looked after collectively. It was the brigade that stocked the big pond with fish fry and tended the tree nurseries.

The commune also ran a number of collective undertakings. These were naturally on a larger scale than the individual teams or brigades could have run economically. There was a brick-kiln that turned out bricks in bulk when some major construction was to be undertaken. There was the big grain store that stored grain, wheat, rice, and maize, as well as vegetable oils for thousands of people. There was the supply and marketing co-op network that also served the whole commune membership as well as shoppers from a considerable area around. Every commune, and even some brigades, had its own co-op store, but the larger had better stocked shops.

Our commune's most ambitious undertaking was the tractor and farm-machinery park and tractor repair workshop. This was financed by a loan from the county and contributions from the brigades.

The brigades and teams paid for the use of the tractors and their tools when they used them. The cost was one yuan one mao a mu, so the teams used tractors only when they had a large area to be plowed or cultivated and limited time in which to do it. They all had to budget carefully and were not inclined to throw money around. The commune as a whole had a certain area it cultivated collectively. This included experimental fields and the alkaline flats to the south which were being reclaimed. It was here that the tractors were really needed.

Upper Felicity's brigade was not so well off and was not at the stage where it could use tractors on a large scale economically.

"How about land and manpower in the brigade?" I asked.

"We have enough land," was the reply. "There's enough land for everyone in the brigade to live well on. All our manpower is kept busy. It's only sometimes that we need the help of a tractor. When we get richer we'll use more machines and use our manpower for other productive undertakings."

There were only a few weeks in the year that they were so pressed for manpower that some of them had to work nights. One time was in early spring when because of the drought they had to keep the wells going all night with men out in the fields to direct the water into the proper channels. A man working beyond the normal eight-hour day is entitled to extra work-points.

Another time was during the harvest. There was a threat of rain and the threshing-floor teams had to work all night, threshing, winnowing, and bagging the grain. When they had really got their existing fields into proper order with mechanized wells and thoroughly reliable irrigation and drainage channels (they were still engaged in leveling a large area), they would go on to tackle their alkaline land in the south. Then they would need tractors and more mechanization to make up for lack of manpower. Though that stage was still some years away, the commune was considering this problem and doing quite a bit of preliminary experimental work. A state farm had already opened one area, then given its land and buildings to the May Seventh Cadre School run by the translation bureau for its cadres. The school was wealthy enough to bring in its own tractors, trucks, fertilizer, etc. The commune watched these efforts with deep interest. It was generally felt, however, that reclamation of this salt land would need a very big joint effort or two or three communes. Certainly the brigades or teams could not tackle it. A very large

irrigation and drainage system was needed, with large amounts
of water for leaching out the salts. Water would have to be
brought in from somewhere or pumped up from deep wells.
The area also needed windbreaks and approach roads; altogether a big undertaking.

The commune's tractor repair workshop was on the high
ground along which the main road ran south of our hamlet.
It was a big compound of new one-story brick buildings with
red tiled roofs. It could give a complete major overhaul to a
tractor or a combine (the commune had one combine) and,
of course, handle any repairs of farm tools or implements.
Besides its staff of qualified technicians it had a well-equipped
toolroom, foundry and smithy. A carpenters' workshop was
tooled up and staffed to undertake any sort of carpentering
needed in the commune. When I needed a new handle for my
hoe I brought it here to be fitted. Another small workshop did
all kinds of small repairs for the commune and commune members, and travelers along the road as well. Ta Sao went there
to get her pots and pans repaired. I took my cycle there when
I had a flat tire. An old veteran tinsmith and tinker presided
over it with three apprentices, including one bright-eyed girl
who didn't know much about the job yet but was bubbling
over with eagerness to try out what she did know on my crippled bicycle. On the workbench waiting to be mended were
sprayers for insecticides and a handpump. A handcart that
needed a new axle stood outside waiting its turn.

The veteran in charge, like the other workshop workers,
received 34 yuan a month. The lowest wage was 24 yuan. Six
yuan of this was given to his team, which credited him with
30 work-points. At the year-end distribution, he received the
net worth of these work-points in cash or kind. A young ap-
prentice told me he got the usual rate of ten work-points a
day, but he also got a food allowance and pocket money of
eight yuan a month for cigarettes and other small expenses.
However, the food allowance and pocket money were practically enough to keep himself on so that most of the ten
work-points a day went to his family. Families whose sons or
daughters had been recommended by their teams or brigades

to work in the commune industrial undertakings were well pleased. Their youngsters were not only getting training in some industrial skill but making a sizable contribution in ready cash to the family budget.

Wage Earners 🌿

amilies that had industrial workers or other wage earners were noticeably more affluent than those that depended wholly on farmwork. Families and their youngsters were excited when a call came for volunteers for work on a new railway project in the province. Several young men responded. They would see and learn new things and get good wages to boot. With frugal living, they could contribute something extra to the family budget. Some men were needed for a short time for guard duty. These were chosen from the commune's militia troop. While on the project they too received their usual ten work-points a day, plus food allowances and pocket money. When the line moved on farther most of them would come home and new batches of workers would be recruited from other communes.

Families that had one or more members working permanently in an outside industrial or construction job, a city office, or a state farm were even better off. One family had a first cousin, a bachelor, working in a mine in the northeast. He sent home a regular allowance each month for his mother and a hundred yuan or more a year to the family. Visiting the old home, these outside members give their relatives a living contact with the big world outside. In accordance with immemorial custom, those who can invariably send part of their wages back to their families. Only in exceptional cases will the home ties be cut. This still remains part of the traditional family "social insurance" of the Chinese people.

One former landlord had a well-educated son working in a

county town office. He and his wife had proved themselves over the years to be progressive and active people and their landlord origin was never held against them. They gave financial help to their father, who naturally, though not working "under supervision," suffered various social and economic disabilities because of his personal history of exploitation of others.

There was also the case of a former rich peasant's son. This young man had also proved himself to be loyal to the people and for many years before liberation he had been independent of his father. The label of a "rich peasant" had been taken off his father because of his good behavior and attitude to the new society, and now the son was able to help his parent financially as well as ideologically, which had been the more important.

There were other ways in which the peasants could make a bit of extra pin money. Many of them were skilled handicraftsmen. If you had broom plants in your yard you could cut them, dry them, and make small brooms, which had a ready sale at the co-op or at the fairs. One family in our second team had a couple of willow trees. They would cut the long, supple branches in the autumn, soak them in the pond, and weave baskets out of them, mostly rough affairs for carrying earth or packing eggs. Nearly every woman in the hamlet could, like our Ta Sao, weave thick sitting mats out of koaliang or wheat straw. These they used themselves or sold. Ta Sao sat on her mat in her cottage or courtyard as she spun or reeled thread, or sewed. But all these handicrafts were now very decidedly subsidiary occupations. The peasants of Upper Felicity had learned the hard way that unless they concentrated on their collective agricultural labor, and that meant chiefly cereal production, their economic life could have no really solid basis.

They all remembered the time they had taken advantage of a favorable market situation and gone in heavily for vegetables. They had eaten well of vegetables and sold some profitably for ready cash, but when the neighboring communes had all organized their own self-sufficient vegetable production and had made big strides in developing cereal production, leveling their land, reforesting, and so on, Upper Felicity had found itself in the unfortunate position of the grasshopper in the fable of the grasshopper and the ant. The lesson had been well learned and now the peasants here were determined not to repeat the same mistake: subsidiary occupations must remain subsidiary. First things must come first.

Bachelor Life 🌿

As you can see, a bachelor, if he has no family, is at a decided disadvantage in the hamlet. Of course, finally it all depends on the man. If he is revolutionary and active and puts the public ahead of self, he finds a great richness of life and companionship in collective endeavor. In the village such a man is not alone for long. He will soon have wife and family. Chinese society takes a rather pragmatic view of marriage. If the bachelor is too old to marry a young woman, his friends and neighbors will be very willing to introduce him to an eligible widow. There were two men who enjoyed good marriages of this type in our hamlet. One of them was Kao. He was strong but a bit lethargic. His mother had put off getting him married for one reason or another and then had died. He himself had done nothing about this important question and was well on in his late twenties when his relatives took the matter in hand and he was married to a good widow with two children. She was an experienced woman, a resolute character, and this was good for Kao. She had changed his lethargy into disciplined, steady work, and Kao became a better man, a good father, and a prop of the collective. His wife kept him at it, and, truth to tell, he was a bit henpecked. Once his wife thought he was lapsing back into the old ways and she gave him a tonguelashing that echoed over the wall: "If it weren't for the children would I ever have married you?

Would any virgin marry you, you lout!" (Her reference to a virgin, we all agreed, reflected a somewhat backward ideology.)

But then there was old Pao. He had been press-ganged into the Kuomintang army and had lost touch with his family. When the army he was in had been defeated by the P.L.A., all the rank-and-file in his unit had been given the option of joining the P.L.A. or going home. He had opted for home, but by then his family had disappeared without trace. No one knew where they had gone to. Later he had got land in the land reform and belatedly got married. But his wife had died childless and again he was alone. He got married again, this time to a widow with two children. He told me that his wife had died and so had the children. I learned later that she had packed up and left with the children. I never found out why. Probably he could not shake off his bachelor ways. Anyway he was alone again and now lived in a small two-roomed cottage without even a yard before it. There was no need for it. He had no one to look after hens or pig, goat or sheep for him. While family men had wives and daughters to cook and sew, pickle vegetables, wash clothes, spin, weave cloth, plait mats, make clothes, and engage in the many activities that make for life and happiness in a home, he, poor bachelor, had to return of an evening to a cold cottage and cook his own lonely meal.

One evening he asked us rather hopefully if we knew of any widow who might be thinking of getting married again, but we had to confess that we didn't.

He was looking after the sheep and goats of the hamlet at that time and later grew increasingly careless of his appearance. By the summer he was really rather unpresentable. This made him even less welcome to the neighbors than he had been before. He was not a very jovial companion even at the best of times. His health declined and he grew more and more withdrawn. His was not a happy fate.

In such personal matters the community will not interfere until it feels it has to because the situation has become more than a personal or family affair and touches the collective. For instance, there was a little boy who had got sick and raised a high temperature. When he was able to leave his bed it was found that his mind had been affected. The brigade had offered to get him treated, but with that terrible conservatism that still afflicts some peasants, his parents had refused. "He'll be all right," they said. For a time his feeble-mindedness was not very noticeable. He played and skylarked with the other

children at their childish games. But soon he began to grow into a youngster and one of his tricks was to pull all his clothes off in the summer. His parents tried tying his trousers on him with intricate knots but it did no good. Off the trousers would come. This was a public scandal, so the brigade raised the question of treatment more urgently, and with the help of public opinion finally got the parents to agree to send him for proper treatment in a children's hospital.

Honored Families

A quite special social status is enjoyed by families who have members serving in the armed forces. When sons or daughters join up, such households are presented with a bright yellow wooden tablet about eight inches long and three inches wide with one end cut to a point. On this is inscribed in red letters: "Glorious Army Family." It is nailed up outside their door on the righthand side. On Army Day, August first, such families are honored by name at mass meetings and visited, as they are also on other big national days, by representatives of the commune sent to inquire especially after their health and well-being. It is unthinkable that such families should suffer difficulties that could be avoided.

Near our cottage was the home of a sturdy-looking man who had fought with distinction in the ranks of the Chinese Volunteers in the War Against U.S. Aggression and to Aid Korea. But unfortunately his physical sturdiness was only apparent. He had been wounded and crippled in the war and invalided out of the army. Any heavy exertion caused him to spit blood. Fresh difficulties came when his wife died, leaving their six children motherless. But this was a family of great spirit. The eldest daughter, a handsome, buxom girl of eighteen from her mother's first marriage, was like her stepfather in build and courage. A thoroughly capable housewife, she had taken over her mother's role in the home. The second girl was fifteen, a child with the beauty of a Botticelli angel in Chinese style; then there were two more girls, a small boy who was a model pupil at school, and finally the baby. All those over seven went to school. Yet the house was always tidy and well ordered.

Such disabilities as this family faced would have crushed them before liberation. In the commune, they were a model family, well respected, well fed and clothed. The father did all he could in the way of work. The commune did all it could for him. Evident pride, respect, and real affection for them was expressed when the comfort group I joined went to greet them at the Spring Festival.

In the old society, the oldest girl would probably have gone back to the home of her father's family after her mother's death. In the new society the two families got together to discuss the matter and agreed that she should stay with her stepfather's family. She was a girl of fine character and had a feeling of genuine filial duty and affection for her stepfather and for her new family. Her elders also thought that it would be advantageous to her future because she would be treated socially as the daughter of a wounded and honored defender of the country with the priorities in work and study that went with that status.

Spring Comes and a "Barefoot Doctor" 🌿

*T*he winter had been surprisingly mild. All through November and well into December the weather was chilly, but the pond was still unfrozen, and it was pleasant to be outside in the warm noonday sun. There was little wind. The peasants remarked regretfully on the absence of snow but were not unduly worried. They had complete confidence in their deep, mechanized wells. It was only in January that the air really became nippy and we went into full winter outfits.

Then one day soon after the Spring Festival we woke to a day that seemed to promise spring. The sun shone in a glorious blue and cloudless sky. A spring warmth was in the air. The twigs of young poplars shone like burnished copper. Feeling the warmth, the tough sprouts of winter wheat marked deep green lines on the yellow-brown fields, merged into a faint carpet of verdure in the middle distance, and lost themselves in the dun haze of the far fields. We congratulated each other: "Spring is coming!"

Young know-it-alls said, "In a week the trees will be in leaf!"

But next day the radio announced a cold front approaching from the north. The spring promise of the morning faded. That very afternoon the north wind began to blow cold and hard. For a time there was an unequal contest as it beat back the mild spring air from the south. Mist enveloped the hamlet, followed by a fall of sleet. All that night the north wind blew, driving flakes of snow before it. By the third day a winter cold had gripped us again and a thin film of snow covered everything, giving a strange loveliness to the place. The pond froze. Warm clothes were hastily donned again. The hamlet seemed deserted as children and grannies clustered round the stoves.

There were complaints of colds and hurried calls to borrow medicine. One evening a round-faced young man called on us and asked us whether we had any anticold medicine. At first we thought he too had come to borrow some, but then we found out that he was the brigade's young "barefoot doctor." He was making the rounds of the hamlet and advising everyone to try a good home preventive for colds.

"Heat up a large metal spoon," he said, "and when it is red hot, drop some vinegar into it and inhale the vapor. If you have no other cold cure and you feel a cold coming on, that's as good a preventive as you'll get!"

At this time "barefoot doctors" like himself were spreading such homely medical lore throughout the villages. Their remedies were cheap and effective and easy to remember. Most of them were culled from the peasants themselves, home remedies that had not only stood the test of centuries but had been tested out anew by modern scientific methods in the country's medical institutes and by trained doctors working in the countryside.

Our "barefoot doctor" was a local lad who had shown an interest in healing and had been sent for a short course for paramedics at a county training center. Here the students had received training in first aid, in the principles of environmental hygiene, in the use of the common drugs and tested packaged medicines anyone could buy in the local druggist shops. He also studied elementary acupuncture and home remedies for illnesses common to the area.

These youngsters got their name of "barefoot doctors" because when they were not healing they did their stint of work in the fields with their trousers rolled up and their shoes off like other workers. They form part of the multitiered medical system that is being extended all over China's rural areas and that makes maximum use of China's still-limited number of general practitioners and specialists. "Barefoot doctors" cure what they can, taking quite a load off the better-trained doctors. They are also trained to recognize more serious complaints. These cases they refer to the commune hospital with its fully trained Western-type doctors and several experienced Chinese herbal doctors and acupuncturists. More serious cases, demanding specialist treatment or major surgery, are sent on to the well-equipped county hospital.

The establishment of this rural medical network is a result of the successful struggle waged against the deposed President Liu Shao-chi's ideas during the Cultural Revolution. Liu argued that since China had so few well-trained practitioners (thirty thousand Western-trained doctors at the time of the Liberation in 1949), these should be concentrated in a number of showplace medical centers in the cities, where more doctors would be trained to staff the rural areas later. Mao Tse-tung argued that it would be more rational to develop this widespread, multitiered medical system using paramedics like the "barefoot doctors" and all available medical knowledge among the 500,000 herb doctors and acupuncture practitioners, backed up by mobile teams of specialists.

After practicing what he had learned for a time, our bare-foot doctor would go back for more training later on, and bit by bit increase his medical skill.

Not many days after this last winter flurry, the north wind was driven back again by a more determined onslaught of spring from the south. In half a day the hamlet roads were dried with a hard, firm crust, and once again we were talking jubilantly of spring. We threw the door open wide to let it in. A swallow swooped through and perched chirping with high spirits on the big middle rafter. He looked round, head cocked appraisingly to one side, and then flew out. Not long after, back he flew with his mate, and together they considered the place as a likely spot for their nest. But they must have found some better spot. Later we saw them perched side by side on the electric wires strung along the lane. They and two other pairs that year became well known in the hamlet, chattering in the trees and on the wires or swooping joyously over the pond waters and the courtyards between the cottages.

Walking by the vegetable plots, we noticed that the slender onion leaves were putting on weight.

What We Wear

In the North China winter you have to be warmly dressed. From December to February the pond is frozen. The peasant men and women wear a very thick cotton vest and long cotton pants next to their skins. On top of this they wear a suit of thick black homespun well padded with cotton wadding. Woolen socks and homemade padded black cotton shoes with thick soles, half an inch thick or more, and a fur cap or padded cotton cap with earflaps complete their outfit. The younger women and girls also wear padded trousers and jackets, but these are usually of colored or patterned homespun or printed cotton. To wash a cotton-padded jacket you have to take it apart first and extract all the cotton wadding. This is a troublesome job, so to keep their padded jackets clean, they usually wear a loose covering jacket of some dark color. The children are dressed like the girls but usually in much brighter colors.

When a man goes out carting on the road, for extra warmth he puts on either his own or a borrowed sheepskin. When the wind blows hard they belt their long jackets tightly round the waist either with a wide leather belt or cotton cummerbund, and tie the bottoms of their trousers with a short length of cloth. When so dressed they make a strong figure. I didn't like the way some of them wear a towel on their heads tied under the chin for warmth on the road. This gives them an "old woman" look. But a towel-turban, knotted in front, is a manly, locally characteristic touch that looks good.

Women's jackets don't button down the front like the men's, but at the neck and then under the right or left armpit and down the side. The older women catch the ends of their trousers with a bright-colored ribbon tied just above the ankles. This gives an attractive touch of color to otherwise sober garb. The girls like to wear headkerchiefs, in plain bright colors or with floral patterns or checks. They are folded from corner to corner, thrown over the head, and tied under the chin so that the point hangs down the back. They also like to wear bright-colored nylon socks with their black cloth shoes. The co-op always has these decorative articles of wear stocked in enough patterns to satisfy the female taste for individuality in dress.

The very old women draw their hair sedately back into a bun above the nape of the neck in the old-fashioned style. Those whose hair is thinning wear a false bun. The middle-aged married women like Ta Sao have a different fashion. In the 1920s, when they were growing up, bobbed hair was the sign of the revolutionary emancipation of women. I remember how women propaganda squads of the 1924 Northern Expedition went out with scissors as part of their equipment. Of course, in those days the queue, or pigtail, was still worn by many men of the Han nationality. This was originally a sym-

bol of subjection and differentiation from the Manchus, the reigning Ching dynasty which had already been deposed in the 1911 Republican Revolution, but it had become traditional and many still clung to it. So the pigtail was also a target for the revolutionary propagandists' scissors. It was at this time that bobbed hair became the fashion in Upper Felicity and thereabouts. Ta Sao and other women still wore their hair bobbed, but it was a shoulder-length bob with a generous tress of hair caught up with a comb or ribbon on the upper side of their heads. The long, rich black fall of hair gave them a youthful, graceful look. The younger women and girls either wore short bobs or long single or double plaits. Many of them had cut off their plaits during the Cultural Revolution when some people argued that such a hair style smacked of overmuch vanity and furthermore was extolled by Teng To, one of the arch-revisionists. The controversy had finally died down with the consensus that long plaits were nothing much to worry about. While their hair was growing back the girls tied it close to the head in two bunches that stuck out cutely like little spouts of hair on both sides of the backs of their heads.

Quite a number of village cadres, both men and women, wear khaki. Sometimes this is a loose-fitting jacket cover and trousers over their padded cotton suits; often it is a khaki padded uniform like that of the P.L.A. (in fact, sometimes army surplus) with army-style peaked caps or round padded hats with artificial fur fronts and earflaps. None of this clothing is extravagant or showy. The peasants are always frugal. The cadres, if they had not learned frugality before, had certainly learned it in the Cultural Revolution. In fact, while the peasants think it no loss of propriety to wear patched clothes, the really heavily patched clothing—seats, knees, elbows, and wrists—is most to be noticed on the clothes of cadres spending time in the hamlet as part of their "labor training," "going back to the grass roots," or among the cadres at the May Seventh Cadre School.

In this, as in all things, there are those who carry things to an extreme. One day on the road I was surprised to see a terribly ragged, patched, and unkempt man approaching me with outstretched hands. "A beggar!" flashed through my mind. "How could this be!" But it turned out to be an artist whom I knew from Peking doing a stint of work in the commune, helping them to set up an exhibition of "Old and New." Apparently he thought that a multitude of patches and non-patches showed he was "learning from peasants." None of the really patched outfits were local.

I myself had a pair of cotton padded trousers, but their covering was of thin cotton, not homespun, so inside I wore cotton shorts, two pairs of long cotton underpants, and, when the weather was really cold, a pair of knitted woolen "longs." I wore two pairs of socks, one nylon, one wool, inside my padded cotton shoes.

On my body I wore a cotton undervest, a cotton and wool long-armed vest, a soft woolen sweater, a thicker one over that, and a very thick one over that. Even so I got cold, so I topped all this with a jacket padded with silk floss, and a blue cotton cover to keep this clean.

Thus clad, I was usually warm enough both inside and outside the cottage. If I attended a meeting outdoors or in the commune assembly hall, which was unheated and had open windows and doorways, I wore my padded winter overcoat and hat of artificial fur with earflaps.

Such was my dress that winter that as the weather got progressively warmer, I shed my vests and sweaters one by one till by midsummer I was going around in shorts and a straw hat and nothing else.

When I first came to Peking I used to change into pajamas for sleeping, but successive bouts of colds finally convinced me that you can't do this and survive in Peking-style houses or North China peasant cottages. Now, like the peasants, I take off my outer clothes but keep most of my underwear on. But while most of the peasants are content with one quilt, I find that I need at least a blanket on top of that and sometimes even another quilt to boot. I found that I was by no means the only "softy" in the hamlet. There was one oldish city cadre who was very earnest about not coddling himself. But after getting a run of colds and sore throats, he had finally compromised to the extent of wearing his big woolen scarf even in bed. Since the stoves have no chimneys, it is not possible to close all the cottage doors and windows at night for fear of carbon monoxide, so the rooms have plenty of air circulating and sometimes quite a breeze blows over your pillow.

Unless it was to change my inner cotton underwear, which

gets dirty first, I never undressed completely. I did not have a bath with a soak in water for four months. I took sponge baths, washing my body a bit at a time. There was no bathhouse in the hamlet. I wasn't too keen on the one in the county town. To take a bath there meant a round trip of seventy li, going one morning by bus and returning the next day. Besides, this was the old-style bathhouse. It had a single heated pool and as they joked, "everything goes in." So Ta Sao and Lao Man advised me to wait until the bathhouse goes modern and puts in showers. Later I didn't need to go anyway. When the weather grew a bit warmer I bought a large sheet of plastic, upended the table, and draped the sheet in it so that it formed a deep bath with its sides supported on the table legs. This made a luxurious bath. The plastic sheeting was cheap. Made especially for the farm market, a large, double-bed-sized length cost just over two yuan.

Customs differ surprisingly in China. Down in Chekiang taking a winter bath is no problem. Every hamlet has several bathhouses. Inside each is a brick and clay structure forming two large steps. A huge, shallow cauldron is let into each step. You fill the top one with water. The upper step is hollow beneath the cauldron and into an opening on its side you feed fuel to heat it. You feed the fire from outside. The smoke comes out of a vent on the opposite side. When the fire is going the bathhouse is warm as a sauna. You sit inside in the lower cauldron and dip warm and then hot water from the upper cauldron. But Chekiang was several hundred miles away. I told the Upper Felicity lads hopefully about these Chekiang baths.

Raising Chicks

We had no hopes of raising chickens for eggs, but when we heard that spring chicken is good to eat at four or five months we bought seven chicks from a commune peddler.

Just around *Chin Chih,* the time of Awakening Insects
(March 6), he had visited our hamlet on his bicycle with two
panniers filled with twittering chicks. When we bought them
all were lively little balls of yellow fluff. But after a few days
we noticed that one little fellow was droopy. He would stand
still and seem to dream on his feet. Ta Sao diagnosed his
ailment as acute constipation. She docked his tail and put oil
on his bottom. But it did no good. Then he could not eat or
drink. One day as he crouched listlessly, too weak even to
draw in his outspread little wing, his sturdier companions
started to peck at him cruelly.

I separated him from them and put a saucer of water just
under his beak. Not long after he dragged himself into the
saucer, closed his eyes, and died. I buried him deep in the
compost pit.

The other six were frisky. I fed them millet and after a
few days water, then chopped boiled turnip, spinach, and
lettuce and the remains of our dinner rice. Within a week
they were foraging for themselves in the yard, busily scratch-
ing, sharpening their beaks on the ground, preening themselves. With no mother hen, they taught themselves everything
they knew. They soon learned to come at my inexpert call.
I let them run around the yard by day, but at night they came
in of their own accord and huddled all together in a corner,
each squeezing to get himself into the center of the crowd.
Then I would put them into a basket covered with netting
and hang it on a hook from a rope tied to a rafter. Here they
were safe from mice or rats till morning.

As I grew fonder of the chicks, I could not stomach the
thought of eating them. And then they made a bit of a mess
in the room and I grudged the time needed to look after them.
Anyway, they had lost their cute looks completely. They grew
wings, inordinately long legs, and scrawny necks and became
unlovely caricatures of hens, with strange mannerisms of
pecking, stretching, eating, and relieving themselves.

All of us cadres had bought chicks. All but the Yuans, that
is. I think that Yuan had some vague idea that this abstinence
would mark him as more progressive than the rest of us who

were going in for a private sideline occupation. Though that saved us the necessity of going into competition with him, we all felt that the purchase of the chicks should be the subject of one of our study sessions. We agreed that while raising our future meals we should not spend too much time on them, as that would display greed. We should also be careful not to spoil our relations with the peasants. For example, if our hostess' chicks or hens ate our chicken feed we should not make a fuss. On the other hand we should not let our chicks eat our hostess' chicken feed. With Yuan on our mind, we expressed the hope that raising our own chicken meat and perhaps eggs would be an example of self-reliance and lessen the strain on the local chicken economy.

The Tangs bought ten chicks but ill luck dogged them. Their neighbor's cat made off with four. Then two others fell into the latrine. A seventh disappeared mysteriously.

The Lings were no luckier. The Tans disdained to buy any chicks. They got their son to bring them an enormous white Cuban hen from Peking. Twice the size of any Felicity hen, she always made me think of a dowager duchess. For a few days she laid eggs regularly, to the enormous satisfaction of her mistress. Any day I was expecting Mrs. Tan to fly on-to the roof and crow. Then the egg laying stopped. Mrs. Tan fussed around finding the reason. She reported that the weather was not suitable and that her hostess' spoiled hens were eating her Cuban hen's food. Finally she decided that the hen must be revisionist and did not like coming down to the countryside.

The Tsangs looked after their chicks as conscientiously as they did everything else. They fed them scientifically and allowed them to strengthen themselves and build up muscle and meat by walking round the whole village. Every evening Tsang went out clucking to get them home.

All this was a lively topic of conversation in the village, and also in our OSD Team. Mrs. Tan was carrying on a feud with the Yuans and asserted that the latter had no need of chicks because they were secretly buying eggs from their host-ess. She had also seen chicken bones on their table. For a few

days our team was rent with discord, and finally the matter
had to be brought up in our study group.

It emerged that the Yuans were on innocent terms of inti-
mate friendship with their hostess, just as most of the better
adjusted cadres were with their hostesses. But since their hostess was somewhat better off than most in the hamlet the exchanges between them were a bit more elaborate. Where Ta
Sao brought us a bowl of steamed locust leaves and we gave
her a dish of radishes in return, the Yuans had sometimes presented their hostess with a dish of meat after having received
an egg or two for their son or a cockerel their hostess did not
want to raise. Thus the Yuans were exonerated, and Mrs. Tan
was reprimanded and shown the error of her ways. We told
her at length and in nine different voices that she should not
only talk about spreading Mao Tse-tung's thought but follow
it herself. After this flareup, the group had a better understanding of each other and so was more united than before.

When my chicks had grown insufferably scrawny I handed
them over to Mrs. Ling. I never got broth, but I got some
good sketches out of them. That led me to draw hens and
cocks and in the upshot I used one of these sketches to
make a good cartoon of a bureaucrat looking like a ridicu-
lously proud cock. In this way my chicks helped the Cultural
Revolution.

Spring Building 🌿

By May 6, the time of *Li Hsia*, Summer Begins, Upper
Felicity looked very different from when I first saw it
in its winter bareness. The fresh green of new leaves
gladdened the eye. Children played lustily in the open. They
played a sort of hopscotch, and danced ring-around-the-rosy.
The pond sparkled in the sunlight. There was much activity,
but it was not rushed—hoeing, cultivating, preparing and

spreading manure, irrigating. A great deal of building was going on not only in our hamlet but in all the surrounding villages. Field work was not so urgent, and it was good building weather.

In our Third Team, the winter wheat, the main crop, was doing well. This was the time of *Hsiao Man,* when the wheat plant fills out and stands firm in the soil. Wheat, with some barley, took up three hundred of the team's four-hundred-odd mu then under crops. According to plan half the crop would be sold to the state. Most of the other one hundred mu (excluding the vegetable plot) had been deep-dug and would be planted to cotton. The rape fields caught the eye with their bright yellow carpet of flowers. Slips and seedlings planted thick in the tree nurseries had sprouted well. Eggplant, onions, oil seed and red flower, peas, squashes, cucumbers, and early maize had been planted. The older men tended these, so

IMPORTANT
BUSINESS

there was plenty of able-bodied manpower to spare for building. A strong team was assigned to making brick and concrete
sections for lining the new mechanized wells. The rest built
houses. The air was dry and warm with light breezes that ran
in and out of the unfinished rooms. Adobe walls dry quickly
and well in such weather.

Twenty rooms in all were to be built in Upper Felicity.
Some were for sons due to be married soon. Two were for the
old ballad-singer and his wife, whose ancient cottage needed
such a thorough overhaul that it was thought better to pull
it down and rebuild it. Four rooms were to be built for the
barefoot doctor, his little clinic, a brigade handicraft workshop,
and office. New babies in some households made the demand
for more living space urgent.

Though the ties between Lao Man and his cousin living
next door were not as close as in the 1950s when they lived
together as one family, they were still very close. The cousin
and his wife were called uncle and aunt by Lao Man's children. Both farmyards had two cottages, and they were growing together. When we left and Lao Man's eldest boy, Ching
Chun, got married, he and his wife would live in our cottage.
In the cousin's farmyard, the two parents slept in the large
east-facing cottage and the daughter slept in the south-facing
one. When Au Chiu got married he would live with his wife
in this cottage. The two families were still bit by bit building
up their double L-shaped compound. This year the cousin
planned to build a good outside kitchen to complete one leg
of his L. He did practically all the work himself. He dug up
bricks from the foundations and a half-remaining wall of an
old abandoned cottage in his yard and with them built the
new foundations and half of the walls of his new kitchen.
Clay and chopped straw mixed with water was his cement.
Then he shoveled off about three inches of topsoil from his
own courtyard and mixed this with chopped straw. With his
daughter and nephew helping him, he cast this into big adobe
bricks which he dried in the sun. When these were ready, he
used them to build up the kitchen walls. He sawed off a
branch of the locust tree in his yard to make a stout main

beam and cut smaller branches and twigs to form the rafters and wattle foundation for the roof. On top of the wattle he plastered a thick, eight-inch layer of adobe. He divided the chamber inside with a curtain wall half as long as the outside wall and two-thirds as high. Only half of the whole area was roofed. The curtain wall and the half-roof gave shelter from wind and rain to the stove, which he built himself out of clay-like loess mud. The smoke escaped through the uncovered portion of the roof and the clay chimney he constructed. Since he looked after the cattle shed and stable on a night shift, he could devote part of the daytime to his building. The team had given him permission to do this. So he lost no work-points on it and the whole thing cost him nothing but the labor he spent on it.

Some communes have set up Homes of Respect for the Aged where the old people, too old for work, live together, looking after themselves as much as possible but with someone assigned to help them keep things clean and see to their meals. Here they engage in a bit of gardening and their hobbies or sun themselves as they gossip in the sunshine. Upper Felicity, however, had found that the old people liked it better when they lived at home with their relatives. But there was one old couple who had no near relatives in the hamlet. Their only daughter was married to a farmer in another village of the commune about six li away and they preferred to live on in their old home visiting and being visited by their daughter and her family from time to time. The husband, Old Chao, the ballad-singer, was now in his seventies, his wife just a little younger, but they were both full of spirit. When the call came for all hands to be out in the harvest, old Mrs. Chao turned out too with her well-worn sickle. She could no longer bend to the work, so she took along a little stool, and seated on this and moving it along, she cut her row of wheat along with the rest of the reapers. Usually she stayed in the hamlet looking after her neighbors' children and seeing after her own cottage chores, but at harvesttime all the children except for the very small babies went out to the fields and played there while their parents reaped the crop.

Old Chao also kept himself busy. He still received work-points for his job of looking after the roads and roadside trees. When our OSD Team sallied out to work he often went with us to help and advise us. He showed us how to clear the ditches, prune the trees, plant slips of poplar or willow, and collect seeds for the next season. He usually carried a light scoop and a shallow basket, and wherever he saw some dung on the road he would deftly spade it up and deposit it in his basket "for the people's good." Every so often, although he knew some of the new revolutionary songs, he would break out into one of the old local folksongs. As likely as not this would be some lyrical and, in the Chinese style, circumloc-utory tale of love. Despite the fact that he had often been admonished for singing about "men and women relations," he could never remember that this was an aspect of the old life style that had to be got rid of.

Old Chao had lived in his cottage for the past thirty years and more. It hadn't been too well built in the first place and was clearly in need of repairs. He put in an application to the team which was okayed by the brigade. Soon after the Spring Festival, Lao Man and three others were sent to rebuild his cottage for him. First they tore the old place down completely. Since it was so old and impregnated with the salts of time and the carbon and phosphorous fumes of the innumerable fires, its walls, stove, and roof were broken up and used by the team as fertilizer. This paid for the labor on the new house, and Old Chao only had to provide two meals a day for the builders while they were on the job. They didn't ex-pect anything very elaborate, just pancakes or millet porridge, cabbage, and a bit of pickle.

While the new house was being built the old couple lived in their outside kitchen and storeroom. Most of their furni-ture lay in their little yard in the open. The weather is very stable at this time of year; it might get colder or warmer, but it would certainly not rain.

The builders spent nothing on materials. Like Lao Man's cousin, they made large sun-dried bricks and reused the bricks and beams, doors and windows of the old cottage. All the rest, adobe for the walls, new wattle and straw, came out of Old Chao's own courtyard or the nearby field. In a few days the job was done.

The building of the brigade's new office and workshop was a bigger project. Here too the first task was to pull down the old structure, part of the former landlord's old house that stood on the site and the dilapidated ancestral hall that for the last few years had done service as a sheepfold. In one day the roof was dismantled and the great roof beams, rafters, and tiles were all carefully stacked away. Then the walls came down, bricks, and adobe. The bricks were sorted, cleaned, and stacked away according to size and so were the cut stone doorsills and cornerstones. Our OSD Team was given the job of cleaning, sorting, and stacking. While this went ahead on the second day, the brawny members of the Third Brigade carried on with the work of demolition and dug the lime pit.

The third day we were not needed. A few men went on cleaning the site of rubble, the lime was slaked and left to settle, and the master builders marked out the foundation lines. There were no plans, just a few indications chalked on a board. The brigade's carpenters took over the brigade's club and meeting room and here planed the wood and knocked together the roof joists, the windows and doors. A dozen men dug the trenches for the walls' foundations. These were filled with a mixture of lime and clay, and a crew of six tamped it down. For tamper they used a square block of stone weighing over one hundred jin. Through its center was thrust a vertical handle, a heavy shaft of wood. Two men, one of them the chant leader, used this to guide the tamp. Four men pulled and slacked four ropes tied through holes cut in the tamp's upper corners.

Lao Man was chant leader. He sang an age-old tamping chant with modern words to fit the new times. Each line was repeated by the work gang and punctuated by the falling thud of the tamp.

We're building a new house.
We're building a new house.

Build it strong!
 Build it strong!
Build for the people!
 Build for the people!
Build, build it better!
 Build, build it better!
Learn from Lei Feng!
 Learn from Lei Feng!

Lei Feng was a young People's Liberation Army fighter who is highly eulogized as a man who served the people unto death.

I asked Lao Man where he got the words of his song. "Some I know," he said. "But most I think up as I go along." Sometimes the tamping went on for forty-five minutes and he never repeated a phrase.

Once the foundations were firmly laid and the lime and mortar ready, the work went ahead rapidly. A dozen or more brigade members could do bricklaying and the walls rose swiftly, with other men and girls bringing up mortar and bricks. The next day our OSD Team was busy again. More twigs were needed for wattle for the roof, and we went out along the highway pruning the lower branches of the poplars. As soon as a large enough number of twigs was cut, one of us would tie them together with a stout rope and drag the leafy bundle along behind us back to the building site. By the fifth day the roof was going on and the best bricklayers were forming an arch of bricks over the main entrance. After that all the strongest workers were withdrawn for the well-digging and only a few men, with boys and girls, remained to do the plastering and cleaning up. The plastering was done with a mixture of finely ground loess clay, chopped straw, and lime mortar. Finally, when the stronger men were free again, they tamped down the earth floor inside the rooms. Then the building was left for several weeks with doors and windows open to let the hot summer weather dry it out thoroughly.

The building of the other rooms in the hamlet was done to the same pattern. Those who could afford it used kiln-made

brick throughout for the whole of the north wall of their new
cottage as this had to bear the brunt of the cold north winter
winds. A new three-room house, with new bricks, rafters,
beams, windows and doors, could be built for 400–800 yuan
($200–$400 U.S.), depending on quality.

Spring Really Comes 🌿

*L*ong after the pink blossoms of the plum had first
graced the hamlet, the willows around the pond were
the first trees to put out leaves, fountain sprays of yellow-green.
Then came the brown-green of the poplars and the buds and
white flower sprays of the locust. In April, the frogs in the
pond began to croak and chatter furiously at night. But our
cottage was far enough away for us to enjoy the cheery sound
when we opened the door or to shut it out at will. By mid-
April, after *Ching Ming*, Clear and Bright, the countryside
was tender green where the winter wheat and barley sprouted;
bright buttercup yellow where the rape seed grew; brown-
yellow where the fallow land was being tilled, turned, or
plowed ready for the new crops.

Here and there grave mounds were still scattered over the
fields. In the 1920s it was estimated that 2 per cent of China's
arable fields were taken up with these relics of the dead. This
year some more of the older ones were plowed under without
fuss. The hamlet had long since forgotten who was buried
there. In these cases small coffins were provided into which the
remains were placed and then buried elsewhere, without regard
to half-forgotten *feng-shui* (wind and water) superstitions,
where they no longer interfered with producing food for the
living. In the old days, when all cultivation was by hand, it was
no difficult job to dig or hoe around a grave mound, but dotted
as they are haphazardly about the fields they are incompatible
with tractor plowing and cultivation.

The spiny date trees were the last to put out their new leaves, and when they did the whole hamlet was covered with green. Then the wheat turned a deeper, cooler green, entirely covering the earth. The rape lost its bright yellow flowers and it too became a thick carpet of green.

In early May our OSD Team pruned all the trees along the roads we tended. We began to weed the less-traveled sections of road, where scattered ears of wheat dropped after the last harvest began to sprout along with tough weeds and daisies.

By the end of the first week in May the maize and kaoliang were sown. Only a few patches of field still remained fallow brown, waiting for seed. For the sowing of the maize all hands were called out, men, women, and older children. There was work for everyone. I went out with the Third Team members, all our near neighbors. Arrived at the field, the team broke up into pairs. My wife and I formed one pair. We took our place in the line of sowers spread across the field. Like all the sowers, she carried a basin of maize seed, and as I dug a hole she threw in a couple of seeds which I covered with earth. In this way, with the whole line advancing abreast, we quickly sowed a good-sized field.

Later we went out thinning the sprouts. Where two sprouts had come up, we uprooted one. Where there was a patch in which no seed had sprouted we put in a spare seedling. Where a stray shoot had appeared between the rows, we pulled it up. And as we went, we weeded rank growths that would take away nourishment from the crop.

Once the shoots had taken firm root, we went out again to give them fertilizer. This operation we only watched. Chemical fertilizer is precious, so the work-team leaders did this job themselves. They filled plastic bags with the phosphate fertilizer and at just the right pace walked along the rows of plants, letting the liquid fertilizer pour onto the plants through a small hole cut in the bottom of the bag.

The next job was done when the maize was already a couple of feet high. We each filled a small basin with insecticide, DDT powder mixed with fine sand, and taking two rows each,

poured a pinch of this into the topmost cup of each plant
where the new leaves were still in the bud. This was light
work so it was given to the older women and younger girls,
most of them in their early teens. They were a gay group,
chattering like magpies as they worked. Some seemed to work
at an incredibly rapid pace, and this brought a sharp rebuke
from Lao Tsai, the veteran farmer who was their team leader.
While we all sat and rested after finishing two rows, he gave
them a harangue about wasting insecticide. "You must put
the insecticide right into the heart," he admonished them.
"It's no good doing things fast in a slipshod way. If you don't
bend down and put it in the heart, the wind just blows it
away and wastes it. Then the plant suffers."

By the time he had finished not a few ears were burning.

"Learning from Tachai," the Third Brigade had for the first
time tried out vernalization of sweet-potato seedlings to get a
quicker and larger harvest. Our Third Team had dug a pit,
built a mud stove in it, and carried the heat through two
chimneys running parallel under a four-by-seven-foot rectangular bed of manured soil. They sowed the seed potatoes
thickly in this bed and, carefully regulating the temperature
from the stove, kept the soil at around 86° F. A keen young
team member was in constant attendance during this experiment and from time to time took the soil temperature. It was
important that it should not rise above 97° F.—otherwise the
sweet potatoes would be cooked and not vernalized. Two other
beds of potatoes were sown alongside as controls. After thirty
hours the experimental bed was already getting green with
sweet potato sprouts, while the control beds were still dor-
mant. After three days the difference between the three beds
was astonishing. While the vernalized bed was thick with
green, the other two beds still only had scattered sprouts.
When the time came, the vernalized seedlings were set out
in the fields specially prepared for them. These were arranged
in a series of flat-topped ridges with sloping sides. The troughs
between the ridges were about six inches wide at the bottom.
The tops of the ridges were about a foot apart. The seedlings
were planted in the sides of the ridges in finely raked earth.

The whole experiment finally proved a great success and following this convincing demonstration of its efficacy was incorporated into the regular farming practice of the brigade.

It was a month or so after the Spring Festival. All those who had come home for the holiday had returned to their work places. Ta Sao, Yuan-tsung, and Auntie from next door were chatting in the sunshine while Ta Sao and Auntie, seated on a kaoliang mat, were doing some cutting out. Soon they were joined by some passing neighbors and the pretty young woman whose husband worked in a factory at the provincial capital. "With their heads together like that," I thought, "it's surely some women's question they're discussing." And of course it was.

When my wife returned I asked her. "Hsiao Ting is pregnant. But she's not sure she wants another baby just now. She already has three and is still nursing the youngest."

"What will she do then?"

"She is going to ask the doctors at the commune hospital for an abortion. They'll do it if she wants and her husband agrees."

"But why don't she and her husband learn about family planning? That's much better."

"They think about it but then they know that the mother-in-law doesn't hold with it and they are scared of a family row!"

We found that Upper Felicity is somewhat backward in this respect too. Complete information about contraception and family planning is available at the commune clinic and county hospital but few of the young married couples avail themselves of this medical knowledge, mainly because of the objections of the old parents. Two or three young wives who already had three or more children came to Yuan-tsung to discuss the matter, but only one decided to do anything about it. The power of the matriarch is still very strong and so is the old urge to have grandsons. They all say, in the modern way, "a daughter is as good as a son" but they know that the girls finally go to some other home. The boys carry on the family.

These conditions differ, of course, from place to place. Family planning is practiced widely in the cities and in the villages around the big cities, particularly in the more advanced eastern areas. But in Upper Felicity the young women still hesitate to discuss the question openly. They admitted to Yuan-tsung that it was embarrassing to talk to a doctor about it. She laughed at this and asked them why it was not embarrassing to go about big with child, since everybody knew then how the child got there! They saw the point and sometimes said that they would discuss the matter with their husbands.

As a cadre my wife was quite right to help them carry out the policy of the government to limit families. But this was an area inhabited by Hans, the majority nationality in China. If it had been an area inhabited by a national minority such as the Uighurs or Mongols, she would have been violating government policy if she discussed this question with them unless they had asked her specifically to do so. The People's Government policy is that since before liberation the national minorities were oppressed in many ways by the Hans, and in some cases, like the Mongols, their numbers were actually declining, it would be wrong to suggest that they limit their numbers.

Combined with contraception, abortion, and sterilization, the government instruction that marriages should be contracted at a later age is reducing the birthrate. In the old days young people married at seventeen or eighteen. Now the girls marry later, at over twenty-one.

Tragedy

A shout went up and was echoed from cottage to cottage: "There's a child in the pond!"

A woman going to rinse clothes saw a "bundle" floating in

the water. Looking closer she realized that it was a baby's legs in cotton-padded trousers. The air caught in the trousers, which were made like thick stockings, was keeping the little victim afloat, but upside down. At her agitated cry people rushed to the pond. The father dashed into the water and brought the child, dripping and muddy, to shore. He carried it home. The mother lit a fire in the middle of the floor, stripped the child, and tried to warm it back to life. Smoke soon filled the room and the sympathetic neighbors crowded around, anxious, inquiring, and offering suggestions. I had little more knowledge than the peasants about what to do in this emergency. I knew that artificial respiration should be applied —but how? Agonized at the loss of time, I thumbed through an encyclopedia and found the necessary entry. Calling some of the visiting cadres to help, I rushed to the stricken cottage. Quickly we put out the fire, cleared the room, brought hot-water bottles, and covered the little body with a quilt. Yuan, following the instructions I read out to him, began to work the child's arms back and forth to force air into and out of its lungs. But it already looked like a hopeless task. The child had been submerged too long. It was one of the two-year-old twins. They had been playing, as usual together, and wandered by the pond when she had slipped and fallen in. Her sister, not noticing, had simply wandered off and said nothing.

By the time we learned this story the doctor had arrived from the clinic. Mrs. Yuan had immediately peddled off to fetch him and he had come posthaste. He too tried artificial respiration, more expertly than we, but also without avail. Finally he pronounced the sad verdict. The mother heard it without a word and sat for a long time in silence. Then suddenly she gave a cry that shook her all over. Sobbing, she buried her face in her hands. The crowd of women and children outside stood silent for a time, then drifted away to leave the two parents alone with their grief.

We went off to work pruning trees but had not been gone long when Ta Sao came running to us in great excitement. The mother had noticed froth on the child's lips and the stomach had seemed to relax. We suspected that this was a false sign of life—probably gas escaping from the young one's belly—but three of us hurried back to see what we could do. We soon saw that it was as we had guessed, but the Yuans labored at artificial respiration for more than an hour, although it was quite hopeless. The hamlet's barefoot doctor came. He used his stethoscope to find if there was any heartbeat. Finally he inserted a fine silver needle at a spot in the tiny arm. There was no response. He showed us his book on acupuncture where it stated that there was definitely no hope of life existing if there was no reaction to stimulation at this point. We all went sadly away. Mrs. Yuan was crying. Her eyes were red with weeping, but she offered us water to drink and thanked us. The father sat disconsolate. Out in the sunshine of the yard, the remaining twin with the heartless innocence of babyhood was playing with a red ball which someone had given her. Only a few weeks ago they had been taken, brave in bright new clothes, to see the Spring Festivities on the threshing floor.

Ox, Horse, and Tractor

*L*ooking up one day from thinning the maize, we saw a team of three horses from our Third Team pulling a cart up a slight rise in the road. They had a heavy load: several sections of brick and concrete lining for the new mechanized wells. They tossed their heads, arched their necks, and strained at the traces. At the urging of their driver, they made a supreme effort and looked fine as they pressed forward over the ridge in the ground. Behind and around them trotted a long-legged chestnut foal with a white flash on its forehead.

"I love to see a horse and cart," said Mrs. Yuan. "But those oxcarts make me sick!" The oxen plod along at a snail's pace, heads lowered, empty-eyed, lunging knockkneed from side to side. Their heavy iron wheels dig deep ruts in the road and leave a sleepy cloud of dust behind. The horsecarts have pneumatic tires and sometimes make a spanking pace. The horse teams seem vastly alive. Tractors are another thing again. Intellectually we see them as the symbol of mechanization, of a modern socialist agriculture, the wave of the future. But emotionally they leave us cold. Brave with red paint, chugging relentlessly over the yellow earth, they seem too impersonal. It is only when we catch sight of their blue-overalled drivers, young men who wear peaked caps and sport white towels knotted like scarves around their necks, lithe and energetic, confident in every action and nonchalant as they probe the tractor's innards, that we sense transforming power—something that even the beautiful horsecarts do not proclaim with such assurance.

Changeable Weather 🥦

*T*he first Monday morning in mid-April dawned like a day in early summer. We saw a lone fly buzzing around the stove and swatted it, rejoicing in this harbinger of warm weather. Later that morning I took off my outer pair of woolen socks and felt hot even in the single pair of nylons I kept on. Since we were riding to the fair in the next village I changed my flannel trousers for a pair of grey cotton trousers bleached almost white by long wear. When we left, looking up at the blazing sun, I put on my large cartwheel straw hat. The heat streamed down; the air was heavy. But soon after we arrived at the fair, a fifteen-minute ride away, a gale-force wind was blowing. Clouds of loess dust hid the horizon. I left my cycle on its stand unattended for a moment. It was blown down. The swirling eddies of cold, dust-laden wind quite spoiled the fair. By evening the whole vault of the sky was hidden in a yellow dust haze. After slackening off for a bit, the wind continued to blow all night from the north.

This was the time of *Ku Yu*, Grain Rains (April 20). The

next morning was so cold that I resumed my woolen socks and put on two sweaters again and a cotton jacket. That afternoon a steady drizzle came from a leaden sky. But this turned out to be a bit of luck. One of the mechanized wells had conked out. It was some time before a technician from the commune tractor repair workshop came to help our brigade electrician repair it.

Home Gossip

In April the commune members got another allocation of raw cotton and soon the spinning wheels and weaving machines were clattering away busily. Ta Sao had already woven the black homespun for next winter, so this time she dyed her white thread pink and blue and wove *hwa pu*, "figured homespun" colored pin stripes and linings for the girl children.

I drew her as she spun patiently, expertly operating the wooden loom that she shared with other housewives. It had been repaired again and again over decades of use, here a new piece and there a patch, so that this was perhaps the twentieth reincarnation of the original machine. When the thread broke, she stopped winding for a moment, with her left hand deftly made a join, and then with face impassive, wound on. She never seemed worried for long. Sometimes if the children were overly mischievous, if the pig broke out and caused trouble or an outside hen came to gobble up the feed for her own birds, she would blaze up and use words not usually used by women but that strangely enough passed without comment in Upper Felicity. Her anger always evaporated quickly. Perhaps that was why even the years of care in the old society had left her face so relatively unscathed. Her long bobbed hair gave her a youthful look, and there was always a half smile on her lips, ready at the slightest chance to break out into a chuckle. She was naturally dignified and polite and tactful. Her presence put us all at ease and made us feel masters of all household worries, whether it was a dying fire, a leaking roof, or a chick that drooped and looked unsteady on its legs—and that died anyway even after her ministrations.

Unfortunately, her eldest son, Ching Chun, didn't take after her or Lao Man in the least. He seemed not to know what politeness was. He would come abruptly into the room. True, the front door was always open, but other people would poke their heads in tentatively to see if we were busy or did not want to be disturbed, or shout loudly, "Anybody home?" to announce their coming. But he would come in and stand about three feet inside just staring at us without a greeting. Or he looked round to see if the bicycle was there, so that he could borrow it.

I supposed that as the eldest he was a bit spoiled. Since he was their first grown child Lao Man and Ta Sao probably didn't know how to handle him. Well, neither did we, at first. We chaffed him gently that he only came to see us when he wanted the bicycle. He came then to see us a couple of times without asking for it and then dropped back into staring again. After I had cleaned the machine up several times after he had used it, I got fed up, so I took it out into the yard and cleaned it right there in front of him with a great flourish. But the hint was completely lost on him. His bad manners were part natural thoughtlessness and the rest awkwardness. I remonstrated with him straight out. I asked him *why* he thought I should clean up the cycle after he had taken his ride. He listened stolidly and I wondered if he felt insulted. But no. He said: *"Tsung-ah, tsung-ah!"* (meaning: "Okay, okay, I'll clean it up in the future!"), and I never had to bring the matter up again. The cycle was shining new from Shanghai but at first, until it was explained to him, he treated it like he treated his hoe: just flicked the worst of the mud off it and put it aside until he needed it again. I explained at length that such a machine wasn't like a hoe, that the bolts needed tightening if you heard them rattle or you would lose your brake or rear light; that the chain needed cleaning or it would get rusty and make riding harder and so on. He learned.

Schooling the Youngsters 🌿

*W*e later heard that Ching Chun had learned to give inoculations to the animals and was taking on this job at the stable. This was typical of such matters in the commune. Any capable youngster—and every youngster had some capability—was given a chance. Some were sent to the tractor repair workshop; some after getting a short course in electricity took care of the mechanized wells or mills; some were sent to be builders, carpenters, or "barefoot doctors." In this way the commune was enlarging its cadre of technically or professionally qualified men, but they still remained farmers.

All these youngsters got their education at the elementary and middle school. They learned reading and writing and math there, with a smattering of geography and history. They studied Marxism-Leninism, and the ideas and teachings of Chairman Mao, mainly from life, partly by going through the famous quotations, learning many of these aphorisms and mottoes by heart, and also studying a selected list of articles from the *Selected Works*. These included the "three good old articles": *Serve the People,* which is an exhortation to do just that; *The Foolish Old Man Who Removed the Mountains,* about the value of collective labor and perseverance; and *In Memory of Norman Bethune,* the famous article about internationalism and the Canadian doctor who gave his life for the Chinese people. They also studied such key philosophical writings as *Where Do Correct Ideas Come From?, On Contradiction,* and *On Practice,* excellent summaries of the dialectical materialist view of the world and how to use that viewpoint to change the world.

Another of the important essays they studied was *On the Correct Handling of Contradictions Among the People.* The theme of this is that contradictions, problems, or conflicts among the people forming 95 per cent of the population—the workers, peasants, revolutionary intellectuals, and other revolutionary elements—must be settled by democratic means. The methods of dictatorship, of coercion, should only be used in settling antagonistic contradictions between the people and their enemies—the recalcitrant remnants of the exploiting classes, landlords, rich peasants, foreign imperialists, and other reactionaries. There was, of course, regular political current-affairs education as well.

At the time in 1970, the controversy in the Great Proletarian Revolution was still raging around the question of how education should be organized in a socialist country, what pedagogical methods should be used, the role of the teacher—in fact, on every aspect of education. Most of these questions had as yet no final answer. As a result, at that time while it was generally agreed that it was good that these great works were being studied, many thought that the pupils had not received enough background education even in the upper classes to take them in thoroughly enough. But perhaps it is not possible for youngsters to take them in "thoroughly enough" at one go anyway. Perhaps in school, even high school, all that could be done would be a preliminary study of them, linking up their contents as much as possible with practice and leaving it to further education in society, in the activities of the social struggle, in productive experimentation and activity, to provide a "postgraduate" course.

Small Au Chiu went to school when he was seven. After a few days learning "Be resolute, fear no sacrifice and surmount every difficulty to win victory," he came home singing his next lesson: "The world belongs to you. China's future belongs to you." He was learning to write these characters. He did not understand their full significance, but of course he understood some of it, and some held that this was so much gain in the right direction. Others held that it would be better if he learned characters that he would use more generally at his age, as this way he would learn faster and what he lacked in depth at the start he could make up for later at greater speed. They were usually criticized as wanting to go back to the "c-a-t, m-a-t" method (or what corresponds to it in

Chinese) by a roundabout way. The truth of the matter seems to lie somewhere in between these two extremes. (When I returned to China in summer 1972, it was pretty generally held that the rational way to educate the children did indeed lie "somewhere in between these two extremes.")

Whatever the merits of these various arguments, the commune had its big middle and elementary schools and practically all of the school-age children were going there (though too many dropped out before completing their middle-school education). They were learning their basic reading and writing and math and science and other useful knowledge, all intimately linked with their profession—farming—and also with the moral values of the socialist revolution. That was a great advance over education in the villages before liberation, and no one doubted that the school, like everything else, would improve steadily as time went on.

It was clear that Lao Man and Ta Sao had succeeded very well in bringing up their three other children. Ta Hsiang, though much too small for her age, was growing up with all the necessary housewifely virtues. Unfailingly cheerful and handy at all household tasks, she had helped us bury our carrots for storage, make dried turnips, and care for our chicks. She was a general favorite with the neighbors.

Au Chiu was boyishly mischievous and high-spirited but just like Ta Hsiang in the matter of household tasks and helpfulness. He was always planting things in odd corners of the courtyard. Some of them actually grew. He reared innumerable small birds that had fallen out of nests, and this was much appreciated by the cat next door. But he was never disheartened. In the summer he was alternately very clean and very dirty—clean just after he had doused himself under the machine well spout or taken a plunge in the pond, dirty when he had rolled around in a tussle with some other boy in the dirt. He and Hsiao Ching had a strange habit. When the weather was swelteringly hot in summer they would lay a piece of sacking out in the yard after supper and go to sleep. But though they couldn't sleep there all night because of the mosquitoes and the dew, nothing would induce them to get up and go in. Unless they were lifted up bodily, they would not budge. The only alternative was to shout in an alarmed voice: "It's going to rain!" At this the two of them would get up, pick up their sacking, and slowly, like sleep-walkers, make for the cottage. But sometimes halfway there the urge to move would wear off and they would stand for minutes immobile and asleep like two statues until roused again by a fresh cry—or a smack from an exasperated Ta Sao.

Hsiao Ching was too young to show her full character, but there was no doubt about her spirit of independence. Once we put her out of our room for some misdemeanor. For a week afterwards she simply refused to visit us. "That room is too hot!" she would say when called. It took an abject sur-render on our part, coddling with sweets and endearments, to get her back. We told the two youngest that our home was their home, and they acted in that spirit. They ate most of their winter meals with us. They often brought their young friends in to see my drawings and kept their pals in order if they got too boisterous.

Deep-Well-Digging

We're not afraid of drought now and we'll soon be able to say: 'No more drought in Upper Felicity!' " declared Lao Man one night.

"How come?"

"Listen to that!" he replied, pointing through the paper-covered window.

For a moment there was silence in the cottage, and then we became conscious of the steady throb of a nearby electric motor. We knew its sound so well that we no longer noticed it. It was working at the mechanized well at the northern end of the hamlet. It was pouring out a heavy stream of water from its four-inch pipe, and the cold, clear stream was running fast down the channels cut for it to the surrounding fields.

"Our Third Brigade has four and a half of those now. We're soon going to dig the two more planned for this year and some more after that. When they are all dug, even if we don't get a drop of rain the whole year, we'll still be able to water our fields and get a good harvest. That means an end to drought!"

We knew enough about local history by then to realize that this final guarantee against drought freed the peasants' minds from an ancient and constant nagging anxiety about flood and drought, the twin calamities most feared by the peasants. Even in the short time we had been there we had noticed the shallow surface wells sinking lower and lower and the ponds around the hamlet already visibly drying up. There had been little snow that winter, just a few flurries that had barely covered the ground for a couple of days, and there had only been a few days of drizzly weather the whole spring. The unirrigated earth was as dry as powder where it had been broken by the tread of feet or the wheels of vehicles. In untouched spots it was as hard as brick. Since the summer rains last July and August, the area had been drought-stricken. Preliberation, the peasants would have been anxiously discussing what to do. Now the brigade leaders simply gave the order: "Switch on the pumps!"

Water had been run into the tree nurseries, and the saplings, cuttings, and seed we had sown had quickly responded, putting out leaves and pushing up through the loosened soil. The rape was a sparkling green and dazzling yellow; the onions were doing well. Day and night, men were on the job channeling the water section by section all over the winter wheat and barley fields. The tough, tufty blades of wheat were a healthy dark green, although the surface ponds around the hamlet were nearly dry.

The four and a half mechanized pumps were hard at it day and night. Their creation had been no small matter. The new wells had had to be dug down to the great reservoir of subsoil water that stretches like a vast underground sea over

加深 加深！
　加快 . 加快！

a large part of the North China plain. The existence of this underground reservoir had not been known or even suspected before liberation. It was the People's Government and the communes that had put the geologists to work, and their wide-ranging surveys with modern methods had resulted in this astonishing discovery. This deep-lying reservoir, formed millennia ago, was perpetually renewed from an even vaster area. At Upper Felicity it was between 100 and 130 feet beneath the surface. That meant sinking a four-foot shaft to a depth equal to the height of an eight- to ten-story building, lining it with brick and concrete, and installing the equipment of a mechanized electric pump, powered by electricity from a substation many miles away. While a few hours of heavy pumping were enough to exhaust a shallow surface well, the mechanized pumps were getting water from a well-nigh inexhaustible source. These things had only become possible for Upper Felicity after the formation of the communes. Up to that time geological science was a mystery to the people of the hamlet; electricity was something they only dreamed of using, and

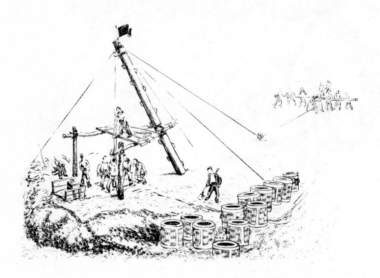

agricultural machines, even the simplest, were newfangled things.

It was with the communes that the big changes came. What had gone before—victory in the Liberation War, land reform, the start of cooperation—was the necessary preparation. With the communes came the first large-scale schemes to rid the area of drought and flood. These two evils, which had thrown the peasants every few years back to where they started, had to be conquered. Unless they were, nothing really effective could be done to improve their livelihood, let alone marching forward to socialist prosperity. This was the time when the Communist Party, leading the People's Government and the big communes in a mighty effort, began to build the three big reservoirs and widen and deepen the channel of the Wei. As the young worker had told us, this construction, with auxiliary channels and dikes, effectually solved the problem of flood. In the process a strong cadre of peasant workers and technicians was trained, men who knew how to organize labor on a big scale, how to use machines and electricity and modern construction methods and think scientifically. It was these men who, coming back to Upper Felicity, took on the big job of digging the first deep mechanized wells that would solve the problem of drought.

The commune had pioneered a technique and method of work that was extremely well adapted to digging deep into the loess soil. This has no top stratum of gravel or rock. Its loose consistency, however—it caves in easily—demands a long, continuous, and arduous effort on the part of the peasants, combined with speed and clockwork precision of activity that the old ways of farming had no precedent for. Peasants taking part in these efforts were taking the first steps to the disciplined labor of the industrial proletariat. It was no wonder that every youngster in Upper Felicity wanted to be in on the new project of digging the two new wells.

Lao Tsen was an experienced well-builder and one of the thirty- to forty-year-old veterans who, like Lao Man, had worked on the big reservoir projects. For some weeks now a

work team under him had been busy on the unused threshing floor of the Second Team, making well linings. For this
they used special kiln-baked bricks, made by the commune's
own brick-kiln, slightly curved so that they could be laid to
form a ring about four feet in diameter. These rings were
cemented together to make a four-foot-tall cylinder with top
and bottom of concrete and four strengthening staves of concrete on its sides. Enough of these cylinders were made to
line the two new hundred-foot wells.

When the cylinders were ready, the work site for the first
well was prepared. This was about thirty yards northeast of
the hamlet. As the sketch I made shows, a big tripod of
scaffolding was raised with a working stage set about eight
feet from the ground. At the top of the highest leg was a
pulley. Over this and connected to the drum of a winch was
a steel hawser. This was to raise the well-digging drum-drill
when it was filled with earth. Other paraphernalia was
brought and a channel cut to bring water from the nearest
mechanized well. Plenty of water was needed. The well shaft
had to be kept full of water while it was being dug.

When all was ready to start the digging, two teams of
eighteen excavators each were formed. They would work for
a week in two shifts around the clock. The well-digging equipment was provided by the commune. It was loaned out to
the various brigades as needed. All the labor was provided
by the Third Brigade's three teams. This was definitely work
for young men in their prime. No one much over forty was
in the teams, and these few were veterans who had charge
of the work and shared as much of it as they could. It was
a good time to start. The house building was done. The
weather just before the *Hsia Chih*, Summer Solstice, and the
start of the Heats of July was warm, but not too warm. Each
team worked six hours and then went off to sleep for six.
Most slept and ate in the hut on the nearby threshing floor
of the Third Team or under the trees there. The brigade
provided all the food for those engaged on the job. The equipment was simple. Winch and drum-drill were both worked by
human muscle power.

First a shallow shaft was dug under the tripod, the same diameter as the well. When it had gone down a meter it was flooded with water from the nearby mechanized well and the drum-drill lowered into it by means of the winch and pulley on the top of the tripod.

The drum-drill is a drum or container with a shallow, cone-shaped bottom. The sides are about two feet deep and the whole made of heavy steel plate. Its diameter is the same as that of the projected well. Two openings in the lower part of its sides opposite each other have hinged covers held closed by two bolts each. There are two slot openings in the cone-shaped bottom. Forward of these project rows of stout, hardened steel teeth about four inches long. Each slot is like an oblong mouth with teeth projecting beyond the lower lip.

The drum-drill has a vertical six-foot hollow axle rising from the point of the cone. It has a screw thread at its upper end and is held in place by crossbars set at right angles over the top of the drum. As the drum-drill cuts its way down into the soil, a new length of pipe can be screwed into the top of the axle. This too has a screw thread inside its upper end and can be similarly lengthened. Many lengths of drill pipe, each about six feet long, were now stored ready to hand on the work site.

The drum-drill was lowered into the excavation and two steel bars were fitted crosswise into square-cut sockets on the upper end of the axle. Then a gang of sixteen men, four men to a handle, began to rotate the axle and the drum attached to it. Two men looked to the winch and lent a hand as necessary, sometimes on the drilling, sometimes regulating the flow of water, seeing to it that the working was full of water but not overflowing. The teeth in the bottom of the drum bit into the soft, sodden loess soil, forcing it through the two slots into the container.

When the container was screwed full of muddy loess, fourteen men began rotating the winch to draw the drum-drill to the surface. When the drum was drawn up about a meter above the well opening, a two-leaved wooden cover made of roughly hewn planks was dragged over the opening, a wooden

box shaped like a big capital u on wheels was pulled under
the drum, the bolts holding the hinged mouths and side openings were drawn, and through the openings the loess mud
fell or was pushed into the u-shaped trolley. When the drum-
drill was thus emptied, the trolley was pulled away and its
contents were emptied onto a pile that would later be used as
fertilizer. The drum-drill ports and slots were then closed, the
bolts hit firmly into place, a few spadefuls of earth were
thrown into it as ballast, and it was lowered to fall back into
the excavation until it touched bottom. The steel bars were
inserted into the slots on the axle, the team took its place, and
with a chant from the work-song leader, they again rotated the
drum-drill and its steel teeth bit farther into the earth. Again
it was Lao Man who led the song:

One man's strength is little.
United our strength is great.
           Push hard!   Do your best!
CHORUS: Deeper! Deeper! Heigh-ya!
                      Heigh-ya!
Grasp revolution!   Get production in hand!
Follow the Party policy!
           Push hard! Do your best!
CHORUS: Deeper! Deeper! Heigh-ya!
                      Heigh-ya!

The drum was filled. As the last hard pushes drove it down,
men peeled off from the axles and raced to the winches so
that not a moment should be lost. The drum was raised,
emptied, lowered again, a new length of axle piping attached.
The process was repeated again and again without pause until
the required depth was reached.

On the fifth day, when commune experts had confirmed
that water had been reached and the well was of the required
depth, the lining of the well began. This too was carried on
without pause. The drum-drill was moved aside. A section of
lining was raised and suspended with cables from a pair of
large hooked feet attached to the winch cable. Four uprights

of bamboo were secured by kaoliang ropes to the sides of the section, and it was lowered into the well until about half of it remained above ground. A second section was then readied to fit on top of the first. The bamboo uprights served as guideposts. Each section had outside flanges for easy grips in maneuvering. Cement was then plastered on the top rim of the first section and the second section lowered carefully onto this. The two sections were cemented together and the join covered with tough builders' paper and bound with kaoliang rope. Four more bamboo upright guideposts were raised and tied to the second section and the whole two sections lowered farther into the well. A third section, a fourth, and so on were added until the first section rested on the bottom and the well was completely lined with cemented brick.

Most of the work team were now free to leave. The mechanics took over. They placed a four-inch pipe in the well, set up the pump and motor, connected the latter up with the switch and wires from the nearest power main, eased on the belting, and when everything was shipshape turned on the current. At first muddy water poured out of the L-shaped pipe into the trough that had been built below it, but soon the clear, cold water of the deep substratum lake began to gush out.

Completed in less than seven days without a hitch, the digging of the deep mechanized well was a job to be proud of. And the peasants *were* proud of it. They were delighted when I made a watercolor painting of the completed well and a series of sketches of its building.

It was very clear from the way this well was dug, from the making of the brick and concrete lining sections to the actual digging, lining, and installation of the pump and motor—all done by members of the Third Brigade, with only minimal assistance from the commune cadres—that the young peasants could quickly accustom themselves to the scientific, systematic, rhythmic speed of work that is characteristic of the modern industrial proletariat. I was often on the work site. There was speed, terrific exertion when needed, complete discipline at all times, and always an infectious cheerfulness, never a word of grumbling, always a rush by everyone to get first onto any job that had to be done.

Toward the end of the work, Lao Man paid a visit to us. But he wouldn't smoke. He just took a sip of warm water. His voice had grown hoarse and then faded out completely after hours of chanting. Another chant leader had had to take over. This was the only casualty of the well-digging.

Soon after the sixth deep well was dug, all the equipment was moved over to the site of the seventh and last well to be dug that spring. This was a mile or so to the east of the hamlet, in the middle of the fields where wheat and maize were usually grown. Work there went with the same spirit and efficiency as at the sixth. I was nearing there one morning when I was hailed by a shout:

"Lao Chen! We've something to show you!"

I hurried over. The something turned out to be a pottery shard. It was the base of a bowl, vase, or jar, three-quarters of an inch thick and about three inches in diameter. It had been dug up at a depth of thirty meters. What ages of history had rolled on while it was being buried by ninety feet of packed loess silt brought down in countless floods! The edges of the shard were well worn. The pottery was of fine quality, but what made it particularly interesting was that the inside was thickly glazed with a brilliant crackle glaze. This was clearly not peasant ware, but from a well-to-do household. It seemed unlikely that it could be the only artifact to be found at such a depth. This was the area in the catchment basin of the Yellow River that had been "the cradle of Chinese civilization." Not so many miles away was a known site of one of the cities of the Shang-Yin, the first historically authenticated ruling dynasty in China. The brigade gave me the shard and I promised to get it to the Peking scientific circles concerned with such things. Peasants and workers everywhere in China have all been told to hand in any artifacts they find.

From the time they were built, the deep wells were used steadily. No rain fell until well into July, and without the wells drought would have shriveled the early crops. With the wells supplementing other measures, Upper Felicity not only weathered the spring drought but raised a record summer harvest.

When no rain fell all the ponds went dry. The big pond's level was sinking so low that the weeds in its bottom could be clearly seen, even at its center. Only a few years back this pond had been deepened and stocked with fish fry. Then the whole thing had dried up in a similar drought and practically all the fish had died. This year, however, a channel was dug from one of the deep wells and the water turned on. In a day the pond was full of water again. The commune plans to get some new fish fry to restock it. This will make a valuable addition to the protein diet of the hamlet.

How We Ate in Spring

Upper Felicity is not very calorie-conscious. The villagers eat enough carbohydrates. These they get from their millet, maize, sweet and white potatoes, and wheaten noodles, *mantou*, flatcakes, and *chiaotze*. The vitamin-deficiency diseases like scurvy from which they suffered in the past have all been banished since they have been able to grow and stock turnips, carrots, and cabbages for the winter and eat their fill of summer vegetables like onions, peas, lettuce, spinach, cucumbers, and pumpkins from their vegetable plots and fruit from their fruit trees. They get their protein from pork, beef, eggs, and goat's milk and, very occasionally, fish. They sell most of their eggs but occasionally, to make a change perhaps once a month, make a dish of eggs. Meat they eat once a month or less, but always on the big festivals like the Spring Festival, National Day, at feasts for weddings and births and betrothals, and sometimes when a neighbor kills a pig for one of these occasions and there is some left over to be sold. Once or twice Lao Man came home with a rabbit that he had chanced on and killed with a blow from his spade. There is one huntsman who finds it worth his while to go out every now and then with an ancient hunting muzzleloader. It has a barrel about four feet long and he is reputed to be an exceptional marksman. A regular meat diet would need ready cash, and this is something that Lao Man and most of the team members are still a bit short of. Most of them have savings, but these are set aside as a result of great frugality and are usually earmarked for something special.

I found it difficult to live on their largely vegetarian diet, and I used to buy canned pork at the co-op (1.4 yuan a can), or bicycle into town or to one of the neighboring communes that kept more livestock than we did and there buy pork or beef at around seven mao a pound, or Yellow River cod at about the same price. I also ate an egg a day. As a special favor, the members of our OSD Team were allowed to buy the slightly cracked eggs at the co-op, or even a jin or two of the good eggs if we were sick. One brigade of our commune whose land ran along the banks of the Wei River raised a large flock of ducks. The one hundred fine duck eggs we were able to buy from it lasted us a long time. We ate them every day, and since the weather was already turning warm, put about fifty in brine. This kept them until we had eaten them all. Not a single one was spoiled.

This sort of feeding—or rather feasting—was regarded by the peasants as luxurious. They tolerated it in me because of my age and health. But they would not have countenanced such ways of living among themselves. Frankly they could not afford it. When they had extra heavy work to do, like harvesting or threshing or transporting heavy goods over long distances in the very hot summer months, they increased the amount of wheat they ate, replacing millet with wheat. Normally Lao Man ate millet nearly every day. When he was doing transport work in the summer he ate wheaten *mantou* every day, sometimes two to three jin a day.

Movies and Operas 🎏

One day in early spring we got news that the county's mobile-cinema team would put on a show that night. In the casual, word-of-mouth way of the hamlet, we were told by Au Chiu, in such matters the most reliable source of information, that the show would be on the main road in front of the commune office. As evening descended, all the roads and paths leading there were filled with streams of peasants, some carrying their babies and others stools or trestles to sit or stand on.

The screen hung athwart the road, held up by ropes tied to trees on either side of the highway. The audience, sitting on both sides of the screen, took up about fifty yards of road. Carts or trucks coming down the road had no way of passing and they simply stopped to see the film. Those who sat at the back of the screen weren't as crowded as those in the front, but of course they saw all the action in reverse, including the titles. This doesn't give much trouble to a proficient reader of Chinese characters, however. Once you get the general direction it is easy to go on. Many of the older peasants didn't have any difficulty about this since they couldn't read anyway. The audience this side of the screen was therefore mostly either non- or highly literate.

The projectors and the films were very good, and both sound and image came over clearly. The film was *Underground Warfare,* and it began as soon as darkness fell. It told how the guerrilla fighters of the Hopei plain had dug a labyrinth of tunnels under their villages and by means of these outwitted the Japanese invaders, at the same time giving the lie to "specialists" who had argued that it was not possible to wage guerrilla warfare successfully in a plain area that had no hills, forests, or other natural cover. It was not a new film. We had seen it at least six times over a period of as many years, but it had great relevancy here in a plain area exactly similar to that of the locale of the film and at a time when the local militia were being trained to deal with any enemy invader.

We had a number of cinema shows that year, about one every two months. In February, on the anniversary of Lenin's death, there was a showing of the fine Soviet film *Lenin in 1918*. Some episodes of this, like the scene in the Marinsky Opera House in Petrograd during a performance of *Swan Lake*, must have seemed bizarre to the audience on Upper Felicity's main road, but others definitely clicked. This was particularly so with the scene where a rich peasant, a *kulak*, comes to complain to Lenin about Soviet policy and gets ordered out for his pains.

The cinema team never seemed to choose the same place twice for its performances. The second time I saw one of their shows I went to a threshing floor in the commune's central village. Another time it was amid the ponds in front of the supply and marketing co-op. This had the advantage that it was easy for everyone to get a good seat on the many levels of the banks of the ponds. Another time it was in the large commune assembly hall. This was really the most unsatisfactory of all. The hall is a large barnlike structure built by a troop of P.L.A. sappers when they were quartered in the area. But it has gradually lost all its glass windows and, unlike the open-air shows, is full of drafts.

Two other films I saw were a documentary on the great Cultural Revolution, and a film version specially made to popularize the revolutionary Peking opera *Taking the Bandits' Stronghold by Strategy*. In the former, of course, the main interest for the villagers was seeing the most recent shots of the central figures in the epoch-making campaigns that had smashed the "bourgeois headquarters" of the renegade Liu Shao-chi and reestablished the political line of Chairman Mao in the Revolution, the line of continuing the socialist revolution and preventing any revisionism, any relapse into capitalism and semicolonialism. There were excellent sequences showing Chairman Mao on the Tien An Men Square reviewing millions of young Red Guards, of Premier Chou En-lai,

Kang Sheng, members of the Standing Committee of the Political Bureau of the Communist Party's Central Committee, Chiang Ching (Chairman Mao's wife), Yao Wen-yuan, and many others.

The second film, *Taking the Bandits' Stronghold,* particularly delighted the children. This opera has already been widely popularized. The story has been told many times on the radio and in a straight film version based on the original best-selling novel. Many of the children have heard the arias from it sung on the radio and stage so many times that they can hum the melodies and sing the words. Now seen in full color in a film taken of a performance by one of the best companies producing it, the Shanghai Peking Opera Company, it was the talk of the village for several days.

At the Spring Festival, on the night after the big mobilization meeting to discuss the plan to raise 25,000,000 jin of grain a year, and again on the occasion of the countywide meeting of Activists in the Study of Mao Tse-tung Thought that was held in Great Felicity Commune center, there were full-dress shows of local or Peking opera or agit-prop performances by the commune's Mao Tse-tung Thought Youth Propaganda Team. This group put on songs and recitations to music with acting and sometimes in costume. Some items were quotations from Chairman Mao's writings set to music, others illustrated quotations or slogans in dramatic form. The peasants liked these because they could follow everything. They knew the quotations themselves or at least were familiar with them. But they had seen or heard so many performances of a high professional standard both on the screen and radio or by visiting professional troupes that they were more than a little patronizing to their own lads' and lasses' efforts. They were quite critical too, but also appreciative, when the county dramatic troupe came down and put on a performance of another of the model revolutionary Peking operas—*The Red Lantern.*

This is a story from the time of the Japanese occupation of China's northeast. A revolutionary railwayman has been given the task of passing on a code from the main Party organization to the guerrilla detachment operating in the nearby countryside. But before he is able to carry out the task he is betrayed and arrested by the Japanese. He bravely defies both their threats and blandishments. His mother and his adopted daughter are then rounded up and all three taken to the execution ground. He and his mother are shot, but the daughter is spared. The Japanese rightly suspect that she has inherited the revolutionary task of her father, and they think it will be easy to follow her when she gets the hidden code and goes to deliver it to the guerrillas. Nevertheless she outwits them. The guerrillas attack and wipe out the enemy.

The Peking Opera conventions of acting, singing, and declaiming are admirably suited to the elevated and heroic tone of this story. There is no doubt of the story's educational impact. For days afterwards the youngsters in Upper Felicity were striking heroic attitudes in Peking Opera style. But it was also certain that these were not merely attitudes of body and gesture. Something of the steadfast revolutionary courage of the railwayman and his daughter had entered their souls. This is an exceedingly fine piece and the peasants enjoyed the intriguing story.

The music of these operas is still in the traditional style of Chinese music played on traditional instruments, but what with the public radio broadcasts and the many home radios in Upper Felicity, I found many peasants quite at home with the entirely Western-style music and orchestration of the popular new revolutionary ballets, *The White Haired Girl* and *The Red Detachment of Women* and also *The Yellow River Piano Concerto.*

Summer

A TIME OF GROWTH AND MATURING

*W*arm May glided into warmer June and the time of *Mang Ch'un,* Grain in the Ear. The tempo of work quickened in the hamlet as harvesttime drew near. There were many things to do, and they all had to be completed so that when needed every available man and woman could be called for the harvest and threshing.

Hours and minutes are crucially important in the days of the harvest. Reaping, gleaning, bringing in the crop; threshing, stacking, winnowing, and bagging the grain all have to be done as swiftly as possible, because it is the time of year when the warm, dry, sunshiny days change into the moisture-laden monsoon days. Then come sudden storms and showers. In the morning the weather seems fine. The reapers cut the crop, but while the sheaves are lying in the open, dark clouds will cover a sky that only a few minutes before was cloudless and of a dazzling blue, and down will come a thrashing wind and a torrent of rain that will scatter the sheaves and wreck months of labor. The team leaders keep in constant touch with the weather reports on the radio and on the phone. But they must also have a weather eye cocked to the skies and

the signs that a countryman reads to tell him what the
weather holds for him. If they guess wrong and a threshing
floor is cleared of grain because of fear of a downpour that
does not come, hours of precious time may be lost. And if
they guess wrong and say there will be no rain when a
torrent is brewing, bushels of precious grain can be ruined.

As harvesttime approached, unfinished houses had to be
hurried to completion. Roofs at least had to be put on. The
vegetable plots needed constant attention: weeding, hoeing,
planting out, pruning, watering. The maize had to be thinned
out, and the first hoeing done there. The teams' best workers
prepared the threshing floors. These had to be given new

facings of sifted loess and chopped straw and rolled flat and hard with a proper slope for drainage. Sacks for the grain had to be repaired, sickles sharpened, and carts and trolleys for the roads and threshing floors put in order. Rakes, brooms, and flat spades for winnowing all had to be readied and turned over to the leaders of the threshing-floor work teams. Mobilization meetings were held to remind team members of the importance of full and prompt attendance at work.

Brigade and team cadres met often to plan out their work and check up on how preparations were going ahead.

One morning Kao, the Third Team's leader, rang the bell over the mortar stone earlier and with greater vehemence than usual. It was the start of the harvest, and he was determined that that day should go well. The men were still busy building, so he was calling out mainly the women and youngsters to begin on the small field of barley. At nine o'clock sharp he was ringing again for the after-breakfast shift. It had been agreed to shorten the time for meals.

"It's already nine o'clock!" he scolded in a loud voice so that every courtyard could hear. "And how many are here? One, two, three—ah, another two are coming. Still, that's only five! Hurry up! Hurry up!" And he clanged the bell again. There was a flurry of movement as more and more reapers hurried out, wiping their lips, adjusting their coats, testing the cutting edge of their sickles.

When he finally got a respectable body of reapers together he moved off at their head without bothering to wait for the late stragglers.

It looked like a very large family party. Kao, brawny, strode along in white homespun shorts that left his massive calves free; his jacket open and flapping; his round head shaved and shining. In a bunch just behind him were the bigger girls, chattering, giggling, joking. Bringing up the rear in larger or smaller groups were the mothers with their children. In the last of the groups was old Granny Chao, with bound feet, determined to answer the call for a record turnout. Ignoring custom, which ordains that men in such a company should walk in their own group of males, I went along with Yuan-

tsung and Ta Sao and Lao Tang's pretty young hostess. Her little girl, and our two youngsters, Au Chiu and Hsiao Ching, gamboled along together. She carried her smallest in her arms. She would put him in a shady place by the barley field where he would be handy for his next feeding.

When we reached the field we spread out in line along the furrow ends that bordered the road. Each took one, two, or three rows, depending on his strength and ability. I took two rows, which was one too many. Ta Sao showed me how to use the sickle. You grasp a handful of wheat stalks in your left hand, pull them slightly backward, and give a sharp chop at their base where they are bent. After you have cut a good

fistful you lay this behind you and to the left at right angles
to the furrow so that all your sheaves have their ears in the
same direction and can be picked up readily by the gatherers.
Then you advance to the next series of cuts.

A good reaper bends to his task and moves steadily forward,
leaving behind him a three- or four-row swath and a neat trail
of sheaves. This is hard on the back muscles and some prefer
to hunker or crouch as they reap. Old Granny Chao sat on
her little stool and cut three rows before moving on and
sitting again. She and some of the other oldsters were several
rows behind the rest toward the end of the shift, but those
who had finished their rows first began at the end of hers

and then worked their way down the rows to meet her before the team leader gave the word for rest.

It was surprising how the big stand melted as line by line the barley went down before the sickles. Some of the younger women got up a competition for sheer joy of work, and as they slashed their way forward, heads bobbing and arms flying, it was so exciting that we all stopped to look and cheer.

Later that day, since the horses were being used with the old cart to fetch coal and the oxen were all plowing, the whole team of over three dozen men, women, and children went out with the new horsecart to haul the barley harvest back to the threshing floor. We pulled the empty cart to the middle of the field and then scattered in all directions to bring the sheaves to it. When it was loaded high, even with some pulling on the ropes in front, others pushing at the rear, and a few at the wheels, we had a hard job getting it back to the road over the furrows and the ditch. Usually this carting job would be done with a team of three horses, two in the front on traces and the third, the strongest, between the shafts. It would be driven, stop and start, about the field, with two men throwing up the sheaves to another who arranged them on the cart, building himself up higher and higher. It was always a glad sight to see a cart laden high with barley or wheat slowly coming home to the threshing floor under the brilliant sunshine.

The next day we began harvesting the first of the wheat fields. I had come a bit late but I pitched in right away among the women and children and worked for some time in what I thought was fine professional style.

"Lao Chen!" sang out a cheeky girl. "How many stalks do you cut an hour?"

I had been working with a will, head down, and concentrated on the job. Now I looked up and found myself well behind the children. There was a general laugh at my expense.

The "Small Doctor" had set up his bed and medical equipment in one of the rooms the brigade had built for its new office compound. But true to the style of barefoot doctors he was usually out in the fields, either at work himself or making

the rounds of the work teams with his Red Cross kit. In a sterilized aluminum box he had his set of acupuncture needles. In his pocket he had his handy first-aid booklet and his well-thumbed copy of Chairman Mao's *Quotations*.

During a work break he would take a seat a bit apart from the main group of resting and chatting harvesters, and open his book. In a minute the youngsters and children would gather round him to hear some appropriate quotations, and when that was done he would tend their hurts. During the harvest these were mostly cuts, scratches, and splinters. With the older people it was usually a matter of stiff and aching joints or muscles, and he gave them acupuncture treatment. The cadres from the city often got mild sunstrokes and he gave them either APC or tiny silver pills of an herb concoction.

Yuan-tsung and I were good friends with him. He had dropped in on us with some substance which looked like old wood and which, on his instructions, we had put into our water butt during a mild flu scare. The next morning Yuan, seeing this brown thing floating in the water and forgetting what it was, took it for a rat and let out a screech that brought Ta Sao running in.

When we complained of mice, our barefoot doctor brought us some white powder which we sprinkled in all the corners of our cottage. Our mouse, however, was well fed and would have nothing to do with his white powder. At that he helped us rig up a simple and most effective trap. He upended a small bowl on the stove and then placed another, larger bowl, inverted on the first, delicately balancing it so that it would fall at a touch. A bait of meat placed under the rim of the small bowl completed the scheme. That night our mouse tugged at the meat, shook the small bowl and the large bowl came down over him and the bait. Next morning I edged a sheet of paper under the large bowl. Inside was the trapped mouse. Never having caught a mouse before, I took it down to the pond and threw it into the water to drown. Well, he was cleverer than I. He had never been in water before, but he swam like a champion and scampered away.

When the summer rains came and the surface wells grew muddy, our barefoot doctor gave us some white substance looking like chalk to put in the water butt, which caused the mud to settle at the bottom. I never had the wit to ask him what all these various things were, but he assured us that they were all local methods. Later I found out that the water cleaner was alum. They were all free and certainly effective.

When Yuan-tsung and I reached home at the end of that first day of the harvest, one of the old veterans who looked after the vegetable gardens was there ahead of us. He had two large cucumbers in his hand that he wanted to give to us. We refused politely, as normal courtesy demands, but he wouldn't take no for an answer. These were our share as team workers in the regular handout of vegetables, he explained. With this explanation we accepted the cucumbers. Then Yuan, seeing his little grandson with him, offered him a sweet. The little lad refused politely and the old man explained that he had been given the task of delivering our share of vegetables regularly and could not possibly take any present for it. This was said with so much dignity and gravity that we felt ashamed of our tactlessness.

In this way throughout our stay we were kept in vegetables. When we left Upper Felicity it was a hard job to persuade the team leaders to let us pay for them.

It was far pleasanter working as a regular if somewhat erratic part of the brigade's work teams than on our own as an OSD Team. We wondered why we hadn't insisted on doing this before. Originally, of course, the leadership of our OSD Team had been worried that if we worked with the peasants as part of their own work teams we couldn't stand their pace. This was true, but the peasants are not such sticklers for etiquette as the team leadership imagined. When they saw we were tired they simply packed us off. When we lagged, one or the other of the stronger ones came over and gave us a hand, just as they gave any other of their weaker teammates a hand. Furthermore, in any collective job there are various tasks and there was always some light work—

even if it was only going to fetch drinking water—that I could do and yet be part of the team.

The leadership had also been worried that the fact that we couldn't do a full shift might reflect on team discipline. But we found that the teams had different degrees of discipline. In such jobs as well-digging or building, where the team had to work like clockwork or mess up the job, discipline was strict and was conscientiously observed by all. Although no "foreman" bellowed to keep them in line, such work teams were composed of veterans and the most active and toughest young lads and lasses. They were nearly all activists and took a pride in working in "the Tachai spirit." The heavy nature and close coordination of their work precluded my joining them. But in the more mixed work teams, where the older women and even the grannies and the older and younger children worked, discipline was interpreted with a lot of lee-way. When the baby cried too insistently, even if its mother was in the middle of a row she knocked off and fed it. Some-one took her place and finished the row. We were not much of an addition to the labor power of even these teams, since the most we could manage was a stint of about two or two and a half hours, but they welcomed us gladly anyway.

"Here are the two Chens!" they would greet us as they saw us coming up. Many were amused and a bit puzzled because both our names were Chen: Chen I-fan and Chen Yuan-tsung. Husbands and wives always keep their own names after marriage, and a marriage between two people of the same surname here is unknown. My wife was known very formally as Chen Yuan-tsung but more familiarly as "Lao Chen's wife" or "Au Di's mama" (Small Brother's mother). In Chinese this is "Au Di-ti Mama," and it rolls off the local lilting tongue very nicely. So important are the children here that even I was often called "Au Di-ti Papa."

Another of our special, amusing eccentricities was that we were "always together!" That was perhaps an exaggeration. We never even touched in public, and of course never dreamed of a public kiss or similar show of affection. But we

were very often together. One day we were walking together
to the harvest field and we passed a solitary plowman. In the
act of turning his yoke of oxen as the furrow ended by the
roadside, he stopped, contemplated us for a moment, and
said, "Lao Chen, you and your wife are always together! It
seems that you are in love with each other! The Lius go about
together, but they are old. The Tangs go about separately.
[The Tangs stick to the conventions. When they walk out,
Old Tang walks three yards in front of his wife.] But you
two are like Liang Shan-po and Chu Ying-tai!"

We laughed at his comments, and he grinned.

"Do you know that story?" he asked.

He gave us a brief account of how these two young people
of Old China had fallen in love and fought the old feudal
marriage customs to unite their lives. They had perished, but
a kind fate had turned them into two butterflies, and they
had thus lived happily ever after. Still musing, he went on
with his plowing after waving us a cheery good-by.

We passed Ta Sao, Auntie, and the two small ones sitting
on the grass by the roadway under the shade of the maize
plants. Au Chiu held a string tied to the leg of a tiny jack-
rabbit. It was too small even to be frightened. Its fur was
tawny brown and streaked white, perfect camouflage for the
loess plain, and I wondered at the hardihood and cunning
of these creatures who had dwelled and survived for so many
millennia on these formerly hungry plains.

We passed a plodding bullock cart piled high with wheat
sheaves. Sitting on top was a pretty girl under her broad-
brimmed straw hat. She gave me a beaming smile-for-the-
old-man.

"Lao Chen's on the job!" commented the driver. He was
referring, of course, to the sketchbook that I held in my hand
to make a quick sketch of the scene.

We did our afternoon stint with the First Production
Team, which was gleaning. This team was short on manpower, so they reaped their wheat with a contraption that
was only used in certain areas of North China. This was a

straight-bladed scythe wielded with two hands: the left hand held its handle and the other hand held a cord attached to the far end of the scythe and to the back of a shallow cord basket fitted on a bamboo rim and attached to the back of the scythe. The reaper swung the scythe in a broad sweep from right to left. The wheat fell in sheaves into the flat basket back of the scythe. With a follow-through swing, the reaper emptied the basket of sheaves into a corded trolley that was pushed conveniently behind him by the second member of the team. Such a two-man team could replace four ordinary reapers. Its disadvantage was that it left many stalks still standing and much on the ground. But these could be gleaned by women and even very small children. In this way the team, despite its lack of fully able-bodied manpower, was able to complete its harvest in time.

While we worked the men spoke little, concentrating on the job. The women and children, however, scurrying hither and thither as they gleaned, were like a flock of chattering sparrows. The children had been let out of the school for the gleaning and even those of seven and eight were there earning their work-points, so many work-points for so many pounds of wheat stalk weighed on the spot and noted down in a book by a couple of schoolchildren, a girl doing the sums and a boy doing the weighing.

This was our first time with this team, so they were very curious about us—how old were we, how many children did we have, where were our parents, did we have brothers and sisters, what was our work in the city, where did my wife get her socks, did she make her own clothes, why was I making all those drawings?

In the countryside a young mother has no hesitation about nursing her baby in public, but the unmarried young women and girls are always neatly buttoned up to the neck and never roll their trouser legs up higher than the knee. My wife, in city style, in summer wore a halter brassiere that was clearly visible through her light cotton blouse. This intrigued them, and they were interested to know the cut of this garment that evidently they themselves did not wear. Since she was married and "from the city," no one was shocked at all by this. Had she been unmarried I suspect it would have appeared to them as rather scandalous.

Summer Wear 彩

With the summer heat upon us, the men of the hamlet wore white homespun shorts or trousers rolled up above the knee and loose, unbuttoned jackets. Many discarded their jackets when they worked. Their large-brimmed straw hats or traditional flat, cone-shaped sun hats protected their heads, but soon all were sunburned dark brown. Some of the youngsters wore drill shorts tailored in modern style and nothing else and looked neat and fine as they plied their shovels and hay forks on the threshing floor. The older men's clothes were cut by their wives in traditional fashion, very baggy and loose-fitting. The girls too wore large, cartwheel straw hats, but some of them preferred a white towel loosely put on their heads with the fringed edges dangling on either side. In their light printed cotton jackets and trousers, they brought bright touches of color to the green fields. Au Chiu and the other little boys simply threw off all their clothes and went around without a stitch. Au Chiu had to dress himself properly for school, however. Next year he would have to wear shorts. Hsiao Ching, at five, wore flowered cotton shorts that always seemed to be slipping down from her waist to somewhere around her hips. Other tiny girl toddlers wore triangular aprons. One corner had a loop of tape to be put around the neck, the two middle corners were taped and tied at the back, and the third end hung down decorously, concealing their tummies. Some of these aprons were beautifully embroidered with flowers and gamboling lions.

Most of the time I went around in shorts and a cartwheel straw hat. On more formal occasions I put on a white vest.

On the Threshing Floor 🌿

*F*rom June through July the wheat and barley fields and threshing floors became the focal points of the hamlet's life. As soon as the two crops were harvested and cleared from the fields, the plowing teams went into action and the same fields were sown in maize, kaoliang, beans, and cotton.

There was plenty of work for everyone, old and young. Besides the reaping, binding, and carting, there was the gleaning. This was mostly done by the children. Then the maize plants had to be thinned and hoed. The vegetable plots needed ceaseless attention. For a time most of the light womanpower of the Third Team was sent to the large red flower plot, east of the hamlet, and up to the team's threshing floor. The girls brought baskets of harvested petals and spread them in thick gorgeous carpets on the threshing floors to dry. The brilliant orange-red and yellow petals are used to make the medicine that traditional doctors prescribe for various women's complaints. Later the seeds are collected and pressed to make fine oil, and finally the hemplike stems are used for making cord or bags.

Up through the times of the *Hsiao Shu* and *Ta Shu,* the Small and Big Summer Heats, activity on the threshing floors never ceased. Most of the brawniest men of the teams were concentrated here. Sometimes they worked in shifts day and night.

During the hot morning hours and until three in the afternoon, most of the open area of the Third Team's threshing floor was spread with the wheat to be dried and threshed that day. At that time most of the men were sleeping in the hut that had been repaired and cleaned for them just beside the floor. At three o'clock the stone threshing rollers were brought out. These are about the same size and shape as small beer barrels. Their sides are grooved to get a grip on the wheat, and they are mounted on frames with the axles running through holes bored through their centers. The team had four rollers in operation, drawn by animals in concentric circles over the wheat laid on the ground. The outer circle was taken by the strongest, fastest team of two mules; inside them and just behind came an odd team of a mule and an ox; inside and behind them came two oxen; and last, on the innermost circle, came a single plodding bull. The driver stood in the middle holding the four reins and his whip, urging the animals on and keeping them on course. Hovering around was a helper holding a scoop, who apparently could predict when any of the beasts was going to present manure. His job was to catch the precious stuff before it had time to fall and soil the wheat. He also had a broom of thin bamboo handy to keep the wheat under the course of the rollers.

The rolling threshing went on all afternoon till the winnowing began. The winnowers were armed with large, very light, flat wooden shovels. They tossed the threshed wheat ears high up into the air, where the evening wind caught and carried off the chaff, letting the heavy, red gold grains of wheat fall straight back to the ground. The winnowers moved steadily forward over the threshing floor. Behind them came men with large whiskbrooms who pushed aside the chaff and swept up the grain for the winnowers to give it a second, third, and fourth throw. Other men with large, light bamboo rakes pulled away and stacked the straw.

Soon the electric lights went on. The work went forward in the pool of light they made in the immensity of the dark plain under the purple vault of the sky. Above was the astonishing arch of the Milky Way and the stars of the Bear and the Centaur. Winnowing and stacking went on from the early hours of the morning until the end of the first morning shift. Then the wheat for the next day's threshing was spread on the floor and the night laborers went to sleep.

Lao Man was in charge of our team's threshing floor, and he took this responsibility with the utmost seriousness. Only a few weeks before he had been selected one of the team's delegates to the local conference of Activists in the Study of

Mao Tse-tung Thought. This three-day meeting, held in our commune, had been called by the county Party committee. It was one of hundreds being held simultaneously all over the country to propagate the study of Mao Tse-tung's ideas and teachings among the peasants. Its keynote was the practical application of Marxism. They studied how Lenin had used Marxism to lead the Russian Revolution and how Chairman Mao had used it to lead the Chinese Revolution, with particular reference to conditions in China's countryside. The conference was at once a place for practical study and a lively exchange of experience. It also enabled the local county and commune leaders and the stalwarts of the brigades and teams to get to know one another.

Lao Man might not understand too much of the historical analysis, but he had a wealth of knowledge both of the problems of the Honan countryside and the experience of the co-ops and communes in solving them. In a small discussion group he could describe that experience well. I often saw him going into plenary session. I also saw him sitting in the shade of trees or haystacks with small groups of conference delegates, discussing problems that could be better handled in such a small group or chewing over the discussions and resolutions proposed at the plenary sessions. Later, with the help of one of the visiting cadres, he wrote an article for the provincial daily summing up what he had said. The conference had discussed many questions, from planting beans to marriage. Its members had gone out to see how neighboring communes and brigades and teams had successfully solved certain problems like irrigation, reforestation, or the planting of new crops.

Fresh from the conference, Lao Man was appointed to be a threshing-floor leader. Since like the other delegates he had pledged himself to do a good job in the approaching harvest season, he was on the job day and night. He slept in the rest hut right next to the floor; and Ta Sao often brought his meals to him there. If it rained or threatened rain, it was he who, in consultation with the other "old heads," decided whether to stack and cover the wheat spread on the threshing floor or wait a while. If it rained at night, he sprang up and was the first to see to the stacks. He received no extra work-points. It was a post of honor. (One of his relatives, however, raised the question of allotting him extra work-points, and the team leaders finally agreed it should be discussed at a coming meeting.) At the height of the threshing we rarely saw him at home. He would sometimes drop in for a meal and to see how things were getting on and then would rush off again. Ta Sao was solicitous for his health and gave him extra large and good meals with wheaten *mantou* instead of meal porridge. But sometimes her patience was sorely tried. One evening she had kept Lao Man's *mantou* and vegetables hot for him long after the time he was expected. Finally she sent Au Chiu to fetch him. He too did not return. It was near ten when they both straggled in, and angry words were exchanged. Lao Man came to eat in our cottage. "Can't she understand?" he complained. "This is the most important harvest of the year. What if there should be a fire or other accident on the threshing floor? Anyone would think that I liked to work on an empty stomach."

"But why didn't you send Au Chiu back with a message?"

"We go to eat by turns so that there is always someone on the floor. The two young rascals who should have come back to relieve me simply went on eating and chatting and forgot me. When Au Chiu came I sent him off to call them, and he couldn't find them. Now you see why the team wants old heads like me to do this job. If I hadn't made a promise at that conference, I'd never have taken on this responsibility. But a promise is a promise."

"But you have to consider Ta Sao too," put in Yuan-tsung. "You know she won't rest until everyone has eaten. Those two young men should be criticized."

After the threshing and winnowing, the clean grain was bagged in narrow, four-foot-high sacks that were handy for carrying on a man's shoulder. As they were filled they were stacked in the threshing-floor shed. The peasants like to eat fresh wheat, so some of it was shared out right away among the team members. Lao Man, smiling broadly, came home one day with a big sackful.

As soon as possible the team piled the new horsecart with

sacks and with a red banner atop carted it off to the grain-collecting center as Upper Felicity's share of the state grain tax. Every day you could see the lines of grain carts making their way to the state granary in the commune center.

Summer Storm 🌿

A shower of rain fell in the afternoon of the first day of reaping and talk in the hamlet was all about the weather. In the old days, said the veterans, this hinge in time between the dry, clear days of early summer and the coming of the summer monsoon with its sudden showers and downpours was called the time of "snatching the harvest from the jaws of the dragon." But that night it cleared up, and from then until the end of the reaping it was fair. The wheat was all stacked around the threshing floor and a large part of it was already threshed before the dragon made another snatch with his drooling maw.

We were just coming in from the fields when we saw a bank of dark, thick clouds gathering over the mountain mass that stretched in a semicircle west to north. It truly was like a great dark, gaping mouth that would devour the plain. The clouds spread upwards. The mountains were completely hidden. Only the most northerly pyramid peak remained visible. Half the blue dome of the sky was covered. The thunder rolled and lightning flashed in great jagged stabs. Then it seemed as if a whole quarter of the cloud mass between us and the mountains dissolved suddenly in one spectacular deluge of rain. Through the translucent veil that was left we could see with startling clarity range after range of mountains, stretching farther than we could ever see on a clear day. "It's like a movie!" shouted Mrs. Tsang as we ran.

The black cloud mass moving toward us seemed to shift direction and veer over toward West Board Bridge Village.

Then we felt the first drops of rain and hastened our race for
shelter. But the full fury of the storm caught us. First came
the lash of wind that moved ahead of the clouds. It dashed
a riot of dust and pellets of earth, twigs, and straw against us,
stinging our faces, arms, and legs. We clutched our broad
straw hats tight and covered our mouths and noses with our
hands against the swirling dust. Then came large, cold drops
of rain, which a moment later were pelting down in solid
sheets of water. The howling wind drowned our voices,
tossed the trees. For fifteen minutes and more the rain poured
down, filling the ditches, turning the road into a slithering
quagmire. Then it passed. Where we were the sun shone,
but we could see the storm tearing away to the southeast.

Within half an hour under the blazing sun, the high
ground was still damp but baked hard enough to walk on
without slipping. The deeper ruts in the road were still
quagmires that quickly put weights of mud on your shoes
or squeezed squelching goo between your bare toes.

It had been a relatively mild shower, swift-moving and, so
we were told, "not so heavy." It could have been worse, much
worse. It could have come three days earlier and gone on
for hours or days. Then it would have left a trail of disaster
in its wake—acres of flattened wheat, shattered stacks, damaged houses, and impassable roads. Such storms, sometimes
with hailstones as big as peas, had been known to cut a
harvest yield by 20 per cent or more.

Summer Heat 🌿

By the end of June, the summer heat was upon us. By
noontime it was oppressively hot and like the rest of
the villagers we were glad to "go to ground" inside
our cottage and sleep till midafternoon. The afternoon work
shift began well after two and sometimes not until three, at

the height of a heat wave. To make up for this, the peasants began work very early. They were out in the cool of the morning around four-thirty, and they worked late until twilight came around at seven-thirty.

Inside our south-facing cottage, it was usually cooler by many degrees than outside. We used to open the doors and windows in the early morning to cool the place off then shut the door to keep the cool in. By noon the temperature soared. On such days I found I couldn't keep awake and like several others, particularly the older people, began to feel the beginnings of heat prostration. It was then that I rigged up my table-and-plastic-bath to cool myself off in after work. In the evenings as the sun went down and the breeze began to stir, we opened the door again. We only really began to suffer from the heat when there was a prolonged spell of very hot weather with no rain. Then the walls and roof of our cottage got thoroughly baked and inside it was like an oven. Luckily a heavy shower of cold rain finally came to cool off both us and the cottage. The peasants didn't bother to close and shut doors and windows as we did. They left the doorway open, covered with a bamboo screen to stop the pigs and chickens from entering. They tore the paper covering off the windows, and brought kaoliang mats out at night and slept on the ground or up on the roof.

We didn't sleep outside because there were still a few mosquitoes around—not many, but enough to annoy. Their relative absence was partly because the breezes kept the insects on the move, but the main factor was that the hamlet had sanitation well in hand. We never used a mosquito net. We found that a stick of antiinsect incense burning in the bedroom was enough protection. We never saw a bedbug in our cottage, and, despite the existence of numerous outdoor latrines around us, there were few flies. The hamlet had succeeded brilliantly in its antifly drive and never let down its guard. The latrines were regularly emptied and cleaned. Each farmyard had its compost pit. Into this the refuse of the yard was swept daily, and every few days a layer of loess was swept or thrown onto the muck. The ponds, too, were well looked after, and there were no small stagnant pools in the hamlet for mosquito larvae to breed in. Those who know what pre-liberation North China villages were like will appreciate what a revolutionary change all this represents.

By this time we had extinguished our big inside stove. Since we had no outside kitchen like the peasant households, I put our Japanese-style "beehive" stove against the wall just outside our door, and we used it to do our cooking on. To protect it from the rain I built a low wall of adobe brick around it. From two hooks in the wall I hung a roof of corru-gated iron sheeting about three feet by two whose lower end rested on the wall. This withstood any normal rainstorm.

The "beehive" is an admirable invention. The stove itself is simply a cylinder of thin iron about five inches in diameter, with a sliding door over the lower vent to regulate the intake of air and a cover for the top. The "beehives" are placed into this from the top. These are three short cylinders of pressed coal dust about four inches in diameter and a two and a half inches tall, each pierced with ten half-inch holes. Once the bottom cylinder is lit, it will burn away slowly and then burn the one on top. When the bottom one is burned out you add another beehive to the top. Two will keep burning without attention the whole night through. In the morning you open the lower vent and in a few minutes you have strong hot flames roaring through the holes in the upper beehive. It is a very efficient and cheap form of heating. In the cities, where gas ranges and gas supply are still rare and the use of elec-tricity is not yet encouraged for cooking and heating, it is widely used.

Upper Felicity was greatly intrigued by our beehive stove. Every neighboring family came to inspect it. It had one draw-back from their point of view—while it was quite adequate for a family of four or even five, it was too small to heat the kind of pot needed for a family of six to eight, which is what many of the households wanted. This point was discussed, and it was agreed that possibly larger beehives could be made. The question of making the pressed coal could be easily overcome. The county's communes were already discussing the opening of a local coal mine, which would bring pithead coal to within a distance of forty li.

This plan to open the coal mine throws some light on how such things are done in China. Only the construction of big-scale enterprises demanding capital investments of twenty million yuan or so are planned by the central state planning organizations. Smaller-scale enterprises needing only local funds can be started by the provinces, counties, or communes themselves to satisfy local needs. They will naturally report what they have done and what input and output are involved, but when it is a matter of spending local funds they do not need to ask permission from anyone except their own constit-uents. This method encourages self-help and local initiative. Seven million tons, or half of China's chemical fertilizer, were produced in locally established plants in 1970.

If the commune wants to set up a small enterprise such as a mill or mine, it can raise the necessary capital as a loan from its constituent brigades or, since it is a local authority, get an allocation of funds from the county government as part of its budget. The agricultural tax would be the source of such an allocation. Labor would be supplied by the brigades. The brigades contributing capital can be repaid out of the profits of the enterprise.

A brigade can similarly get funds to establish an industrial or other enterprise by getting contributions from its constit-uent teams. These contributions are then repaid out of the profits of the enterprise. The brigade is then the collective owner of the enterprise.

Between Harvest and Sowing 🥀

*T*he summer harvest was fairly good, but the peasants of Upper Felicity, while confident, were also cautious in ven-turing final forecasts. They planned this year to raise income per member in their brigade to an all-time record, a big 30-

per-cent leap over the previous year, and they knew that there might yet be a stiff fight to raise and bring in a good autumn harvest. There could be no relaxation of effort at this time. In fact, right after the summer harvest they plunged into strenuous work with all their manpower to get the autumn crops sown in good time to benefit from the summer rains.

The weather following the harvest was very changeable. This was the time of the Summer Heats, from the *Hsiao Shu*, Slight Heat, to the *San Fu*, Third Heat—the "Autumn Tiger." One day would be tropically hot and the next cool enough to have to wear a jacket over your shirt. After one prolonged shower, the rain began to soak through our thick earthen roof and in the middle of the night I had to rig up a contraption of ropes and string and plastic sheeting and an umbrella over our bed.

The next day Ching Chun patched that part of the roof. The hay stored there had prevented the rainwater from running off, so it had formed a pool and slowly trickled through the six inches of ceiling. But only a small patch was affected. Ching Chun threw all the hay down and announced that the whole roof would have to be given another layer of earth if it was to withstand the summer rains.

First Aid and Beansprouts ✿

One day Big Son came to our cottage, followed by a crowd of children. He held a bloodstained rag to his skull. He had been completing the building of the new brigade office when a spade had dropped on him. Luckily its blade had only gashed his head. Though only skin-deep, the wound was three inches long and pouring blood. We had some reputation for our knowledge of first aid and so he had come to us first, just across from the building site, instead of going to the clinic, which was a good ten minutes away.

We bathed and cleaned the wound with antiseptic fluid,

and then the young barefoot doctor ran up with his first-aid kit. He put some antitetanus ointment on the wound and bandaged it up with clean gauze. We gave Big Son a basin of hot water to clean off the blood on his face and hands and washed his bloody handkerchief for him. He was feeling a bit dizzy, so we advised him to go home and take a rest. It was a small matter, but since it was a dirty wound, it might have proved dangerous. We dismissed it from our minds. The next day Big Son was back on the job doing light work.

Some days later Big Son's old mother came to us with a large bowl of fine beansprouts, and she pressed them on us, refusing to take no for an answer. We learned later that it was the third batch of sprouts she had raised for us. The first two batches hadn't satisfied her. We had succored her only son, and she was determined to express her thanks to us in a really spectacular way.

Of Pig and Sunflowers 🐖

With the coming of spring the vegetables grew thick in the plots around the hamlet. And Little Pig (no longer little) was confined to her sty. It was her own fault. She had nosed into a vegetable plot and eaten the spinach seedlings. This, of course, was a heinous crime, because the vegetable plots all belonged to the collective. Ta Sao imprisoned her before she could do any more damage, and for days thereafter her wailing, grunting, and complaining were continuous. When I went to comfort her with some succulent cucumber peelings she started up from her bed of dust and straw but sullenly refused to eat or even look at the cucumber, a favorite dish of hers. She simply stood, legs spread, and glowered. After a few days, however, she got used to being in the sty and lazed around all the time, and grew fatter and bigger day by day.

I was really rather pleased that Pig was kept incarcerated.

There were few flowers in the hamlet and I resolved to grow sunflowers as I had in Peking. I dug up two small plots just outside our cottage door and put in the seedlings that I had raised in a couple of jam jars. There were fifteen seedlings and I pictured my cottage bowered in sunflowers. I built a low earthen wall around my plots and covered the seedlings with prickly thorn, but in a twinkling pigs and chickens had wrought havoc among them. Only seven were left.

I replied to this attack with reinforced protection, and Ta Sao's imprisonment of Pig was added help. Still two more plants were nibbled. Another succumbed to a downpour that flooded out my walled plot. The drain-off from the roof dripped straight into it and I had left no opening through which the water could run out. That left four. One night another mysteriously disappeared. The three survivors grew fast and well under the summer rain. They were three feet tall but still frail when the huge porker from next door tried to squeeze through between the wall and the innermost plant. Down she went, and the next-door pig nibbled off the topmost leaves so that it was useless to replant the stem. I put all my defenses round the last two and these grew a splendid eight feet, bursting into glorious flower in September. When I left I bequeathed them to Au Chiu and Hsiao Ching as a memorial to my learning why Upper Felicity did not grow beds of flowers along the highway.

The Old Men

One day several of the oldsters in the hamlet blossomed out with red metal lapel tags issued by the commune proudly proclaiming that they were in charge of road-mending "for the people." They were all well over sixty. They were not enrolled in any of the regular work teams, but received their rations of grain and other allocations as commune members and worked more or less when they liked. One of their jobs was to prune the trees and weed and do light repairs on the roadway. If any serious repairs were needed they told the team or brigade and a work group was organized for the job. Like the ballad-singer, a lot of the oldsters carried baskets over their shoulders and light scoops with them wherever they went. They used the scoops to collect manure along the roads and lanes. All received work-points for their work.

Most of the older men who were still able-bodied but not well and spry enough to keep up with the regular work teams were assigned to the vegetable plots. All these were near the hamlet, so none of the old men who tended them needed to walk far to work. The jobs here could be done in more leisurely fashion, each individual working at his own pace, and it was always possible to call in help if necessary.

During the rainy season our OSD Team was also mobilized to repair the roads. If a tractor or heavy bus or cart went along a road just after a shower, huge ruts were left in the surface, and if the ruts dried hard it made rough going. Our job was simply to smooth down the ruts. Simply? It is extraordinary how many complications such a simple job can cause. Yuan wanted to finish the work off in a rough-and-ready way because the next downpour would undo it all. Tsang disagreed; his theory was that we should do as thorough a job as possible, rain or no rain. This argument raged with increasing heat. It was only the latest of a fundamental disagreement between their two natures. Yuan was a good cook and liked to cook. He had argued only the day before that it took at least one hour to cook a meal and so the persons cooking for the family (and he was one of them) should be allowed to return home an hour at least before the rest of the team knocked off. This horrified Tsang, who was in charge of organizing our work. "A simple meal cannot take more than half an hour to prepare," he argued, citing the Party's exhortation about frugality and simple living to back up his argument. Lin, who tried not to take sides, worked sometimes with Yuan, roughly leveling the road, and then went back to work alongside Tsang, who was left far behind meticulously filling up every crack and leveling every pothole. Old Tang worked quietly and hard by himself, refusing to be involved in the argument. He messed things up in his usual impractical way. I had been working with him, but I could not stand the preposterous things he was doing. He would fill up a pothole with gooey mud and then cover it over with dry earth scooped up from under the trees so that it looked as if the pothole was completely filled up with firm earth. If he had been intent on making a trap for some unwary traveler he could not have done it more efficiently. If I had been Lao Man, I would have told him, "Comrade, this is the way to do it!" and showed him what Mrs. Tsang, Mrs. Yuan, my wife, and I were doing, and what any person of ordinary common sense would do. We were leveling the sides of ruts and filling the trough in with the leveled sides; we were filling in potholes with the sand that other road-keepers had left ready stacked by the sides of the road.

Ling, the artist, as usual buried his frustrations in concentrated work. His wife never turned out for these chores. Tan leaned tiredly on his spade, staring out into the far distance, completely oblivious to what was going on around him. His wife was thoroughly enjoying herself. There was nothing she enjoyed better than a good row to watch and talk about later. This was a pity. She had seemed to be making ideological progress but now she was backsliding.

Summer Food 🌾

By July Upper Felicity has vegetables aplenty and in great variety—large succulent cucumbers; eggplants of three colors, dark purple, light green, and white; Spanish and spring onions; very tasty tomatoes; garlic; and fat and very long French string beans. Yesterday I ate new potatoes and the day before that, vegetable marrow. For

some time before that we were eating the early summer vegetables: lettuce, spinach, and *tcho tsai*. Upper Felicity folk eat
eggplant raw but are not very fond of tomatoes, a relatively
new crop for this area. They were amused when they saw me
going to a great deal of trouble to make salads. I put the
tomatoes and lettuce in sterilizing purple permanganate solution and made the dressing with fragrant vegetable oil, pepper,
and salt, with a dash of soybean sauce. With a draft of icy
cold water from the mechanized well, this is a wonderful dish
on a hot afternoon.

Sometimes we boiled noodles, then cooled them off in the
pure well water and ate them cold. The hamlet housewives
rarely go to so much trouble in making everyday meals. Usually, along with the staple meal porridge, pancake, or *mantou*
they will hand the family raw or plain cooked eggplant or cucumber and that's that. But sometimes Ta Sao made everybody savory *mantou*, stuffed with finely chopped mixed
vegetables and garnished with onion or garlic. Yuan-tsung
made these too but usually added some finely chopped meat.
This transformed the *mantou* into a *baotze*. Sometimes she put
a filling of dark brown Cuban sugar into the *mantou*, which
made them *tang baotze* (sugar dumplings). Something else
we all enjoyed was chopped spring onions and *do fu*—soybean curd.

We were also eating more fruit. There was no need any
longer to eat expensive bottled pears or peaches from Shanghai. (The peasants never touched this sort of luxury. They
were kept by the co-op shop exclusively for the cadres from
town.) First, in June we got a big allocation of twenty jin
of lovely red plums from a nearby fruit-growing brigade. The
children all enjoyed this windfall, and so did we. Then other
local fruit ripened. Outside the co-op shop on most days you
could find a member of one of the neighboring communes
selling apricots, peaches, or, later, watermelons and *mien gua*
(cotton melon) for his brigade or team. The most frequent
seller there was a big, serious-faced farmer who disdained to
use any of the wiles or come-on tactics of the old fruit-sellers.
He had been chosen primarily for his honesty and not for his

"salesmanship." He had his own technique. He would display
his fruit, dust them off with a little brush, put the damaged
ones aside for sale at a cheaper price—and wait. Customers
soon learned to trust his description of his fruit implicitly. If
he said they were sweet, they *were* sweet. And with that assurance you bought willingly. It was always a pleasure to buy
from such sellers.

The local plums were exceptionally good. Upper Felicity
grew no fruit at all except dates. They said that the soil just
didn't produce good fruit. But I expect that will be changed
in the future. It was not till early August that the first corn
began to be distributed in our team. It was good corn for
grinding and eating as meal, but since they harvested it late,
it did not roast or boil well.

If there was no fruit-seller at the co-op or traveling around
the villages, I rode to one of the county towns or fairs to get
fresh fruit. The county revolutionary committee supervised the
fairs, but they were held in one village or another, according
to a long-established tradition. At least once a fortnight at the
outside there would be one in a nearby village, within a
distance of five to thirty li. Our hamlet was too small to
qualify for the honor, but during a period of a year there
were two fairs held in West Board Bridge Village, four in
Great Felicity, the commune center, three in East Li Village,
on the main road between two big county towns. A special
fruit fair was held at a place some twenty li away. These were
the ones I visited to buy a brush, a mat, a part for my fountain
pen, handles for our spades, twine for Ta Sao's shoemaking,
eggs, fruit, and vegetables.

The fairs sold many other things. There were always a
number of tinkers plying their trade, with an array of pots
and pans, buckets, and what-not for sale, baskets of all kinds,
small shopping baskets and big grain storage bins three feet
wide and as deep, farm furniture, tools, building materials,
beams, rafters, windows, doors, dressed and undressed timber.
Sometimes these things were being sold by the handicraft
teams of some commune. Sometimes a peasant commune
member had pulled down an old house or cut down a tree or

a branch and wished to sell for ready cash. The old grannies who took their eggs to the fair were clearly novices at trading. On one occasion I bought ten eggs from an old soul. She knew how much she would sell one for but not how much she should ask for ten or one jin. These markets were by no means "free markets." State and co-op trading or trading by the communes, brigades, and teams completely dominated the scene. If a private person sold or bought anything, it was by nature of a once-only operation. Any sort of speculative buying or selling was entirely ruled out. The fairs were a useful auxiliary to the co-op trading network, a center for exchange between the communes, brigades, and teams, and primarily a convenience for the occasional commune member seller or buyer.

There was always one part of the fair set aside for the sale and purchase of horses, cows, pigs and piglets, goats, sheep, and kids, rabbits, ducks, chickens and chicks. You could always locate this part by the prodigious squealing and cackling.

As the cadres say: "The struggle between two lines, two roads, and two policies is ever-present and very complicated." That means the struggle between the socialist way, the new way of doing things, the way of honesty, "serving the people," the way of the new morality born of the Revolution, as opposed to the old way of doing things, the way of calculated dishonesty, of serving oneself, group selfishness, the way of the old morality born of the exploiters' way of life, the way that drags society backward all the time. And this struggle between the two ways came out even in buying watermelons at the fair.

I always got a square deal from the young commune sellers, frank-faced young men who tried their best to pick a good melon for you. But occasionally one of these new men might be accompanied by an old "experienced" seller sent by a team or brigade that hadn't "put proletarian politics" thoroughly enough "in command." And the result would be a two-way struggle. Either the new way of selling triumphed over the old way if the young man was politically keen, or the old way triumphed over the new way if he was lacking in vigilance.

Old Tang fell afoul of the old way of selling. He walked

twenty li to the Li Village fair to buy a melon. With his usual naïve good humor he asked the old chap at a melon stall to "pick a good sweet melon," and without even sniffing the one offered him, put it in his sack and plodded the twenty li back home. The round trip, carrying a twenty-pound melon in the broiling sun, took him half a day, and he was too tired to even think of enjoying it. When his wife smelled and tapped the melon she had her doubts about it. "How do you know it's a good, sweet melon?"

"The seller said it was, and what's more he said that if I wasn't satisfied I could bring it back and get a refund," replied Tang, pleased at his forethought.

"But there's no fair at Li Village tomorrow and you don't even know his name."

Old Tang, resisting the implied criticism, counterattacked. "Don't forget we're living in a socialist country."

"Well, that only means that you should show some socialist common sense," she retorted.

He put the melon in a bucket of ice-cold water from the deep well. He invited us over to enjoy it the next day after work.

When we had washed and changed into clean things we hurried over to enjoy the melon. Tang brought it out, put it on a tin tray, and then paused as he was about to cut it. He scrutinized it carefully. He had forgotten to cover the bucket and a rat had nibbled out a good chunk.

Undaunted, Tang carved off the gnawed part and sliced through the fruit. The knife went through it like butter and it fell into two rotten halves.

Discussing the matter afterwards, we all agreed that the old farmer had not used Mao Tse-tung's Thought in selling the melon and that Old Tang had not used Mao Tse-tung's Thought in buying it.

Summer Nights 🌿

*T*he winter nights had been beautiful, still, cold, calm, and the summer nights had their own lovely charm. After the brazen heat of day, the fresh cool of evening was balm to the body. The azure sky turned to deepest indigo. Night advanced with its heaven-stealing hand and then filled the sky with its galaxies of stars. Overhead, slightly to the west, a thin scattering of stars was dominated by the vast constellation of the Bear. Over on the east stretched the luminous mist of the Milky Way.

Through the tangled embroidery of trees and branches, the pond glimmered like a wraith. The frogs kept up their hoarse croaking until near midnight. Then utter stillness settled over the hamlet. The only sounds would be the intermittent complaint of a restless child, then the muttered solace of its mother—and then again silence.

Wind and Cloud Battles 🌿

*T*he Central China plain is a great battleground of the winds. They blow from northeast and northwest, from south and southeast. Those from the north are cold or cool. Those from the south are warm or hot. To the northwest and west of Upper Felicity stretches the mountain range that alone alleviates the dead level of the surrounding landscape. In the space above them the mighty aerial battles of the winds and the clouds take place that make the weather of Upper Felicity gay and warm, or cold and sullen; breathlessly hot or freezing cold; or tense with expectation of storm, cloudburst, and calamity. From the clash of hot and cold, dry and wet, come spectacular cloud effects and sunsets that dazzle with their beauty and strange forms and colors, from red to orange to yellow and emerald green, and into deepest purple.

In mid-June, a steady southern breeze brought us days of still, withering heat from which there was no escape night or day. The fields of kaoliang and maize trembled. Their scintillating green took on a hard metallic luster. The big pond began to dry up. The tips of the water-weed on its bottom began to show. There was no time to fill it from the wells, which were being pumped round the clock to get water to the bone-dry fields of crops.

Then one day a wind began to blow from the north. At first this northern breeze seemed as hot as the wind from the south. The still, hot air that had blanketed the whole plain was being pushed back south by the cold blast from the north. What we were feeling was the retreat of the south wind.

It was only late in the afternoon that the advance guard of the cold north wind itself reached us. And what a welcome cold that was! In such battles the temperature can drop five to ten degrees in as many minutes.

By the evening of the next day the wind set from another quarter—the northwest. Great banks of dark clouds built up and formed vast, stupendous shapes that grew fantastic as they were reddened by the setting sun. Then, as the high wind blew, these clouds dispersed in all directions over the flat of the plain. Islands of cloud fragments floated over us in a low haze that made them appear even more diaphanous than they were. Rain fell to the north, and we could feel its repercussions: cool breezes that threatened but never actually brought rain. Then the fortunes of battle changed again. The south wind regained the mastery by a gentle, persistent pressure and once again still, hot air settled over the hamlet, and we sweated as we slept so that our straw mats were wet to the touch in the morning.

The summer monsoon should have started in July. In that month, they told me, it would rain steadily sometimes for four whole days together or would pour down in sudden cloudbursts. "The ponds will fill up and you'll see how the crops will grow!" At first it seemed that the weather would follow the usual pattern. There were some sudden showers and once it rained fitfully all day. This did the crops good but failed utterly to fill the ponds. A few puddles formed in their bottoms.

"It'll be a dry year," pronounced the veterans, scanning the cloudless blue sky.

On July 19 the *Tou Fu,* First Heat, was due to start, the hottest part of the year. I rearranged my working schedule. I got up well before six and was drawing or painting by seven. By twelve noon I was tired and wilting from the heat and after eating lunch went to sleep and drowsed away the afternoon. I got up well after three when the bell rang for the peasants' afternoon shift. I found that I could only work in the fields for an hour or an hour and a half. More than that left me so fatigued that I was incapacitated for the rest of the day and hardly recovered even by the next morning. Around six I came back home and washed and supped. Usually after that we sat in the cool of the trees around the yard and chatted till bedtime. It was too hot to read. Our hurricane lamp, so comforting to read by in the winter and spring, now gave off enervating waves of heat. We stopped using it unless absolutely necessary and went back to the little lamps the peasants used—just a bottle of kerosene with a wick in it. You cut a piece of metal about as big as a penny, made a hole in it, placed it over the mouth of the bottle, and stuck the wick through it.

Some days by nine or ten o'clock it was too hot and sultry for drawing. When I pressed my wax pencils on the paper, they bent limply in my hot hand. Then I read instead.

The ponds had dried up completely. Only the big pond had been refilled, a boon to our tired eyes and to the children and young men who swam there every afternoon. In the other ponds all the water disappeared. The frogs burrowed deep and didn't even croak. Many peasants built little open shelters of kaoliang or straw on any high shaded space and slept there during the heat of the day. From noon till after three, the whole hamlet dozed off. Even the pigs ceased to nose around, and the hens and chickens huddled away in some cool corner.

When I forgot to water my sunflowers morning and evening, they drooped and the leaves shriveled at the edges and turned brown in the pitiless sun.

Actually working in the fields and participating in the complex work of raising the crops gave one a new vision of the countryside. Before, I had admired the widespreading fields of crops, but now I had a new feeling of oneness with them as I contemplated the kaoliang and maize fields and the deep green of the cotton plants with their leaves shimmering in the heat like burnished metal.

Heat and Storm 🌿

*T*en days before *Li Ch'iu*, the Establishment of Autumn (August 8), the heat grew more intense. Although the sky was cloudy, there was no rain for several days. The heat weighed on the hamlet. Only late in the evening did a mild breeze stir the hot air out and bring a relative cool to the cottages. This lasted until six-thirty the next morning, when the sun again began to bake the hamlet. In this heat wave the afternoon rest had to be lengthened to nearly four o'clock.

The main work now was irrigation: running water from the mechanized wells down channels and into the fields and then guiding it by strategically placed dams and temporary channels from plot to plot. Hoeing kept down the weeds and preserved all the moisture for the crops. The maize stood shoulder high. It would soon be harvested. Then would come another busy time in the fields for the main manpower of the team. For the moment many men were taking time off to make adobe bricks, shore up walls, repair their roofs, and make things shipshape for the really big rains that were now expected.

After we had mixed clay loess and chopped straw with water to make a thick, gooey paste, Lao Man, Ta Sao, and I climbed up on the roof of the cottage. While Ching Chun threw up spadefuls of the mud to us, Ta Sao and I passed ladlefuls along to Lao Man, who plastered it down with a trowel in a thick layer on the roof. The job finished, the cottage would be waterproof for another year.

Another big team job was cutting grass and weeds to make great compost heaps. Piled waist-high to form an oblong mass ten by twenty feet, mixed and covered with mud, such a heap was built in a hollow and water was allowed to run into it. After being left to mature for several weeks, it was spread on the fields. This method had already been used with good results for the vegetable plots. It was now being used to increase the organic content of the other fields. In trying out these various methods the Upper Felicity farmers were gathering experience for tackling the big job of the future—the opening up of the big area of alkaline land to the south.

Family Tiff 🌿

T he long continued heat frayed everyone's nerves. By the time the *San Fu,* Third Heat, began, children and even grown-ups grew irritable. Suddenly I found my wife nagging at me and me snapping back no less unreasonably. Then I would put the transistor radio on loud or bury myself in my book. A serious tiff occurred next door. Angry words were spoken. When I looked out Ta Sao was standing on the step with Lao Man waving his fist angrily from the yard. Ta Sao had wanted him to repair something and he had kept on putting it off. "All you think about is your everlasting meetings!" shouted Ta Sao. And Lao Man shouted back, just as unreasonably, "What do you do all day?" Before we could intervene both were yelling at each other at the same time, but Lao Man was using very bad language. By this time his niece had hurried round from next door and took Ta Sao's part. "Don't curse people," she admonished him. "Men and women are equal now!"

The old uncle from the other side came and began to upbraid Lao Man. Lao Man, reared in the old tradition of filial respect for his older male relatives, didn't dare answer. He went to spend the rest of the evening with the men who were wont to gather for a chat at the stable. He only came back late that night to find the cottage door locked. He knocked once and twice. No answer. We came out and persuaded Ta Sao to open the door, but when Lao Man entered she came out, crying that she wouldn't "stay in the same house with such a man!" Then the children woke up and cried. Lao Man locked Ta Sao out. Niece, uncle, and aunt came round. The children opened the door and rushed out. Lao Man locked himself in. There was bedlam in the yard. Finally we persuaded Lao Man to open the door and he came out swearing. In the midst of the altercation, he raised his arm against Ta Sao. His uncle stepped between them. There was a moment's stunned silence.

In the old days a peasant in this position would have cursed his wife with impunity and beaten her, too. She would have submitted tamely, not daring to resist, and the whole family and hamlet would have taken it as his right "to assert his authority." But not now. Lao Man found himself censured all round. "Do you know," exclaimed the aunt to the sizable crowd that had gathered, "he even raised his hand against her!" Lao Man hurried off to the stable.

Ta Sao hardly appeared before the cottage all next day. Twenty years wed, she talked of going home to her mother in West Village.

Lao Man came home that evening subdued and contrite. He visited us and for a long time smoked his pipe silently. He answered our questions with a monosyllabic yes or no. For a long time we avoided the matter of the quarrel, but we knew that this was what he had really come to talk about. We were determined not to let him justify himself.

Finally he tried to make a lame excuse for himself. Ta Sao, he said, had also used bad language. "She cursed me and my dead mother! How could I stand that?"

"Lao Man," said Yuan-tsung severely, "I didn't hear Ta Sao curse your dead mother, but even if she did, you were cursing your children's living mother! What will they think of that?"

Lao Man evidently felt even more in the wrong. He was really contrite. Next morning he got up extra early and fetched in a big armful of pig-grass for Pig. (He had said that Ta Sao was neglecting this chore.) He ate his lunch and dinner separately by himself sitting under the locust tree at the side of the farmyard. He and Ta Hsiang did the cooking. Ta Sao still did not appear, but spun cotton thread in the cottage. Only the steady whir-whir of the spinning wheel could be heard.

Only in the evening of the next day was the reconciliation made. Dusk was descending. We were all in the yard eating our supper. Ta Sao sat under the date tree surrounded by the three younger children. Lao Man came home from work, went to the kitchen, served himself a bowl of gruel and vegetables, and hunkered down to eat them all by himself. He ate in silence, listening to the chatter of the small ones. Having eaten, he put his bowl away, fetched a mat from the cottage, spread it on the ground, and lay down in cheerless solitude. Hsiao Ching and Au Chiu came over and lay down with him. This broke the ice. We tried to help by speaking as if nothing had happened. My wife said jokingly: "Children are like little stoves. If both of you sleep there with your father he won't get cool! When our Didi sleeps with us in winter we only need one quilt!" The conversation became general, while the babies frolicked all over him.

The moon had risen and sailed serene and golden in a deep blue sky. The leaves glittered as if dipped in silver. The reconciliation was complete. We were sure that it would be a long time before Lao Man gave way again to summer irritation and used bad language to his wife.

The "Cat" Problem Solved ❧

*T*hings had got so bad in the house of the "Cat" that the team had had to step in to settle a long-standing family row. Everyone in the hamlet knew the story of the Cat. She had married the eldest of three orphan brothers and from the very beginning had made it clear that she was determined to rule the roost. Her husband had made a short-lived effort to assert his authority and build a united, happy family, but he soon realized he was no match for the Cat. The Cat caused so many squabbles that it wasn't long before the next eldest brother left home and went to live with an old bachelor friend. That left the third and youngest brother to endure the Cat's onslaughts. By that time she was raising her own family, and no matter what her neighbors and the commune cadres said to her, she made it clear behind their backs that she wanted the ancestral home for herself, her harassed husband, and her children and no one else. This feudal thinking was much criticized and condemned, but that did not make things any easier for the poor younger brother.

The team first attempted to solve the problem by trying to help him get into the People's Liberation Army, for which he had volunteered. But the Army has strict standards. He was not tall or strong enough. He waited a year before trying again. But in that year his sister-in-law had made things even worse for him, keeping him short of food, and he had grown very little and put on no more muscle.

In this crisis the Tsangs, who lived in the Cat's farmyard, again showed their worth. They resolutely took the side of the younger brother, braving the Cat's displeasure by regularly inviting him in to share their meals. One of the cardinal rules for cadres going to the countryside is to maintain good relations with their host and hostess. Other cadres might have "kept out of trouble" by ignoring the younger brother's problems in order to please the Cat, but they stood firmly by their principles. With them, wrong was wrong. They took the matter up with the team and got the lad recommended for a job on the new local railway that was being built. He was accepted, but so strong was the youngster's family feeling that he actually asked the Cat's permission to leave home. She was the "head of the house" and as the old Chinese saying goes: "Treat your elder sister-in-law as your mother." This was especially to be observed when the mother of the family was dead.

There was nothing the Cat wanted more. She said she did not care what he did and he left that summer for his new job. She hardly said a perfunctory "Good-by" to him, and yet, as the new custom is, he sent home part of his first month's wages for his little nephews. Perhaps that made the Cat think.

Transport Team 🌿

Since there was not much heavy work to do when the threshing was over, the team leaders decided to send out a transport group to earn some ready cash for the collective. Four men were chosen, two experienced older men—one of them Lao Man—and two strapping youngsters. They took two of the team's handcarts, a pump for the pneumatic tires, a change of clothes, raincoats, and bedding and set off for the county town. They would cover the thirty-five-odd li in a few hours and would be ready for work next morning. Each took some spending money along with him and a bag of grain containing enough to last a week or more.

It was going to be hard work. They would hire themselves and their carts out for hauling goods for various factories and organizations in the county and even for private persons. They would be working a good eight-hour day in the broiling sun, hauling one thousand jin a load. Forty per cent of what was earned would be shared out for food and lodging, and the rest would go to the team. In addition, the team would credit each man with twelve work-points a day instead of his usual ten.

I reckoned that living expenses would amount to some twenty yuan a month. Most of this would go for food, the rest haircuts, baths, cigarettes, and lodging. Since they would be doing hard work they would need more food than when at home. Commune peasants are not issued grain coupons like city-dwellers. They get their grain according to their team allocations, so they would have to buy grain at the usual state commercial rate, which was higher than for couponed grain. That meant that they would have to earn about one hundred yuan a month per man to make the venture really worth while for themselves and the team. This seemed a lot to me, as only a well-qualified cadre gets such a wage in the cities. When I raised this question I was told that there is still a shortage of trucks and so rural factories particularly have to do a lot of their carting by manpower. The services of the transport team would be in big demand, and they might even gross two hundred yuan a month per man. They hoped to get a regular job for a period with some factory or shop, and then they could also arrange to sleep and live on the factory premises or in its dormitory. Their wants would be simple: a bare room to sleep in, a tap in the yard for washing, access to a boiler to get boiled water for drinking. They would probably sleep out in the open anyway.

Some men in the hamlet had done transport work as a sideline in the days of private enterprise, but this was the first time the production team had gone in for such a venture. To protect the collective, the team had stipulated that a gross take of less than one hundred yuan a month would mean a cut in their income from twelve to ten work-points a day. If the men saw that the venture could not succeed, they were to call it off.

The four-man team went off in high spirits. Not everyone thought the scheme would be a success, and some thought that the two older men were too old for this sort of job. The day after they left the rain fell in torrents, continuing steadily the whole of that day and the day after. The roads were waterlogged, wheels got caked with mud, and organizations and people all put off moving goods, so the team had to return home to await a change of weather. When the weather changed they went out again, this time even more determined to make good.

They stayed on the road for two months and their gross take was nearly a thousand yuan. Lao Man came back with sixty yuan over and above his keep, and was well satisfied with the results of this venture. But he admitted that the work was tough and that he probably wouldn't do it again the next year.

Beating the Flood

*T*he radio had warned us of a coming storm, but when it came its violence took us by surprise. The day had been stiflingly hot, so we were thoughtlessly happy when the temperature began to drop toward evening. Big storm clouds billowed up over the northwest horizon and formed awe-inspiring patterns of blue, black, grey, and ghostly, dazzling white above the mountain ranges. The vault directly overhead seemed devoid of cloud, but it was filled with a thick, impenetrable mist that obscured every star. Distant rumblings of thunder signaled the coming of the hurricane. Then lightning flashes, forked prongs and contorted tendrils of white flame, bright sheets of cold white lit up the southeastern sky where the storm broke first. Minute by minute the lightning and thunder spread to the south and southwest, then west, north, and northeast. Ringed by intermittent flashes bright enough to read by, we sat in our yard enjoying this cosmic spectacle. At ten o'clock a slow shower drove us indoors.

We went to bed and were lulled to sleep by a gentle drizzle on the leaves that contrasted strangely with the fireworks gashing the whole horizon. Then came a sudden shattering burst of thunder directly overhead and a fury of lightning flashes. Howling wind and pelting rain hit the cottage from all directions. The iron roof over our stove was wrenched off with a clatter and went hurtling down the yard. Ta Sao shouted some unintelligible words of warning. I ran out in shorts and sandals and replaced the stove roof. The rain beat on the plastic net covering the windows, and thin trickles of water began to drip down the inside wall. Beating through every crack in the door, the rain quickly turned the earth floor by our entrance into a sticky morass. Trees bent as if they would snap. The wind, howling like a mad thing, blew in all directions, creating such a din that we had to shout to make ourselves heard. While we were trying to devise some way of keeping the deluge out of the windows and door, another mighty gust took the stove cover off again. The stove sizzled angrily as the rain beat down on its unprotected top. We had either to let it go out or bring it into the cottage. We decided to save it. Throwing our raincoats on, we waded out barefoot and brought it in in a wave of rain. We rolled the paper shutters over the windows, which stopped most of the rain coming in. But I was worried lest the paper become so sodden that it would break and leave us open to the elements. Luckily the first fury of the storm soon slackened and all we faced was a steady downpour that hit the roof hard but left our windows intact. It poured all night.

In these days at the end of July, the days of *Tou Fu, Ta Shu,* and *Erh Fu* (First Heat, Great Heat, and Second Heat), it had rained or drizzled intermittently. Now it rained in torrents. Two days of it filled all the ponds around the village and raised the level of water in the surface wells to ten feet from the wellhead. Low-lying roads and fields began to flood. Though the water poured and gurgled down the ditches and channels, it couldn't get out fast enough. The old moat around the commune center filled to overflowing. As a precaution, the commune opened a new channel to drain away as much water as possible out of the ponds inside the old wall. The children partially blocked the channel with a dam and fished with baskets and string shopping bags for the small fish that were carried down by the swift current.

The Wei River was rising alarmingly. If it broke its banks, despite all the work that had been done to deepen, widen, and straighten its channel and raise its dikes, then many communes, including our own, would suffer damage. A round-the-clock watch was being kept on it and the threatened communes were regularly informed of developments. There was sporadic talk of flood and what should be done. The brigade leaders said they were not worried yet about the possibility of local waterlogging, but I noticed that the big drainage channel cut across the fields of our three teams—twenty feet across and ten feet deep—was already running full and fast.

The May Seventh Cadre School housed in the middle of the low-lying alkaline flats was already marooned by a sheet of water. The students had packed their things and were on a stand-by alert. They had jacked up the lorries and tractors and built big rafts of empty gasoline drums lashed to old house beams. If the buildings went under water they would pile everything movable onto these rafts and ride out the flood.

During a slackening in the rain I went out with our brigade leaders to inspect the fields. Most of the corn was doing well, but here and there rain and wind had destroyed sizable plots. The eggplants had suffered badly and we decided to harvest and distribute the remainder of the crop right away. There was no serious damage yet. But it was clear that another two or three days of heavy rain might cause heavy loss. Beyond tending the ditches and clearing the fields of as much surplus water as possible, there was not much else that could be done.

A telephone call came through warning that a flood crest was coming down the Wei. Added to local run-off, the resultant flow might top the banks. Communes all along the line were asked to send men to strengthen and raise the dikes. Ching Chun and a score more of our brigade's young men immediately shouldered spades and other paraphernalia, wrapped up some *mantou* in plastic bags, and went off.

Some of these youngsters were members of the Young Communist Youth League, the junior wing of the Communist Party. Others were Red Guards who had gone to Peking in the heady days of 1966 and had seen Chairman Mao at the great Red Guard rallies held on Tien An Men Square. The commune school had its Red Guard organization and the YCL members formed the core of its leadership. Membership in the Red Guards was not so strictly controlled as in the YCL, but only good, well-disciplined students could join it. At times like these the YCL and Red Guards were expected to show their mettle—and they did.

The next day Yuan-tsung and I joined another contingent of flood-fighters. We took our spades and set off early in the morning with members of the First and Third Production Teams. Four young men with shoulder poles carried big baskets filled with lengths of rope and canvas squares that could be used as earth carriers. Several large squashes were added for the lunch and supper. The commune would cook gruel or noodles down on the work site and provide boiled water for drinking. Most of us took a couple of *mantou* or pancakes in our pockets to eat during the work breaks. My wife and I would return that same afternoon, so we traveled light. The young men we went with would stay perhaps two days, but they didn't bother about extra clothes or bedding. They too traveled light. By now it had stopped raining and the weather again was broiling hot. They would sleep uncovered in the open on the bundles of straw or straw mats that were used to strengthen the dike.

As soon as we came to the roads leading directly to the Wei we found ourselves part of an immense procession marching in parallel columns to the river. Some groups ambled along, others marched with red banners at their head, singing and keeping in step. A propaganda team passed us, carrying loudspeaker equipment in a handcart and a framed portrait of Chairman Mao at their head. We heard that Li Village

Commune was sending three thousand men and women that day to help raise the level of the dike. Li Village lies on high ground and was well out of danger, but used this fine gesture to show its solidarity with the other communes.

By the time we reached the river we were part of a mile-long procession of workers that had converged on the approach road from many directions. The dike rises some twenty feet above the level of the fields. As far as the eye could see, it was alive with people. Tens of thousands of peasants were at work throwing up a new embankment two feet high and three across to raise the height of the dike.

From on top of the dike we could see how great the danger was. On the river side the swirling floodwaters raced by only a foot below us. Only inches remained between the flood crest and the top of the old dike. On the other side of the river the water had already flowed over the dike and flooded as far as the eye could see. A large part of our own commune lay under several feet of water. Here and there was an islet of higher ground. A lone rabbit sat on a mound that showed a foot above water level, a tiny islet of salvation. In other places the crowns of trees ballooned out of the brown mass of water. A bit to the south we could see a grove of trees, the roofs of a hamlet, and the tops of several haystacks. It looked as if they were all in the water, but actually they were on dry land. The hamlet was surrounded by a round high dike that protected all within its hollow inside. On my trips around the countryside I had seen several such hamlets. In some cases the protecting dike wall was double the height of the houses inside and planted thickly with trees and shrubs to strengthen it. In normal times, openings in the dike allowed easy ingress and egress, but when flood threatened, these openings were quickly blocked up with straw mats, reeds, and earth.

On our sector the army of commune members was extending the new two-foot-high embankment to a width of six feet, enough for the passage of a tractor. Each new team was assigned a sector, planted its red flag there, and immediately went to work. Without asking we took our place among the Upper Felicity team wherever we spotted a lack of hands.

Some of our men were digging earth out from the field beside the dike. Two-man teams with shoulder poles and baskets were carrying this earth to dump it on the top of the dike, where men and girls spread it evenly with spades. Some carriers used squares of canvas tied at the four corners, which served almost as well as baskets. Others had woven makeshift baskets out of willow twigs and rushes cut on the spot.

The soil all around was sodden and heavy. After one or two spadefuls the mud stuck to the spades and baskets like glue. We threw off shoes and sandals and were soon knee-deep in mud. The sun at noon blazed down and the earth steamed. While one shift worked, the other rested on the cool side of the dike or in the shade of trees or straw mats propped up with spades.

At the ten-o'clock break I joined many of the young men as they plunged into the swollen river and swam for fun to the opposite bank, which showed as a narrow strip of grass-covered soil some thirty yards away. The team's barefoot doctor was of course on hand, treating cuts and bruises and sunstroke. The commune leaders came around on an inspection tour. Some were getting on in years, but for a time they too pitched in, taking off their shoes, rolling up their trousers, and digging, carrying, and spreading earth.

Basketful by basketful of earth the new embankment grew. It is amazing what such mass collective effort can do with the most primitive equipment. The commune had come within two days' rain of a considerable disaster. Five days of work with the help of tens of thousands of other commune members had now put it ahead of any possible flood danger. Only a heavy five-day deluge of rain—an unlikely eventuality—or some such disaster higher up the river could put it in such danger again. Yet no one was unduly perturbed. They knew that if the danger had been ten times as great, they could have put forth ten times the effort needed to cope with it at a moment's notice.

I asked Lao Man and the others how the brigade whose fields had been flooded would fare. They said that if the loss was not great, it would, like all self-reliant commune units, just grin and bear it and try to make up its loss by some sideline activity or a shift of crops. If the loss was more serious it would get a remission of agricultural tax. Destroyed or damaged houses and other buildings would be repaired by the team or brigade, perhaps with commune help if the damage was serious. If a family suffered total loss of its belongings, it would be entitled to state relief and money to set itself on its feet again. These regulations were known to all commune members, so in fighting the flood they were rid of the old preliberation nightmare of wondering "What about after?"

The day after our men returned from strengthening the dikes our Third Brigade collected one thousand jin of *nangua* (squash) and sent them off to the Red Flag Brigade, whose fields had been flooded. We also composed a letter of condolence and encouragement and our best calligrapher wrote it out on a large sheet of red paper. Other neighboring communes sent gifts and revolutionary encouragement.

Good antiflood work had greatly limited damage to the Red Flag Brigade. Only the standing crops had suffered badly. The flooded fields had had a rich deposit of silt spread all over them, which would give them added yields this coming autumn and next year too. This brigade, incidentally, depended for a large part of its income on the ducks it raised, and their eggs. Not a duck had been lost.

Following this excitement, the weather was good. The level of the waters went back to normal and we knew that the flood danger was beaten with a bonus. The strengthened dikes were an added guarantee against calamity for many, many years to come.

I thought of the contrast between this disciplined, well-organized flood fighting and the happenings of the past. Then calamity struck without warning. There was panic and each family tried to save itself as best it could. Now there had been hourly reports by radio and telephone from up the rivers. Adequate forces had been mobilized by the communes and people's governments to deal with the danger. The peasants knew that they themselves and the people's state had ample reserves in case of need. There had never at any time been the slightest hint of undue worry. Things were always well in hand.

After the Rain

After the rains of August the crop-covered fields around the hamlet shone clean. My sunflowers grew visibly day by day, putting themselves well out of reach of Pig. She and her colleagues couldn't even see the juicy buds of leaves at their tops. The two plants that were left made a brave show six feet tall on either side of our yard. In late August they began putting out their great yellow flower-heads.

The children reveled in the heat and the water in the ponds. When the heat tried them too sorely they plunged into the big pond. A surprisingly large number of them could swim, a reminder of the swimming craze that had sprung up when Chairman Mao had swum the Yangtze River in his eighty-first year.

The plants all seemed to try their best to respond to the efforts of the peasants. After the rains, stray wheat seeds sprouted on the roadbeds. Where an eater on the road had spat out a few seeds, melon vines curled in the culverts. Maize is particularly tough. Crushed underfoot by some incautious foot when a young seedling, or lodged by a too-heavy load of rain when grown, it will put down a whole new set of roots and twist itself upright again and grow.

Most of the work we did now was on the vegetable plots. The red flower and the cucumber and squash plots had been harvested and replowed and planted with turnips and other late root crops.

Autumn

A TIME OF RIPENING AND REJOICING

Autumn Tiger ✤

*D*uring the time of the north winds' battles with the south monsoon wind and the coming of the July and August rains, there was always a period of cool in the mornings and evenings, but with the "Autumn Tiger" the heat-laden southern monsoon engulfed the earth. The change of weather was rapid. Despite the warnings given me by the weatherwise peasants, "The heat will soon be here!" or "This cool weather won't last!" the mornings had remained pleasantly cool. I thought that perhaps we would be lucky and that autumn, cool, real autumn, would set in after the blazing summer. I should have believed the calendar, the concentrated wisdom of millennia. That very afternoon we sensed a change. The usual cool breeze from the north failed to come. Instead, a warm and then a hot stirring of the air came from the south. As they came in from the fields men and boys plunged with relief into the big pond and we could hear their shouts and chatter and laughter. Women and girls do not bathe in the open as yet in Upper Felicity, so I stayed at home with Yuan-tsung. Only the inside of our cottage was cool. Even the shade of the trees gave no relief. It was useless sitting in the yard thinking that we could enjoy the evening air, so we now gathered inside the cottage to chat.

The next day it grew steadily hotter. The children tried to cool off in the pond but only found the heat outside the water the more oppressive. Only essential work was done during these days. The slightest exertion left one covered in sweat. The heat seemed to drain the energy out of you.

Luckily the main crop, the maize, needed little attention. The ground was sodden and rich with moisture. The maize stood head high and made a wall of green on both sides of the roads. I could well understand why it was called the Green Curtain. Bandits in the old days were known as Knights of the Green Curtain. A whole regiment of men could have been hidden within fifty yards of the hamlet and even a high lookout would not have been able to spot them. In the days of the Japanese War this was the classic time of the year for the guerrillas to begin their depredations on the enemy beleaguered in his armed camps and blockhouses. Small enemy and puppet detachments were scared of moving even a few miles through the menacing Green Curtains of maize and kaoliang.

Even the children grew limp with heat. Au Chiu came home from school one afternoon and threw himself down to rest in the shade of the cottage wall. The sun began to set but still the heat lingered. Soon he fell sound asleep. Hsiao Ching was told to go and call him for supper. She took her time. She looked at him, then went to fetch a small stool, set it down, and sat herself down on it. With the tip of her toes she meditatively raised Au Chiu's chin. He uttered no sound. Hsiao Ching then toed him over and prodded his back. Au Chiu gave a low complaining groan, rubbed his eyes—and promptly went back to sleep. In normal weather he would have been roaming and scampering like a spring lamb around the cottages and pond from the time school got out till he was dragged home to supper and bed.

These days we found no shelter from the heat even in the cottage. After a few days under the blazing sun, its thick walls and roof became heated through. Instead of keeping the inside cool they now gave off heat like an oven, so like everybody else we lived more and more outside, where we cooked, ate, read, worked, and rested. Passersby, seeing our pot on the stove, would ask us what was cooking or remove the lid and take a look. I found myself taking an interest in other people's cooking and doings and peered into bowls as I passed them. Everybody knew what everybody else was eating and doing.

Mercifully, the Autumn Tiger is short-lived. The really insufferably hot, humid weather lasted the usual ten days. By the last third of August it was cool again at night and in the early morning. The calendar warned that August 23 was *Chu Shu*, Heat Continues, but it was still unpleasantly hot only during the day, from around ten to four o'clock. After that cool autumn weather set in. The skies were filled with wonderful cottony clouds that piled up in all sorts of magnificent shapes. Then meandering breezes dispersed them in a wrack of cloud fragments all over the vast translucent dome.

Morning and evening we again wore our cotton twill jackets. At night we covered ourselves with a cotton sheet. The sounds of autumn surrounded us: the ceaseless rustle and murmur of the leaves, the hum of insects.

There were plenty of vegetables for our salads. In mid-August tomatoes and cucumbers were still available but by then were rather expensive. Melons had doubled in price. The local grapes were small and not sweet at all. The pears had tough skins and were neither juicy nor sweet. The apricots were not very large or sweet either, but were fleshy and tasty, so I used to stew them with sugar, a proceeding that was regarded by the locals as altogether wasteful and outlandish. The old singer of Honan folksongs introduced us to one of Upper Felicity's sweetest delicacies. I had not known that the brigade kept an apiary over against the sesame plot. Now he got the team to allocate us some sesame honey, which we enjoyed for weeks after.

We also began to enjoy the results of a successful experiment begun by the defunct state farm and continued by the May Seventh Cadre School—a new strain of apple trees they had introduced and tended gave a bumper harvest of very good apples, green-skinned, hard-fleshed, not oversweet, good for eating as well as cooking.

Discussing State Affairs ✻

*T*he general meetings of the brigade or teams were held very informally wherever it seemed convenient, or sometimes wherever the members happened to gather together. One evening when the weather was very warm, a meeting was called at the new brigade office, but the first-comers happened to seat themselves on the big cut stones outside the archway—and it was there that the meeting was held. As usual, those who couldn't leave the children at home brought them and the youngsters played around or listened to the proceedings. The matter on hand was no trivial thing—the brigade was starting a discussion, then developing nationwide, to hammer out the new constitution of the People's Republic of China.

The first constitution had been drafted and promulgated in 1954. At that time 150 million people took part in the public meetings that discussed and amended and finally approved it. But that was a constitution for the further development of the new-democratic revolution and the initial development of a socialist state. Now the country was building socialism and had experienced over three years of the Great Proletarian Cultural Revolution. Many things in the first constitution were already out of date. A new basic law for the state was needed in tune with the new society that was growing up and the new tasks that society had to do based on the people's communes and revolutionary committees of management and administration that ran the nation's affairs under the People's Government.

These basic premises were discussed at the meeting, first

in a report by the Party secretary and then by some of the
leading cadres. This meeting was in the nature of a preliminary survey of the matter, yet it lasted from nightfall till
nearly eleven. By the time the new constitution was passed it
would be discussed, amended, and kneaded into shape by
many millions more people.

Cottage Architecture

*T*he heat set me wondering about the design of the cottages. Those in Upper Felicity are all of the same pattern.
A two-room cottage (sometimes actually just one large room,
undivided by an inside wall) has one door and one window,
both on the same side. A three-room cottage has one door in
the center and two windows, all on one side. No cottage in
the hamlet has a window in a back or side wall. There are
no two-story houses in the hamlet; even the old landlord
never ran to such luxury. I saw some in other villages. These
too are of the same basic pattern, with the exception that the
top floor is usually one large room with three windows all
on one side. A west-facing cottage gets the late afternoon
sun in winter but is cold during the rest of the day; while
in the summer, just when you want the place to cool off in
the afternoon, it is warming up for a sweltering night. An
east-facing cottage in the summer is cooler in the afternoon
and at night, but it gets heated up from early in the morning,
and in the winter it gets colder and colder from noontime on
till morning.

A south-facing cottage is, as I have said, the most desirable.
Like ours, it is delightfully warm all winter with very little
heating from the stove. In summer it is several degrees cooler
than other cottages. But I could not help wondering how
much cooler in summer all of these rooms would be if they
had even one single window in an opposite wall to give a

through draft. When I raised this point with my neighbors they said that such a house would be drafty and that such a window would open out onto someone else's yard, an invasion of another family's privacy, and against local tradition and custom. But the answer was not so simple. In some cases this building custom had something to do with the old belief that when the head of the house was alive it was "not good" to open a window in the wall opposite the main door. This taboo did not apply if the male head of the house was dead, but it was still observed, because what family did not hope for a new male head of the house? This was another leftover of the wind-and-water doctrine and would take time, argument, precept, and education to overcome. This was one of the "Four Olds" that the Cultural Revolution was sweeping away. I found that none of the younger people knew that the lack of a window in their back wall was concerned at all with anything other than old building traditions. They simply presumed that all old inconveniences such as this would end when "really modern houses are built in Upper Felicity."

One or two of the rusticating cadres from town became close enough friends with their peasant hosts to ask permission to open up such a small window. When such permission was received, what a difference it made to their comfort! Many old, irrational beliefs lingered on simply because they had not been challenged. In the new social atmosphere of the commune the first reasoned challenge sent them flying.

The kitchens were a source of endless discomfort and prodigal of labor. Most of them, like Ta Sao's, were simply square boxes of adobe without chimneys and only a slit of an open window to let out the smoke. When Ta Sao cooked the whole kitchen was filled with acrid smoke that made her eyes smart. Some peasants had themselves designed and built vastly improved kitchens with good ventilation, but they were the exceptions. Most were building kitchens just the way they had been built for centuries past that made of cooking a tiresome, labor-consuming, inconvenient, unhealthful, and unpleasant chore.

This matter of the window or the kitchen is a small point,

but when properly solved it will make an enormous difference
to the life and health of the peasants, so I wondered why the
problem of village architecture had not been taken up. I
suppose the answer is that Upper Felicity's remnant laissez-
faire still made itself felt. In some places, such as Chekiang
Province, several imaginative projects and model homes for
peasants had been born not only on the drawing boards of
architects but in the villages themselves, to the happiness of
the peasants.

On the Road

*I*n mid-August I bicycled in with some friends to the
county town to get a new pair of spectacles, and to replenish
our larder. Yuan-tsung had been there a couple of times, once
to accompany Ta Sao for a medical checkup at the hospital,
but she had taken the daily public bus.

We decided to start at five-thirty in the morning, and
figured on doing the thirty-five li in something over an hour.
That would bring us in on time to queue up for the opening
of the state-run butcher's shop and a chance for a choice cut
of meat. A visit to the hospital and then to the optician
should not delay us long. We would buy vegetables at the
market on the way and be home before the noonday heat.

When we left the hamlet, the sweet odors of night still
hung in the air. It was just getting light and it was a joy to
be on the road. Everything was cool and morning fresh.

Along its whole length the road was bordered with one or
two rows of willows or poplars or both. Few trees seemed
older than ten years, and some were mere saplings. For long
stretches of the road we were hedged in on both sides by
walls of tall maize and kaoliang plants. But some fields were
already harvested or being harvested and here the landscape
opened out to give views of the wide North China plain, flat

to the horizon. In one harvested field a red Loyang caterpillar tractor was at work with its multiple plow getting the soil ready for the winter-wheat sowing.

Few people were on the road. We passed a few cadres cycling into town for supplies, a few peasants hauling empty handcarts bound on the same errand, a few with handcarts filled with pumpkins for the market or with wife or grannie and children going to pay a family visit. We passed some work teams. One was weeding the roadside and repairing the ditches, work which our OSD Team had often done. Another small team of young men was pruning the tall poplars, probably getting twigs and branches for some communal building project. Some solitary peasants and groups of children were busily gathering roadside grass as fodder for their animals. But for whole long stretches we had the road to ourselves and raced on as fast as we could, just for the sheer joy of movement.

The road was excellent though it was just a loess surface over a layer of large and then smaller broken rock. Where it had been worn down by the big bus wheels and had not been churned up by a tractor going to work it was smooth and hard, with very little dust after the recent rains.

For a long stretch the road ran along the top of the dike on the right bank of the Wei. Sometimes the peasants call this channel a river, sometimes a canal. Both designations fit. It was originally a river but after liberation and especially during the years after the formation of the communes in 1958 it had been greatly transformed. I could see how much work had been done on it with the aim of making it capable of carrying even such exceptional run-offs as we had recently seen. Now it could even take care of the more dangerous situation when the Yellow River overflowed and its water sought an outlet to the sea along the channels of other rivers like the Wei. The project was thus conceived on an imaginative scale and involved an immense amount of work. The bed was dredged and deepened and the dredged earth piled on either bank to raise the height of its levees. Sections which were too narrow had been broadened. Corners had been cut off to enable it to flow faster at flood times. Some of the banks at sharp turnings had been reinforced with stone and concrete to take the beating of flood currents without caving in. Where too-sharp s-curves had been cut through, we could still see the old winding channel. Quite a number of big new drainage channels had been cut into it, giving it new tributaries. Graceful bridges spanned it. And all along its course communes had set up stations to pump water from it to irrigate their fields.

All these improvements had turned it into a year-round navigable waterway for quite large craft. Where before tattered-sailed junks found themselves stranded on sandbanks or bedeviled by sharp turns when traveling it, now trim cargo junks always had a good channel with navigational difficulties reduced to a minimum. Only a few weeks earlier I had seen the Wei in flood, a raging body of water one hundred feet wide between its banks that it threatened to burst any minute. Now, its summer spate ended, it had sunk forty to fifty feet and was moving placidly along its basic channel far below us.

As we rode along the top of the levee we saw many junks carrying cargoes of farm goods or coal or building materials between these hinterland areas and the great port of Tientsin on the eastern coast. Some were the usual broad, squat lumbering vessels that one sees on any sizable Chinese river, with a single or tripod mast with single, square-rigged sail. Some were extra long and jointed in the middle for greater ease in negotiating the channel's many turnings. Both kinds used their sails if there was any wind but, because of the impossibility of tacking in the narrow channel, its crewmen always stood ready to tow or pole the vessel along. Each junk had a clear eight-inch gangway running down either side. This was for the polers. Placing their big punt poles firmly on the bottom of the channel or on the bank and then leaning on them, they would walk to the stern in step with each other, forcing the junk forward under them. Dexterously raising their poles just before their catwalk came to an end at the stern, they would swiftly stride to the prow and repeat the process, mile after mile. Other junks had a plank thrown athwart their

bows, forming a stumpy wing on either side. Here two oars-
men stood and rowed with long sweeps. Another crewman
handled the tiller oar projecting from the stern.

The junks were equipped for long trips of several weeks.
Amidships, usually just behind the mast, was a covered hatch
with galley and sleeping quarters. Quilts and clothes were
tucked up on tidy bunks and here more likely than not was
a fourth crewman placidly doing the cooking. It was possible,
if you had the time, to book a passage for a few yuan and
make the slow two- or three-week trip to the coast.

County Town 🌿

The county town revealed itself in the distance first by the
square mass of the old West Gate and bell tower. These were
the only remains of the ancient wall and battlements that had
surrounded it only a decade ago. Then high above the trees
we could see the tall chimney stack, water tower, and glittering silver columns of the new textile plant that had been built
after liberation as part of the plan to bring the textile industry
away from such highly congested industrial areas as Shanghai
or Tientsin or Wuhsi and closer to the sources of raw materials and local markets for cotton goods.

We rode through the dormitory and living complex of the
textile mill. This residential area is wisely separated from the
mill itself, which lies on the other side of the river. A wide,
smooth concrete driveway leads through well-built, two-story
dormitories and flats for married workers and their families.
Here too are shops, the post office, theater and cinema, small
outdoor market area, and a variety of service shops—laundries,
tailors, hairdressers and so on—the whole forming a typical
complex of rural industrial planning and housing in present-
day China.

Many of the mill hands are young textile operatives from

Shanghai who volunteered to come and get the new mill started and stayed on afterwards. As we rode among them, it was clear that they had brought their Shanghai go and sophistication with them. They talked with animated gestures and walked not with the deliberate and tireless plod of the countryman but the quick, jaunty step of the city dweller. Several of the girls had just come from the baths and wore their long black tresses loose over their shoulders, a charming frame for their faces. Many wore tailored shorts, which would have been considered impossibly daring in Upper Felicity. Here nobody took any notice and their legs shone white in the dappled shadows under the trees. Plane trees grew on both sides of the road and formed an arch where their leaves and branches met overhead. The cool here was very welcome after the heat of the ride in the open country.

From the mill complex we rode round a tree-bordered, embanked lake and into the town proper. We threaded our way through a number of narrow lanes lined with one-story half-brick, half-adobe houses, like those in any village, but the roughly cobbled street and the deep drain made of hewn stone on either side made it clear that we were in a town. Then abruptly we came into the very center. Here at a crossroads was the big department store on one corner and another corresponding building on the other. Both were large two-story brick and concrete structures with decorative façades such as you might see in the new residential areas of any big city of China like Peking or Shanghai. Only the ground floor of the department store had been completed, but it was already doing a brisk business while the second floor was being built.

The other two corner buildings of the crossroads looked much as they had for centuries past, but in function they were very different. One was an adobe and brick restaurant selling low-priced meals; the other was an old open-fronted shop selling mainly modern tinned goods: canned pork, pork and beans, tinned bran and bamboo shoots of a famous Shanghai make, melon jam, canned fruit of various kinds, apples, peaches, bananas, condensed milk, as well as biscuits, sweets, and many brands of cigarettes. There were various kinds of locally made pickles and many wines, from mild rice wine to fiery *maotai*, a clear liquor made from kaoliang and stronger than gin or vodka. There is convivial drinking in the town, but, like the rest of China, never any drunkenness.

On the streets adjoining this central shopping place were many other restaurants and shops. You could get good meals in the restaurants. Some served cheap, filling meals; others had in addition a choice of more elaborate dishes costing a yuan or more in great variety with fish, chicken, pork, beef, and eggs. There was a fine, newly built red brick post office and, as in every town in China, a Hsinhua Bookstore stocked with the Marxist classics and the works of Chairman Mao, Chairman Mao badges and portraits, and posters for the current campaigns to "Get a Grip on Revolution and Promote Production!" to develop the defense forces (a P.L.A. soldier, a sailor, an airman, a peasant militiaman, and a worker Communist keeping a watchful eye over the nation's borders), and to "Learn from Tachai!" There was also a section with a great deal of technical literature such as peasant cadres need: on irrigation and building techniques, drainage, reforestation, sideline occupations, mechanization, electrification, tractor technology, and so on. There was a section marked "Literature," but for the moment, due to the arguments still raging in the Cultural Revolution, this was still rather bare except for children's books, texts of the new revolutionary operas and ballets, and exhortatory stories about heroes of the revolutionary struggle.

Other shops sold special goods—dried fish and marine products, farm tools, bamboo products from the south, pickles, ironware, rope, and basketware. Government shops sold vegetables and meat. Conscientious cadres came to these first, before going to the market on the streets.

When we arrived at the state butcher shop, at around 6:45 A.M., there was already a longish line, and after waiting for about an hour we only just managed to get what we wanted. But this was Sunday, when many people like to eat meat for their holiday meal. On other days when I arrived there was just the normal crowd of shoppers, and you could still buy meat even long after eight. Beef was not as popular as pork. There were two state meat shops and they also sent out a seller with a handcart fitted up with a glass-covered top under, which the meat was displayed. He made the rounds of the market streets and residential areas and had usually sold out by around ten o'clock. The town had no ice factory, so traders were anxious to sell perishable goods like meat as soon as possible and did not take out too big a store of them.

The county town market was an impromptu affair. No special place was set aside for it. Peasants and commune sellers just took up a stand on the streets near the department store, the station, and the hostel which the county government maintained for visiting cadres. In August there was a big variety of foods to choose from. Tomatoes, green and Spanish onions, *tscho tsai,* eggplant, all kinds of fruit, apples, pears and grapes. The watermelons had already passed their prime but they were good thirst quenchers in the heat. There were a couple of stalls just on the corner under big cotton awnings where you could buy either whole fruit or large slices for five fen from sellers of a local co-op. Yellow River cod was on sale, still alive in water. These were beautiful silver and black fish over two and a half feet long. They had been caught in the Wei by a lucky peasant fisherman. Another man, a commune seller, had a large tub in which smaller fish were lazily swimming. These were from one of the reservoirs and fish farms of the county. As the day grew warmer, a state seller of iced popsicles began to do a roaring trade.

The sellers came from communes, commune brigades, and teams. Some were simply individual members come to sell a few eggs or the produce of their small backyard gardens or fruit trees. Prices on the market were set in the play of market supply and demand, under the controlling influence of the price set by the state through the supply and marketing co-ops and state shops. There was no absolute prohibition against commune members selling occasional produce here, but of course anyone doing this regularly to the detriment of the collective economy would be criticized and warned against "taking the capitalist road." On the other hand, commune members would go only to this market as an exceptional means of getting supplies. They might want to buy fish, meat, or vegetables for a wedding or betrothal party or some such occasion. None would normally indulge in such a luxurious way of getting food. They would have neither the ready cash nor the time for it. Most of the individual sellers were old men or women or mothers with children. Most buyers were the townsfolk. Some were rusticating cadres or students at the May Seventh Cadre Schools. Among other buyers were cadres or cooks in charge of public canteens of offices or other local organizations and factories wanting to get some extra tidbits outside the normal state allocations. Some would buy up a whole handcart full of vegetables and ask for it to be delivered just as it was to their canteen kitchens. There were some amusing incidents. What was obviously a commune brigade's small group of three men came into town pushing a handcart of very limp-looking lettuce. They stopped on the road on their way to the main market area, and a few housewives gathered round to look at their goods. When they heard the price asked, the women hemmed and hawed and when more and more neighbors came up raised their objections to the price in louder and louder tones. Finally a considerable debate developed between the team's spokesman and the spokesman for the assembled housewives, who exclaimed in a horrified voice: "You want five fen a bunch for that worn-out lettuce! Are you making fun of us?" (Loud rumble of general wonderment and pain at such unreasonable sellers.)

The brigade seller (more and more flustered by the "mass pressure"): "Well! What do you want for five fen! Do you want me to give it away to you?"

Intervention by a town organization cadre in a neat uniform and a long beard (who puts matters on a higher theoretical level): "You're supposed to be doing socialist trading! You mustn't cheat the masses!"

Brigade seller (making a show of anger but at his wit's end and not wanting to be thought of as "not serving the masses"): "All right then! We'll go elsewhere! You don't want our goods. Other people do!"

And he grabbed the shafts of the handcart and hurried away. But instead of going to the market center, he and his comrades pushed their cart up a side street. As soon as they

got out of sight of the housewives they immediately stopped
and held a worried colloquy, and as I cycled past I heard one
of them saying ". . . if we are serving the people, then. . . ."
Presumably economic fact and political theory had both encouraged them to lower prices.

The department store was stocked more or less like any
shop of its size in Peking or Shanghai. In Peking it would
not have rated as high as one of the largest urban department
stores, but it offered a wider range of goods than a district
department store. It had all the common goods of daily use:
clothes, knitwear, rainshoes, scarves, caps, towels and cloth,
and of course stationery, fountain pens, radios and transistors
and parts, plastic sheets, soap, toothpaste, cigarettes, all kinds
of toys and knickknacks for the children, flashlights and
batteries. There was a big selection of tools for carpentering,
metal work, and electrical installation. A whole counter was devoted to "cultural goods," Chinese violins, drums, cymbals,
flutes, phonograph records and broadcasting equipment for
commune radio and rediffusion networks, texts of plays, and
song music. On shelves and in a middle-of-the-floor display
were sports accessories: gymnastic apparatus, volleyballs and
badminton rackets, table-tennis equipment. There was also an
assortment of cameras and photographic supplies. Business
was brisk and the service good, though not up to Shanghai
standards. Prices were uniform, as they are all over China,
whether in Peking or up in distant mountain villages.

I dropped in at the optician's, hoping to get a lens to replace
one I had recently broken. But they pointed out that the
prescription was many months old, so I had better go to the
local hospital, have my eyes tested, and get a new one. They
promised to have a new pair of spectacles ready for me inside
a fortnight.

The hospital was not far away. It was a former Protestant
mission establishment which now, of course, is part of the
state medical service. No longer under the old proprietors, it
is run by the county government. Housed in the old block of
buildings with some new ones added, its very competent staff
of doctors and surgeons is highly praised by the peasants. It
has all the usual departments: ear and nose, eye, dentistry,

gynecology, maternity, and an advanced surgical department.

I paid my registration fee of two fen (less than half the cheapest bus fare in Peking) and went straight to the eye doctor's office. About half a dozen people were ahead of me but the oculist in attendance had three assistants, lively young interns, one of whom tested my eyes. The doctor went over the test and wrote out the prescription. The whole thing took no more than half an hour. I took the prescription to the optician and in a couple of weeks had my new spectacles in the standard mass-produced plastic frames that cost just a couple of yuan. The whole thing cost me about two U.S. dollars.

On our way back, we dropped in to see the hostel run by the county for visiting cadres. This is a modern brick and concrete three-story building. It was clean but had no frills. You could get a single bed here for 5 mao a night or a double room for 1 yuan (U.S. $0.40). Each room contained two wooden beds with clean bedding, chairs, and a table. There were exhortating slogans on the wall and a picture of Chairman Mao. This was all the furnishing, in keeping with the Party's call to the comrades to lead a Spartan life. The canteen provided simple meals at very cheap prices. Cadres arriving by rail in the county stayed here until they caught their buses or other conveyances to their May Seventh Cadre School or the communes, or to settle down with their families for a spell in the country.

Remolding at the Cadre School 🌿

By and large the rusticating cadres were well behaved and did their best to learn as much as they could from the peasants in farm work, in their frugal, hardworking style of living and their simple dedication to the new life. And by and large the peasants were well pleased with their contacts with these cadres. As usual, it was the very few who rocked the boat, either through stupidity or perversity. There was the cadre who after a visit from his wife complained bitterly against her to a peasant and vowed he was going to divorce her. Next time she came down, the peasant proposed that he would be quite ready to marry her himself. There was the cadre who extravagantly bought five pounds of egg cakes at one go for himself and two little children.

One day Mrs. Yuan went on strike. She had labored hard to get us all set up with winter vegetables, coal, and eggs and had gone several times through the winter cold to buy goods for us in the county town, but along with praise and thanks she had got nagging complaints from Mrs. Tan that the meat was underweight and too lean and "someone" had hinted that she had kept the best of the meat for herself. This was too much—she simply went on strike. When Tsang asked who would go to order more coal, she wasn't at the meeting. Yuan said that he had to study; Ling's bicycle had broken down. Tsang was sick but, conscientious as ever, he went. When he came back and we met in his house he looked gaunt and tired. Mrs. Tan was subdued and never complained again. We all felt that in one way or another she was getting remolded.

Each group of cadres was expected to maintain its own discipline, but this depended a great deal on the leadership of the group and the spirit of its members. The thirty families in West Board Bridge Village were for a time unfortunate in their leadership. By various manipulations both at the head office in Peking and down in the May Seventh Cadre School control had been seized by a group of cadres dominated by extremists and "ultra-leftists."

During the Cultural Revolution an extremist organization known as the Five One Six Corps had emerged and with powerful backing from manipulators in high places had made a serious bid to seize power. Only in late 1971 was it revealed that among these was Lin Piao, the Defense Minister, designated as Mao Tse-tung's successor at the 1969 Ninth Congress of the Chinese Communist Party. Its attempt had failed, but it had managed to climb to power in a number of organizations. One of these was the translation bureau. Infiltrating one of the mass organizations, underground Five One Six members actually controlled a number of departments in the bureau and were doing their best to hang on. To do this they had placed complaisant stooges in positions of authority wherever they could. One of these was in charge of the group of cadres in West Board Bridge Village. Several more dominated the May Seventh Cadre School. As usually happens, the stooges took advantage of their positions. The wife of one petty stooge was exposed as spending more than 150 yuan a month for herself, her husband, and their little girl. She went to Chengchow especially to buy such delicacies as preserved mushrooms and shrimps. Another stooge, to the insult of his peasant host, entirely redecorated the room he was renting. These scandals were undermining all discipline in the West Board Bridge Village group of cadres. But the situation in the May Seventh Cadre School was worse because there, isolated as it was from the villages of the commune, the Five One Six gang could keep their wrongdoing hidden, by the same means they were using in Peking. They had instituted a reign of petty terror.

In an attempt to keep people's mouths shut, they set up a regime of jackboot discipline that made labor not a thing of joy and honor, but a punishment. In other May Seventh School farms it was regarded as an honor to do such mucky jobs as looking after the pigs and cleaning out the stys and latrines. In this Five One Six-run school these jobs were assigned to "undisciplined" cadres as punishment.

This situation was one of a number that was dealt with in the final stage of the Cultural Revolution, when all such anomalies were attended to by the Communist Party. First a small number of experienced Party members were sent in to investigate the situation in the Peking bureau. It was not hard to see that something was wrong, and once given a lead the remaining cadres there quickly exposed the Five One Six group that had burrowed themselves into the leadership. The investigation and struggle then spread to the May Seventh Cadre School.

First the wrongdoers were given a chance to "come over to the side of the Revolution." A message was sent down from Peking pointing out that during the Cultural Revolution certain people had tried to disrupt the movement and lead it astray in various ways. Instead of trying to expose the misdemeanors of the revisionists "taking the capitalist road," a small number of leading Party members had used their authority not to lead revolutionary activity and encourage the rank-and-file to express their opinions, but to suppress criticism and, when they could not do this, divert popular wrath against innocent people. The May Seventh Cadre School leadership was asked to investigate the situation.

The Five One Six leaders stupidly tried to cover up their wrongdoing by trying to justify their former actions and instigate the rank-and-file to criticize anew the cadres they themselves had unjustly accused before. They also used strong-arm methods to blackmail their victims into silence. One young man had been vilely slandered as a "foreign agent" because he had received his early education abroad and still, to some extent, lived in "a foreign way." Now he was trotted out again as a convenient target of attack to divert attention from the real culprits. The Five One Six Corps instigated people, particularly its dupes among young and inexperienced ultra-leftists, to write wall posters reviving all the groundless accusations against him.

Wang Pei-yung had been a leading cadre. He had made mistakes, it is true, but had honestly tried to do his job well. He was a veteran of the People's Liberation Army and had been wounded in the battles for the Revolution. Still suffering from the effects of these wounds, he had been invalided out of the army and given an editing job. He was too ill to do heavy exercise, and his doctors advised him to take up swimming or dancing. For the young extremists of the lunatic "left," dancing was tantamount to supping with the bourgeois devil. During the Cultural Revolution, they dragged him out at a meeting and railed and sneered at him, regardless of the fact that they had been running around playing in shorts while he had been fighting bloody battles for them and their future.

Now, in a desperate search for a diversion at the cadre school, they had attacked Wang Pei-yung again. When he complained of sickness they accused him of malingering and drove him out to work in the fields.

Two of his fellow victims remonstrated that Wang was in no condition to walk, let alone work. His face was ashen. This only seemed to infuriate these young scoundrels the more.

"You gang of counterrevolutionaries! Get to work!"

Wang gritted his teeth and marched off. But the effort was too much for him. As soon as the group reached the field of wheat where they were to work, he fainted and fell to the ground. It happened that a doctor was in a team of cadres from another organization working nearby. When he saw Wang fall, he hurried over.

"Get this man to bed as soon as possible," he ordered. The other "evil elements" in Wang's team told him what was happening, and Wang was removed in care of the friendly organization.

At this juncture, the May Seventh Cadre School was visited by a Mao Tse-tung Thought Propaganda Team from Peking. It included members of the group that had originally uncovered the Five One Six Corps activities in the translation bureau and also people who had been duped by the Five One Six into supporting them and had now "crossed over to the side of the Revolution" and exposed the criminal activities of the corps. A great mass meeting was called at the May Seventh Cadre School. Cadres from the bureau throughout the area were summoned. The activities of the Five One Six in Peking were exposed. Their former dupes took the stage to reveal what they knew. The air was electric. Just as in Peking, it was essential that the rank-and-file themselves should expose and clear up this mess. Only in this way could there be any guarantee that the same thing would not happen again. First one and then another braved the black looks of the corps to take the stage and speak out. The Five One Six panicked and in a tumultuous sequel began to pour blame on each other and others. The ringleaders, who had even instigated or perpetrated murders, were arrested—the small fry and their dupes were sent back to their various units to make self-criticisms. It was the duty of their colleagues at work to help them see the error of their ways and get them to turn over a new leaf, first by making a clean breast of their wrongdoing and then by undertaking to win merit by "serving the people" in any way they could. In this way the "front of attack was narrowed to the minimum." Everyone understood that in the confused struggles that had sometimes arisen during the tense days of the Cultural Revolution it was almost inevitable that some weaker or less vigilant souls should be swept into acts that they would never have done in more normal times. Everything possible was done to rehabilitate these people.

There was a great clearing of the air after this clean-up in the cadre school. Elections were held free from the shadow of the Five One Six and new leaders were chosen to lead the cadre school and the cadre communities that had suffered from Five One Six leadership. All their stooges were voted out of office, and in several cases the innocent cadres who had been their victims were elected to take their places. Real discipline in the various communities was restored or established, and the peasants quickly noticed the difference. In some cases the peasants had been genuinely disturbed. A cadre in West Board Bridge Village had been buying chickens and homespun from the peasants in defiance of strict prohibitions. This had come to the ears of Lao Man and he had told us, "The West Board Bridge people say that some of the cadres there are behaving like landlords!"

All such activities were now quickly stopped. Meetings were held to remind all cadres that they were there in the countryside to "spread the Thought of Mao-Tse-tung" and to "learn from the poor and lower-middle peasants."

During these events, I realized better the role that Lin had played, in his unassuming way. He may have hemmed and hawed over how to repair a road or plant a tree, but he had rejected the advances of the Five One Six and when the showdown came he was able to lead a united group into battle for the Cultural Revolution. They sometimes foot-slogged for hours over sodden roads to get to and from the cadre school for important daylong meetings. Rain or shine, they did their bit. Tan ignored his rheumatism. His wife forgot her petty gossip and went in for political issues of major importance. Yuan neglected his cooking. Ling was less phlegmatic. Tang bestirred himself and, of course, the Tsangs and Mrs. Yuan were more active than ever.

Late Summer, Early Autumn 🌿

Right to the end of August the summer heat still made itself felt in the noonday hours. Then the hamlet was silent. After lunch the toddlers slept soundly on mat-covered beds, exhausted by play and heat. In the cool, dim light of the cottages the women went on with their accustomed tasks. I could always hear the chuck-chuck of a weaving frame or the intermittent whir of a spinning wheel.

In many farmyards, the early corncobs drying on kaoliang mats made bright carpets of vivid orange and yellow. They were vigilantly guarded by a granny or a youngster armed with a willow switch to keep the hens off. Some households dried their corn on their roofs, but the hens managed to fly up there even on their clipped wings.

All this time, much to Ta Sao's amusement, we ate cold foods for lunch whenever we could. This was mostly *mantou* and, since the cucumbers were finished, cold boiled squash and tomatoes and new potato salad.

In the autumn nights, the crickets chirped with shrill contentment.

Art Criticism 🌿

*P*ai Lu, the White Dews, came on September 8, and all the planting of the autumn-ripening crops had been done. Temperate, cool weather returned and I was able to go back to my earlier schedule of work for the day: an early rise, breakfast and the whole morning painting or drawing, then lunch and rest, with an early turnout for my afternoon stint of work. It was light until nearly seven, so I could do some more drawing in the late afternoon and eat later. Then we chatted or read and went to bed around 10 P.M.

My peasant neighbors never lost interest in my drawings. Nearly every day, grown-ups or youngsters would drop in for a look at work in progress. When I was out sketching they would crowd round to look over my shoulder. Everyone who could took a look through my sketchbook. They would ask curiously why I was drawing this or that. I explained that I was drawing how a cart was built; that I wanted to keep a souvenir or mental picture of an incident or a movement. This was the simple truth, and they accepted it as such. They would criticize what I had done, if they felt it would help, from that point of view. They would point out that "the harness does not lie that way. It passes through a hole in the yoke," or that "the roller on the weaving frame is higher than you have drawn it." When I was sketching the swing sickle that the Number One Team used, during a pause for the midshift rest, they eagerly explained how it was made.

Whenever I went out with my sketchbook, they shouted gaily: "Lao Chen! Draw me!" Then they crowded round and commented, "Yes, that's just right!" They were specific in their likes and expectations. Quite frankly they expected a drawing to "be right," but that did not mean that they expected a naturalistic, photographic reproduction of reality. When Ta Sao saw my sketch of a girl carrying a basket, she asked, "What's in that basket?" It was a valid question—what was in the basket gave a further clue to the significance of the girl's action. The basket and what was in it were important to the drawing. I learned from that question. Not everyone was so keen, but in general I felt from their reactions and comments that they took my sketches in the spirit in which I made them: comments on their life and work. When Lao Man chanced on the big bureaucratic-looking cock I had drawn, he laughed out loud spontaneously. He quite understood how this grotesquely caricatured cock had evolved out of my realistic sketches.

They were not worried by a quick line sketch that left out all detail and background and concentrated solely on the rhythm of the movement. If the "squiggle" caught the movement, "That's exactly right!" they would cry.

The interest they showed in my work was a constant inspiration and encouragement to me. When I went out sketching and happened on an interesting work team, I always did a stint of work with them first before I started sketching. Though it would not have been taken that way, I felt that to start right in drawing would have looked like coldly exploiting their labor.

The practical-minded peasant cadres thought how to put this drawing ability to some immediate militant use. They asked me to make a series of drawings on the class struggle in the countryside. This would be put on exhibition in the middle school as part of the political education course on the nature of class struggle. I did a series of eighteen drawings for them showing landlord exploitation and brutality, the Kuomintang press gangs, peasants fleeing from famine and flood, and finally a meeting during the land reform with the peasants accusing a landlord of his crimes. They were very pleased with these drawings. Later they asked me to do some pictures to decorate their new office. They understood immediately when I said that I wanted to get to know the local life and people first and then paint such pictures. Unfortunately I had to leave Upper Felicity before I fulfilled that promise. But when I visited them two years later, they still had my drawings at the school.

Foreign Affairs as Seen from a Ditch 🦋

Our OSD Team read the papers regularly, particularly the editorials of the *People's Daily* and *Red Flag*. We also listened to the radio broadcasts. In addition we received regular briefings on current events and Party and government policy from propaganda cadres sent down to us from Peking or from confidential statements which were handed down to us. That summer there was a particularly interesting briefing on foreign affairs. The reporter outlined the current international situation and discussed American policy in relation to Vietnam and China. Soviet policy in the Far East was also discussed. The Cambodian issue had recently come to the fore. The CIA had evidently conspired with reactionary elements like Siri Matak and Lon Nol to take advantage of Prince Sihanouk's absence from the country and stage a coup d'état.

The words "propaganda" and "propagandist" as used in China have a different connotation than in the West. Propaganda work in the Chinese sense means explaining or popularizing policy or ideas. Thus, a Party propagandist explains or popularizes Party policy. A sanitation propagandist explains and teaches sanitation policy and methods. A Mao Tse-tung Thought Propaganda Team disseminates, explains, and puts into practice the ideas and teachings of Mao Tse-tung.

I remember this foreign policy discussion in particular. It was so interesting that later that day we continued it while resting comfortably in a ditch, our backs against one side and our feet propped up against the other. We discussed the Soviet refusal to recognize Sihanouk's new government. We also discussed U.S. foreign policy options, and a number of other questions.

This discussion contrasted sharply with an earlier "discussion" in Peking several months before, when the Five One Six Corps had been in control of the office. It had been not so much a discussion as an intemperate harangue by one of the young ultra-leftists who had been given his head by the Five One Six. With a great show of bravado but not much sense, this young man had called on us to be ready to plant the flag of revolution not only on the spires of the Kremlin but on the top of the Empire State Building.

In contrast to this childishness, which had been thoroughly criticized along with other extremist Five One Six ideas during the recent debates to eradicate the influence of this group, we of the rank-and-file down in the ditch now considered the various foreign policy options before China. The consensus was to reject any demagogic and dogmatic policy that would paint China into a diplomatic corner. We unanimously opted for action that would take advantage of any possibilities in international alignments so that China could press forward a foreign policy based on the Five Principles of Peaceful Coexistence: respect for the sovereignty and territorial integrity of all states, nonaggression against other states, noninterference in the internal affairs of other states, equality and mutual benefit, and peaceful coexistence. Support for these principles was voiced in the joint U.S.–China communiqué signed by President Nixon and Premier Chou En-lai in February 1972, more than a year later.

These foreign policy issues were being discussed in study groups all over the country. Reports of these discussions and the opinions and suggestions voiced were collected and studied in Peking, and in this way Party and government leaders kept their fingers on the pulse of public opinion. This is one of the ways the democratic process and the mass line operate in new China.

When, many months later, I first heard about Ping-Pong diplomacy, I vividly recalled this discussion in that lane near Upper Felicity.

Apotheosis of Pig 🐖

Pig became a notorious escapee. First she jumped over the wall of the sty. It was built higher. Then she burrowed under the cartwheel that served as the door to the sty. The hole was filled in and a thick kaoliang stalk mat was pushed over it. But then she found that she could scramble over the heightened wall by taking a running leap and using the trough as a springboard. Ta Sao gave her a scolding and blocked this way of escape with a second cartwheel. For two days Pig lay moody and sulking. To comfort her I threw her some pieces of eggplant. She nosed them over and, just like Big Pig before her, turned away sulking. Then one day she got a real break that completely restored her spirits.

In mid-August there was a pause in the collective field work and the hamlet's inhabitants went off in all directions to gather in fodder for the winter. The children were let out of school and after working the whole afternoon would come back just before supper in twos and threes so heavy laden with grass that they looked like haystacks moving along on small legs. As they came in they threw the grass down in the courtyards to dry, and soon pigs, goats, and chickens came running up to gorge themselves to their heart's content. When the grass dried it would be stacked in corners or on rooftops over the winter. Meanwhile the animals had a field day. Pig was let out of her sty. She came out with a bound and then stood transfixed in wonder on the edge of that huge blanket of succulent green spread in our courtyard. Pig waded in up to her haunches, tail wagging and ears flapping. She even forgot to go to the latrine for her *hors d'oeuvre*.

The hay is sold to the commune at a yuan per thirty jin. Ta Sao and the children had collected over one hundred jin already and by the end of the autumn would have cut several hundred more. This was useful pocket money.

When Lao Man saw Pig fat and replete, he said: "Pig is really getting big now!" Pig paid no attention to this voice of fate. She went on eating, even more voraciously.

Au Chiu

Au Chiu caught a sparrow nestling and decided to raise it. He gave it a nest of dried grass in a discarded tin, kept it on a windowsill inside the cottage, and fed it scraps. The trouble came when its little wings were strong enough to fly. Then he tied a long kite string on to one of its legs and placed it on the high sill outside our cottage window. When he came home from school, he exercised it by letting it fly around to the length of the string. When he tired of this he shortened the string to a foot or so and tied the unfortunate sparrow to the wooden grating of the window. Next morning he went off to school. I heard the bird fluttering furiously, trying to fly away, until, exhausted, it hung limp, head down at the end of its string. I put it back in its nest two or three times, but as soon as it had recovered its strength it fluttered furiously again, torturing itself in its effort to escape.

Later I was just in time to see the next-door cat make a spring at the sill where the sparrow cowered and fluttered in fear. I gave the cat a clout and he made off over the wall. Then I thought of the birdcage I had seen in Mrs. Lin's cottage. I went to her and after a few words drew her attention tactfully to the cage. "That's a fine cage you have there."

For a moment she looked pleased. But she didn't reply. It turned out that the cage had been made by her son, her oldest child, who was now in the northeast and whom she missed greatly, although she had her two little girls with her. "That cage is like a keepsake," she said. "It reminds me of him. He is so clever with his hands."

After that I didn't have the heart to ask it of her, and returned home empty-handed. I put a network of sticks over the window and thought this would protect the bird. But I underrated feline greed and cunning. Soon after Au Chiu came back from school we heard him wailing. The cat had eaten his sparrow. Only a few feathers lay scattered on the ground. Getting the last big enjoyment out of his victim, the four-footed murderer was playfully chasing what remained of the victim round an overturned stool.

Au Chiu soon stopped crying. He went off with a spade several sizes too large for him, to get more trees to plant in his "garden"—a discarded chamberpot.

Autumn Harvest

With the last of the squashes and pumpkins harvested and distributed, the vegetable plots were plowed up and planted to the last main crop—turnips. The sweet potatoes, carrots, and cabbage had already been put in. Then all attention was turned to the maize harvest. This got going in late August.

There was not the same tense rush that there had been over the summer wheat. The maize had been sown over a period of several weeks, and the stands were cut as they ripened one after another. No rain threatened. The weather was fine. After the harvest there would be plenty of time to plow and sow the winter wheat. The beans and cotton were long ago sown and doing well. That accounted for all the brigade's land. Nevertheless, the brigade's whole manpower was mobilized. There were jobs for all. Even the children and the oldsters could earn work-points, harvesting the crop.

The grown men and youth of both sexes did the cutting. Using their sickles with a free, swift rhythm, they hacked the maize stalk through close to the ground, laid the cut plants behind them, and advanced to the next. Competitions got going, sometimes team against team or three, four, or five harvesters in a row where they found competitors worthy of their mettle. In some fields they pulled the whole stalk up, root and all. Then the children, wielding small mattocks, broke the soil from the roots. The roots would be cut off later and used for fuel. Sometimes the women and children stripped the corn from the stalk in the field; sometimes the whole harvest was brought home and stripped on the threshing floor. This was the way it was done in our Number Three Team. The women and children swarmed over the sheaves of maize as they were brought in, pulled off the glittering cobs, and piled them up on the threshing floor in hillocks, shining in the sun, bright golden yellow or deep golden bronze. Whatever method was used, the husking and shucking were done on the threshing floor. For many days everybody was there. Even the mothers with crawling infants could take part, as the floors were all near the hamlets and the children loved to play over the heaps of drying corn and among the crackling husks.

One day on the road I passed a work group from our Third Team. Most were resting in a field that was being harvested. But jolly Mrs. Kuai was sitting by the roadside with her baby chewing the sweet sap from a length of kaoliang stalk. She gave me a length to chew and as we sat there chatting I noticed a small corncob lying nearby. I stretched over and handed it to her baby.

"No! No! You take it!" cried Mrs. Kuai.

"You take it home and boil it for the baby," I said.

"Not on your life!" she laughed, and took it from the baby and gave it back to me.

"Why not?" I asked.

"Because I don't want to do this," she replied, and she hung down her head like the central personage at a criticism meeting.

"Well, neither do I," I said, and threw the cob onto a pile of cornstalks being readied for carting to the threshing floor.

"But what about this?" I indicated the lengths of sweet kaoliang stalk we were chewing.

"Oh, that," she said and paused, thinking the matter over. "That's all right. We're all doing it."

Upper Felicity laissez-faire again!

Knowing how their members liked to eat fresh grain and that some were probably getting low on stocks, the brigade decided to share out part of the harvest right then and there. The peasants brought their shares of cobs back home in baskets, handcarts, and barrows, the whole family lending a hand. For days the glint of gold and red could be seen on every threshing floor, courtyard, and roof. Ta Sao was on the threshing floor with the two youngest children and they helped her bring the family share home. After they had shucked it she tried drying it on the ground, but it was a constant struggle to keep the chickens from it. Then she spread the grain out on the roof. That was better, but she still had to come out now and then from her spinning to make horrid noises and wave a long stick to frighten hens and birds off the roof.

While the husking was on, the men were laying out the maize stalks to dry in grey-green ranks around the threshing floor. The wheat stalks were already neatly stacked in the shape of cottages with high roof or in circular, domed towers tapering down to a small base.

The children, meanwhile, were restrained with great difficulty from going at the dates, which hung in tempting green clusters on the trees. The lowest bunches had disappeared early. Sticks and bricks had been heaved in vain against the higher clusters. Even year-old saplings had a few fruit. But it would be the end of August before the dates would turn deep green and brown and ripe for eating. Most would be eaten raw. Some would be turned into pastry, cooked between slabs of dough, perhaps, with a pinch of sugar. The Upper Felicity dates were not the sort that could be put into spirits and fermented as they do in Shansi.

The threshing-floor cadres slept on the spot to keep watch and ward. The weather was still quite warm at night and they built wigwams out of the maize stalks to sleep in. By this time the crickets were chirping in the trees every evening like mad things. It was a season of manifest well-being. The maize fields were scenes of busy activity. The threshing floors were bright with color and movement, chatter and laughter. The orange-red of the drying maize cobs shone like lanterns amid the green leaves that bowered our hamlet.

The sweet potato vines formed thick green carpets, so thick that not an inch of bare earth could be seen beneath them. The cotton was in flower and coming along nicely. When I passed it I liked to think secretly that part of this flourishing crop was due to my pruning. Ah! Individualism! How hard it dies!

Evening 🌿

A cloud floats bright pink against a cobalt sky. Then it turns purple and finally fades blue on blue into deeper blue. Music from a faraway commune loudspeaker comes over so faintly, so distantly, that it seems like a memory in one's own mind.

A goat bleats hoarsely. A child cries fitfully. The frogs in the big pond set up their monotonous evening chant, croaking in unison. The moon hangs like a half-sliced melon in an indigo sky. Overhead and to the west shines the Bear and that glorious, bright, steadfast guiding star—Vega.

A soft breeze rustles over the ground. It is the time of *Pai Lu,* White Dews, September 8. The date tree in the courtyard hangs its branches heavily. They glitter with the bronzed, almost ripe fruit. The children have made a troubled attempt at sleep in the open air. They are ordered peremptorily to bed. Ching Chun is going to sleep on the roof. Now and then he can be heard slapping away the mosquitoes that try to bite his legs.

Deep night descends and leaves everyone to oblivious sleep.

Year's End Fruits 🌿

B y early September all the maize was in and by the end of the month the cotton and beans were being harvested. In October all the main harvests were in. *Han Lu* came on October 9. After *Shan Jiang*, Dew Falls, on October 24, the brigade got down to the job of settling up the year's accounts, summing up the year's experience and planning for the tasks of next year. The agricultural tax in kind had been promptly delivered. The division of the rest of the harvest had been gone into pretty thoroughly when the production plan had been drawn up. Part was set aside for investment and production funds and welfare. The rest went as income direct to the brigade members. Part was sold to the state and the proceeds along with the rest of the surplus were distributed, so that each person in the brigade received nearly 30 per cent more grain than the year before, not literally grain, of course, but its equivalent in value, including not only wheat and maize and other cereals, but beans, cotton, cottonseed and other vegetable oils, vegetables, and some ready cash. It fell a little short of their perhaps overambitious plan, but it was a very fair result and certainly a matter for congratulation in any farm.

Mao's Way 🌿

I had lived in the green valleys of Chekiang, south of Hangchow; I had studied the hill communes amid the loess mountains of Shansi; I had visited the Five Star Commune in the fabled Turfan oasis of Sinkiang, and also a new farm being created by men of the People's Liberation Army on the edge of the Taklamakan Desert. Like Upper Felicity, in this former famine bowl of the Honan plain, all were progressing. I was struck by the unity of thought success-fully guiding all these places. In each case I was seeing the living implementation of Mao Tse-tung's ideas and methods of creating a new social and environmental system based on socialist principles.

Each was an example of restructuring both man and nature to solve the urgent problem of man's survival and growth in a finite world with infinite possibilities. In each case the main problem, or as Mao's phraseology puts it, the main contradic-tion, was being grasped for initial solution and, in effecting that solution, the active force, man, was taken as the key. In changing nature, his environment, man was changing him-self. In using his knowledge of nature and of society to effect progressive change, man was achieving the progressive lib-eration of mankind.

It is only a little over a hundred years since man achieved a high enough level in the physical sciences to give him a high degree of mastery over nature. It is hardly a century since Marx provided him with a high enough level of knowl-edge of the laws of social development to enable him to restructure society consciously. Lenin synthesized this knowl-edge into a theory and practice of revolutionary change in a modern world. Mao has developed this theory and practice further with particular reference to the Chinese situation. And now here was this knowledge, this Mao methodology of revolution, being applied successfully and with great imagi-nation by millions of people, millions of peasants who only yesterday were in rags, starving, illiterate, enslaved by feudal landlords and superstition. This is one of the most important achievements of the twenty-one years of leadership of China by the Communist Party and Mao Tse-tung.

The essence of the Mao way is first to make a correct scientific analysis of the problem to be solved. Through this analysis the investigator elucidates its essential aspect and deals with this first, bearing in mind the other, nonessential or minor aspects for subsequent or complementary handling.

Mao stresses that it is necessary at all times to be aware of the limitations imposed by the existing conditions, the environment, while seeking within those limitations the utmost freedom of action. While avoiding wild flights of fancy, one should think hard, be imaginative and bold, carefully considering how a situation may change and how plans must be adapted to that changing situation.

Mao's works abound with advice on how to apply his methodology. He gives concrete examples of both successful and erroneous application and supplies numerous aphorisms to stress one or the other point. Many of these have been collected in his "little red book" of *Quotations*. For instance in his article on improving methods of study he writes: "[With the Marxist-Leninist attitude] a person applies the theory and method of Marxism-Leninism to the systematic and thorough investigation and study of the environment. He does not work by enthusiasm alone, but, as Stalin says, combines revolutionary sweep with practicalness."*

Mao can write with authority because he himself used this methodology to lead seven hundred million people in a successful revolution. After the six-thousand-mile Long March, the Communist Party's Red Army numbered only thirty thousand men. Using his methodology, Mao built this force into an army able to defeat four million troops commanded by Chiang Kai-shek and backed with four billion dollars of American aid. In the following passage he summarizes the method of leading such a campaign, but it can be taken as a generalized summary of his way of tackling any problem, whether the enemy is a hostile army, a hostile environment of drought or flood-stricken plain or mountainside, slum conditions in a city, or postwar monetary inflation.

A commander's correct dispositions stem from his correct decisions, his correct decisions stem from his correct judgments, and his correct judgments stem from a thorough and necessary reconnaissance and from pondering on and

* "Reform Our Study" (May 1941), *Selected Works*, Vol. III, p. 22.

piecing together the data of various kinds gathered through reconnaissance. He uses all possible and necessary methods of reconnaissance, and ponders on the information gathered about the enemy's situation, discarding the dross and selecting the essential, discarding the false and retaining the true, proceeding from the one to the other and from the outside to the inside; then he takes the conditions on his own side into account, and makes a study of both sides and their interrelations, thereby forming his judgments, making up his mind and working out his plans. Such is the complete process of knowing a situation which a military man goes through before he formulates a strategic plan, a campaign plan, or a battle plan.*

The Maoist farmers of Upper Felicity used this methodology to study their situation and then tackled the central fact of their poverty: exploitation of their landlessness by the feudal landlords prevented efficient use of the land and their labor. They solved this main contradiction by confiscating the landlords' land and distributing it equally among the peasants during the land reform. They went on to tackle consecutively the new key problem that arose in the new situation: the inability of their community to cultivate the land efficiently because of lack of tools and manpower on the individual farms. This problem was solved by mutual aid and cooperation in the use of tools, labor, and land by pooling them. They advanced step by step to tackle the major problems of ending flood and drought. This demanded restructuring the land and building great water conservancy works by the cooperative labor of millions of people. By the time they were ready to tackle these problems they had themselves created the necessary conditions for success: new, modern, collectively minded farmers willing and able to organize joint work for the common good, and also powerful commune organizations willing and able to work together and fired with the confidence that

* "Problems of Strategy in China's Revolutionary War" (December 1936), *Selected Works*, Vol. I, p. 188.

unity gives strength enough to perform miracles. In this spirit they built their great reservoirs and channels and ended floods, dug their deep wells and ended drought, and achieved a basic sufficiency where before there had been destitution.

Thus they had changed the social relations of production, the way people were organized for work, and the system of ownership of property, from feudal, to capitalist, to socialist (collective). Now they were tackling the next key question, that of increasing yields, and preparing to solve the question after that: transforming the forces of production, transforming their technology, the physical means of production, bringing about the mechanization and chemicalization of agriculture to produce yet larger yields and so advance to the abundance necessary for a fully rational and efficient socialist and then communist society and the new outlook that must go with living and working in such societies.

In Shansi Province the farmers of Tachai likewise analyzed their situation and were similarly transforming themselves and their environment. Formerly pauperized, scattered individual producers, they had freely organized themselves into a strong collective, laboriously terraced their barren hillsides and gullies, brought water along a new, five-mile-long canal, and raised yields from seventy-five pounds to eight hundred pounds of grain per acre.

In more prosperous Yangtan, by similar methods, the peasants had more than doubled yields in ten years. In Sinkiang twenty-three years ago the Uighur farmers of Turfan were the virtual serfs of feudal *bais* and Kuomintang warlords; most of the men who now comprise the People's Liberation Army Construction Corps there were the bewildered conscripts of the Kuomintang. In the years since then, using this same Mao methodology, they had made the Turfan oasis bloom and the desert around it blossom. In fertile Chekiang, "Land of Rice and Fish," the farmers had likewise overthrown their oppressors, restructured their lives and land, and more than doubled yields. In Tungkuan County, farmers were raising eighteen hundred jin of rice per mu. Every household raised three pigs. In each case, in Honan, Shansi, Sinkiang, and Chekiang, the peasants were restructuring their environment and both man and society in widely differing conditions for the purpose of achieving a more efficient man-environment system, more efficient in the sense of providing a better designed environment for better living and making less give more. No one has yet put forward a more effective methodology for progress in China.

But if man has begun relatively swiftly to apply his new knowledge to solve his social and economic problems and has achieved some success, notably in China, with its one-fifth of the world's population, there can be no denying that there is a growing urgency about this whole question of mankind making more efficient and wiser use of his earth.

As matters now stand, man is well on the way to polluting his world and wastefully exhausting its resources so that it may soon become uninhabitable. This is not a question that one nation can solve. It is a world question. It is not possible to set up national boundaries in the world's air and water. A world divided into haves and have-nots cannot exist without wars or devastation in which both will perish. China's Communists believe that men must solve these man-environment problems. This is what they mean by world revolution. They believe this can be done by application of Mao's methodology.

Mao and his followers want a higher quality of life on this planet. They want to bring about a restructuring of social relations to achieve a proper relationship between the individual, the family, the community, and the world; a new and rational balance of interests that will be complementary and not antagonistic. They do not suppose that such a process can or will be completed without well-planned and arduous effort and struggle against the opposition of deeply entrenched vested interests. This is what they mean by class struggle.

The Communist Party 🌿

How do Party and government directives originate and come to Upper Felicity for discussion and implementation?

The top organ of the Party is the Party Congress, representing all its eighteen million members, which meets at intervals of several years. The last congress, the Ninth, met in April 1969. The Congress lays down the Party's general line and program and specific policies for current activities. To give leadership to the Party between sessions, it elects a Central Committee, which now has 170 members and 109 alternate members. This is too large a body to be in constant session. Many of its important members are heads of provincial Party committees and therefore permanently stationed away from Peking, and they come to the capital or elsewhere only when needed for meetings of the Central Committee called by its Chairman, Mao Tse-tung. Day-to-day Party activities are directed by the smaller Political Bureau of the Central Committee with its twenty-five members and alternates. These men and women are always readily available when needed for consultation by the prestigious Standing Committee of the Political Bureau. This had five members. As elected by the Ninth Congress, they were Mao Tse-tung, Chairman of the Party; Chou En-lai, who is also Prime Minister of the People's Government; Kang Sheng, once a Party Secretary; Lin Piao, then Defense Minister, and Chen Po-ta, who was head of the Cultural Revolution Group under the Central Committee of the Party. The last two were much in the public eye during the tumultuous days of the Cultural Revolution, but Chen Po-ta has since been dismissed from his post, and Lin Piao died in an air crash, a self-condemned traitor.

Beneath these top Party organs are the twenty-nine Party committees of the provinces, the Sinkiang Uighur, Tibet,

Inner Mongolia and other autonomous regions, and the
municipalities of Peking and Shanghai. Beneath these in turn
are the Party committees of the two thousand-odd counties
of the country, then Party committees of the districts and
communes, and the Party branches and groups of the communes' brigades and teams, and of factories, offices, schools,
colleges, and other institutions.

Important policy suggestions, suggestions about what the
Party should do and how, may be initiated by a member at
any part of the Party structure. Sometimes a proposal may
come from an individual or group outside the Party. But
wherever such a suggestion comes from it will eventually be
discussed by the top levels of the Party. Strictly local matters,
of course, are handled at the appropriate levels.

When a good idea comes up for discussion in the Party
it is normally handled by the method of the "mass line."
Chairman Mao has described this method as follows:

> In all the practical work of our Party, all correct leadership
> is necessarily "from the masses, to the masses." This means:
> take the ideas of the masses (scattered and unsystematic
> ideas) and concentrate them (through study turn them
> into concentrated and systematic ideas), then go to the
> masses and propagate and explain these ideas until the
> masses embrace them as their own, hold fast to them and
> translate them into action, and test the correctness of these
> ideas in such action. Then once again concentrate ideas
> from the masses and once again go to the masses so that
> the ideas are persevered in and carried through. And so
> on, over and over again in an endless spiral, with the ideas
> becoming more correct, more vital and richer each time.
> Such is the Marxist theory of knowledge.*

In another passage he explains this even more concisely:
"We should go to the masses and learn from them, synthesize
their experience into better, articulated principles and meth-

---

* From the article "Some Questions Concerning Methods of Leadership" (June 1943), *Selected Works*, Vol. III, p. 120.

ods, then do propaganda among the masses, and call on them to put these principles and methods into practice so as to solve their problems and help them achieve liberation and happiness."*

This mass line is a theme that Chairman Mao comes back to again and again. He pours scorn on people in leading positions in the Party "who think that it is enough for the leaders alone to know the Party's policies and that there is no need to let the masses know them." He adds that "this is one of the basic reasons why some of our work cannot get done well.

"To be good at translating the Party's policy into action of the masses, to be good at getting not only the leading cadres but also the broad masses to understand and master every movement and every struggle we launch—this is the art of Marxist-Leninist leadership. It is also the dividing line that determines whether or not we make mistakes in our work."†

When a good suggestion comes to the leading organs of the state and the Party, they discuss it and a draft resolution or instruction is formulated. This will then go down to the masses, who will discuss it and sometimes try it out in one unit, such as a farm or factory, or perhaps in a whole "experimental area," a commune, a county, or an even larger area. The results are brought back to the leaders. The amended process may then be repeated for a further practical check on the feasibility of the suggestion before final decisions are made. If found practicable, it is distributed for implementation to all the departments of government or Party concerned.

If an important project of national significance has to be carried out, the whole weight of Party and government will be thrown behind it to mobilize the ideas, will, and energy of the people and get it implemented. Formulated as a Party and government resolution or instruction, it will be publicized on a vast scale in the national press, in such organs as the *People's Daily*, the official Party daily, and the *Red Flag*, the

* "Get Organized!" (November 29, 1943), *Selected Works*, Vol. III, p. 158.

† A talk to the editorial staff of the *Shansi-Suiyuan Daily* (April 2, 1948), *Selected Works*, Vol. IV, pp. 242–43, FLP.

Party monthly. The rest of the national and local press will print the instructions and they will be posted on countless walls in town and countryside, broadcast over the radio and TV networks, and distributed in more permanent pamphlet form. They will be read out and studied and discussed in millions of small study groups in factories and offices, schools and universities, and on farms from the commune down to the brigades and teams.

The new draft Constitution of the People's Republic was discussed in this way. After the state committee entrusted with drawing it up wrote the draft, the Party Central Committee discussed it in plenary session and then state and Party sent it down to the masses, to the people. Finally it was discussed by the Third Brigade of Great Felicity Commune. Lao Man, Ta Sao, and the youngsters all sat in on the discussions. That means that the constitution was discussed and commented on by hundreds of millions of citizens. Of course not everyone can make a significant contribution to the discussion, but millions will do so, and the rest have been drawn into a significant act of mass participation that will develop more and more activists in the future and so deepen and widen the foundations of China's socialist democracy. Discussion of the constitution was an impressive measure of democracy and democratic action that paves the way for ever wider-based democracy and democratic action in the future.

Such nationwide discussions can develop into great mass movements. There have been many such movements since the establishment of the People's Republic in 1949. There was the movement to wipe out corruption, waste, and bureaucracy (the *San Fan* or "Three Anti" movement); the movement to wipe out flies, mosquitoes, and other pests; the movement for the socialist transformation of private capitalist enterprises in industry and commerce when these were turned into joint state and private enterprises; the movements to form rural mutual-aid teams and later to form cooperatives and collective farms and communes; and many more.

Each of these movements was a great mass-education campaign in which vast numbers of people of all ages got to thinking about and discussing state policies, and their own relation to those policies. One of the greatest of these movements in recent times has been the movement for socialist education that began in 1962 and developed into the Great Proletarian Cultural Revolution of 1966 and that continues in 1973.

The Chinese Communist Party is the largest party of its kind in the world. Its membership is open to all Chinese citizens, but every applicant is strictly scrutinized and is usually required to serve a period of probation. No one applies for membership unless he is already fairly certain that his life and activities in his place of work have won the approval of his fellow workers and members of his local Party branch. His application is then considered by the whole of the Party branch, and the non-Party rank-and-file are also asked to give their opinion. As a Party member he is expected to be a model citizen and completely dedicated to the policies and goal of the Party—to build communism in China. From the moment he joins he is expected to work hard to master the theory and practice of the Party, and be ready to carry out its instructions at all times like a soldier on active service. Monetary rewards, position, creature comforts, self, all must take second place to service to the people. This strict and voluntary discipline and cohesion among members, the ability of the Party to maintain its close links with the people and move as one man in the service of its revolutionary policy, is one of the great strengths of the Party.

Mao Tse-tung, however, stresses that Party members "must always go into the whys and wherefores of anything, use their own heads and carefully think over whether or not it corresponds to reality and is really well founded; on no account should they follow blindly and encourage slavishness."* He also says, "Communists must be ready at all times to stand up for the truth, because truth is in the interests of the people."†

* "Rectify the Party's Style of Work" (February 1, 1942), *Selected Works*, Vol. III, pp. 49–50, FLP.

† "On Coalition Government" (April 24, 1945), *Selected Works*, Vol. III, p. 315.

The People's State 🌿

*T*he composition of the Party and its leadership has, of course, changed since the Cultural Revolution to bring it into conformity with the new tasks of today. A handful of top revisionist leaders like Liu Shao-chi have been expelled from the Party leadership, along with some very inactive Party members among the rank-and-file, but these losses have probably amounted to less than 2 per cent of the membership. The leaders and rank-and-file members who were guilty of revisionist mistakes and following Liu Shao-chi's line and policies have been severely criticized but most, after temporary loss of their posts, have accepted this criticism in good part and made suitable self-criticisms, acknowledging their mistakes and undertaking to turn over a new leaf. With this they have been restored to full Party activity and in many cases received back their old posts, or been given other suitable jobs. In addition much new blood has been infused into the Party by the admission of the vigorous, bold, and dedicated young leaders of the masses who emerged during the struggles of the Cultural Revolution. In this way the leadership and ranks of the Party have been cleaned up and strengthened, but the Party structure has remained the same as before the Cultural Revolution.

Not so the state structure of the People's Republic. There has been a similar cleaning, renewal, and strengthening of the organs of state, and its very structure has changed besides.

Before the Cultural Revolution the state structure was also pyramidal. At the base were, in ascending order, commune or district, county, and province. The commune, the lowest level of local government authority, had its Delegate Conference and elected Management Committee. The districts, counties, and provinces had their People's Conferences and People's Governments. Each, electing delegates to the next higher level of administration, elected delegates finally to the National People's Congress, the highest organ of state power. The NPC then elected its standing committee and the President and Vice-Presidents of the NPC who were also the President and Vice-Presidents of the People's Republic. The President (who was Liu Shao-chi) appointed the Prime Minister (Chou En-lai) and confirmed his cabinet of ministers who headed all government departments and their subordinate organizations.

All this has now changed. The country's administration is still in a state of revolutionary transformation. Since the last NPC session in 1965, Liu Shao-chi, the President, has been deposed, and a number of his followers, ministers, and heads of government bureaus and departments and offices and other state organizations have lost their jobs. In 1972, neither Liu nor other dismissed members of the standing committee of the National People's Congress had been replaced. Furthermore, all the local governments from the provincial level on down were taken over by the revolutionary organizations of the people formed during the Cultural Revolution, and they have been replaced by revolutionary committees. There is as yet no constitutional amendment or new constitution legalizing these changes in government structure. They exist at the moment simply by virtue of revolutionary legality, the will of the people, people's power. Only when the new National People's Congress is called will the new state structure be constitutionally established.

Revolutionary committees are an invention of the people perfected by Chairman Mao during the Cultural Revolution. When an alliance of workers, peasants, students, and revolutionary intellectuals and employees' mass organizations supported by the local units of the People's Liberation Army took over power from the old and discredited Shanghai Municipal Party Committee and Municipal Government in January 1967, the victorious masses planned to set up a Shanghai Commune on the model of the Paris Commune of 1870. This proposal was taken to Peking by Chang Chun-chiao and Yao Wen-yuan, two Party members who played a leading role in the revolutionary events in Shanghai. In consultation with Chairman Mao himself, they amended the original proposal and jointly, in consultation with the Shanghai masses, produced the blueprint of the new revolutionary committee type of administration.

Today revolutionary committees run all local governments, from the lowest level, the commune, up to the provincial level. This level includes the two big municipalities of Peking and Shanghai, which are directly under the Central Government, and the big autonomous regions like the Sinkiang Uighur, Tibetan, and Inner Mongolian autonomous regions. Revolutionary committees also head the work of all the big and little state corporations concerned with commerce and transport, industry and handicrafts, and all cultural institutions. All schools, universities, colleges, and research institutions are run by revolutionary committees, all factories and handicraft workshops, theaters, film studios, ballet and concert troupes, libraries, parks, and zoos.

The revolutionary committee is a tripartite body. It comprises representatives of the rank-and-file chosen from among the revolutionary mass organizations which at the call of the Party seized power during the Cultural Revolution, representatives of the best of the old cadres in the old administrations or managements, and representatives of the defense forces. These latter representatives may be from the local units of the People's Liberation Army who came in to "help the left," that is, help carry on the Cultural Revolution in the organization in question, or they may be from the people's militia. In the rural areas, P.L.A. representatives only sit on revolutionary committees at county level or above. At the commune level and below, the defense forces are represented by members of the militia. Every farm team, brigade and commune, factory and institution has its people's militia. These are a volunteer defense force that in case of invasion will fight as local guerrilla units in combination with the regular P.L.A. units.

On the farms, the revolutionary committee is admirably suited to manage commune and brigade affairs. When forming a revolutionary committee, the party and rank-and-file are at pains to make it really representative. As in Upper Felicity, they see to it that it includes activists who have really earned the people's trust and understanding by their work and social activities. There must also be veteran cadres who have the know-how of farm management and techniques. There must also be representatives of the women and youth of the farm, and of its technical and intellectual forces. The Great Felicity Commune revolutionary committee, for instance, has representatives of the commune's teachers and the technical personnel employed in the tractor park and the tool repair works. Care is also taken to bridge the generation gap by including veterans, the middle-aged, and youth in proper proportions. The aim is to ensure that the revolutionary committee efficiently administers the human resources of the farm and its land and all other natural resources.

The presence of representatives of the defense forces of the P.L.A. or militia ensures that defense requirements are never lost sight of and that in the event of a war emergency the whole commune or other organization can be swiftly and smoothly mobilized for defense. The revolutionary committee is thus an extension of Chairman Mao's concept of people's war. It can ensure that "every citizen is a soldier," and that when and if the time comes, the defense forces, P.L.A. or militia, can move among the people "like fish in water."

The commune revolutionary committee also has sections to perform all the usual local government functions such as registration of births and deaths, the collection of the agricultural tax, organization of education, welfare, and medical and health services, and so on.

Thus, great care is taken to ensure that the revolutionary committee is representative and democratic and has revolutionary authority. In Great Felicity Commune, as in all others, to ensure that its members remain in close touch with the peasant masses, there is a regulation that they must go down and work with the rank-and-file in the fields and workshops for at least fifty days every year. Brigade and team cadres are, of course, working farmers most of the time.

The Revolution in the Countryside ❧

*T*he Cultural Revolution came as one of a series of mass movements initiated by the Communist Party as part of its overall program to transform China from a backward, semi-feudal, semicolonial country into a modern socialist state with a modern industry, agriculture, science, and culture. Each movement, including the Cultural Revolution, has been part of a complex, coordinated chain of change to carry out this overall design of continuing revolution according to Mao's methodology.

The overall design is essentially simple. China was a bankrupt country in the century before 1949. It was weak economically, politically, and militarily. The miseries that beset the poor peasants of Upper Felicity were the miseries of most of the nation. The feudal landlords and their spawn, the warlords and militarists, used every base means to preserve a system of ruinous exploitation of the people. The result could only be a series of mass revolts and uprisings and continued weakening of the country in face of the attacks of the great imperialist powers, Britain, the United States, France, and Japan, each wanting its "concessions" and "spheres of influence" in preparation for final dismemberment of the "Sick Man of Asia."

Depredations by these foreign powers, the levying of heavy indemnities on China as punishment for resisting their invasions, the forced signing of "Unequal Treaties," and fratricidal civil wars instigated by foreign intriguers further weakened and impoverished the country. Establishment of the Chiang Kai-shek regime in 1927 made matters worse. This regime was a coalition of the old feudal landlord and militaristic elements, like warlord Yen Hsi-shan, who ran Shansi Province as if it were his own estate, and the group of monopoly-capitalist bureaucrats represented by such men as T. V. Soong, his brother-in-law, H. H. Kung, and the fascist-minded Chen Li-fu and his brother, Chen Kuo-fu. These bureaucrat-capitalists controlled the Kuomintang ministries of industry and trade, communications, education, and propaganda and used their positions to increase their economic power and wealth. This militarist-capitalist coalition was aptly symbolized by the marriage of Chiang Kai-shek, himself a militarist and stockbroker, to May-ling, multimillionaire T. V. Soong's younger sister. Because of its inherent weakness as an antidemocratic dictatorship, this regime was forced to depend on foreign assistance, mainly American. Chiang's regime received over four billion dollars in U.S. "aid" to finance its attempt to suppress the exasperated masses of town and countryside, led by the Chinese Communist Party. It became nothing but a *compradore* (commercial agent) of foreign capital and was more and more hated by the people for its subservience to foreign interests. Chinese Communist theory and propaganda pinpointed the feudal landlord system and its main domestic backer, the bureaucrat-capitalist, militarist, and fascist Kuomintang regime of Chiang Kai-shek and its imperialist allies, as the main enemies of the Chinese people's peace and progress.

The first stage of the Revolution led by the Communist Party, the party of China's working class and industrial proletariat, was designed to overthrow the rule of these enemies of the people. It was essentially a democratic revolution of the people against their oppressors similar to many democratic and nationalist revolutions of the past, but it had new overtones. It was designed to establish the prerequisites for the further development of the Revolution to achieve socialism. Hence it has been called the new-democratic stage of the Revolution.

This stage of the Revolution was basically achieved on October 1, 1949, when the People's Republic of China was proclaimed in Peking. Soon Chiang Kai-shek's army of four million had been completely defeated and he himself, with the remnants of his troops and his horde of bureaucrats, secret police, and agents, was driven off the mainland together with his bureaucrat-capitalist supporters and other hangers-on. China, after a century of struggle, was at last a free, democratic, and independent People's China, governed by people's power. Only the island province of Taiwan remained under Chiang's Kuomintang rule.

This first stage of revolutionary change continued for some years after the setting up of the People's Republic. The state-capitalist enterprises run by the Kuomintang government and the great bureaucrat-capitalist enterprises controlled by the Four Big Families of Chiang, Soong, Kung, and Chen were nationalized. These included most of the big banks, steel mills, mines, transport companies, and tea, salt, and other monopolies. These, together with state farms built on reclaimed land, became the basis of the new socialist state-owned sector of the national economy run by the People's Government. In this way the People's state controlled the key sectors of the national economy.

The economy of the war-ruined country was quickly rehabilitated by a people elated by their liberation. Torn up by the people's guerrillas and ruined by the Kuomintang during the civil war, the railways began to run again. Inflation was ended, prices were stabilized, the livelihood of the people improved, and industry and commerce boomed. In 1952, the final blow was given feudalism when the land reform was completed throughout the nation. Feudal landholdings were confiscated from the landlords and shared out among the landless or land-poor peasants. Meanwhile, urban private capitalist enterprises were enjoying the benefits of boom conditions, and so were the handicrafts which play a big role in China's economy. Handicraftsmen make pottery, tools, household goods, furniture, umbrellas, fans, kitchen utensils, jade and ivory items, stone and ironware, silverware, and countless other products. The craftsmen were largely self-employed in small workshops or doing part-time work as farmers.

In 1948, under Chiang Kai-shek's rule, China's economy was dominated by feudal landowners and Kuomintang state, bureaucrat-capitalist, and foreign-capitalist enterprises. These were weak native or national capitalist enterprises, small, scattered handicraft enterprises, and rich-peasant, middle-peasant, and poor- and tenant-peasant farms. Mainly poor tenant farmers and landless agricultural workers comprised the vast majority of the peasant population. They lived like Lao Man did before liberation.

By the mid-fifties this state of affairs had changed. After land reform there were no landlords but hundreds of millions of peasant landholdings (the number of rich farmers and middle-income farmers remained the same); a number of state farms and cooperative farms and handicraft cooperatives; an increased number of national capitalist industrial and commercial enterprises and small handicraft producers; and a sizable state socialist sector made up of new state-built enterprises and the former Kuomintang, bureaucrat-capitalist, and foreign-owned enterprises nationalized by the People's Government.

But the overall program of the Communist Party and People's Government calls for a China with an economy based entirely on state-owned socialist (public) ownership of enterprises and collective (cooperative) ownership of enterprises, in industry, commerce, and agriculture. This meant that the next stage of the Revolution, beginning in the mid-1950s, should be a socialist stage of revolution that would end capitalism in China and transform it into a socialist state with a totally socialist economy.

The creation of a socialist society demands more than the transformation and elimination of feudal and capitalist property and economic relations. Feudal and capitalist ways of thinking must also be cast off and replaced by collectivist, socialist ways of thinking and ways of life. A socialist society demands a socialist culture and art and socialist education. Superstition must be replaced by scientific knowledge. The "free enterprise," dog-eat-dog mentality must be replaced by a collectivist, socialist mentality of mutual aid. The political revolution must engender a continuing economic and cultural revolution.

Economic growth can serve not only the interests of socialism but of capitalism or even fascism, depending on what politics is behind it. That is why, led by the party of the working class, the workers and peasants, the vast majority of the people, must organize themselves to take their destinies and that of the country into their own hands if they want socialism. They must learn to run things themselves and *for* themselves in a socialist way. In the fifties and after, various campaigns were organized by the Party and the People's Government to push forward this program of socialist policy and education all across the board, in industry, farming, politics, social relations, in the fields of ideology or outlook, in education and culture, in foreign relations—among the peasants and workers, the cadres, intellectuals and national capitalists and petty bourgeoisie, among the women, youth, and children.

The Communist Party's program goes further. It regards socialism as only a transitional stage to a communist society. Under the socialist system the principle governing distribution of wealth produced by society is "to each according to his work." Under communism the principle will be "from each according to his ability, to each according to his needs." This demands a high level of productivity and an abundance of goods sufficient to satisfy the needs of every member of society. It also demands a high level of social consciousness and public-spiritedness. Everyone will be motivated by such public-spiritedness, such selflessness, that he will give to society all he has in the way of energy and ability and take from the social pool only what he really needs. In such a world, the differences between town and countryside will end; villages will be cultural centers as well as farm-industrial centers; the towns will not be asphalt jungles but garden cities. Mental and physical labor will receive equal rewards. Democratically run organizations will organize and regulate society's productive efforts, and there will be no need of a state with coercive organs like police, courts, and jails. The universal establishment of communism will mean an end to armies and wars and international conflicts and the establishment of universal peace and international cooperation for the common good of the world because all the nations will be ruled democratically by the people, for the people. "Serve the people" will be the universal watchword. Selfishness will be overcome.

It is clear that the establishment of such a social order will require a much higher level of morality and social conscious-ness and a much higher level of productivity and efficiency than we have anywhere in the world today. It is Mao's view that these must be achieved in the process of building and consolidating the transitional socialist system. In this phase of the communist revolution men have to make the change from private to public or collective ownership, particularly in the rural areas of China, and from private to joint state and private ownership and then to public or collective owner-ship in urban industry and commerce. They must also change from low productivity handicraft to large-scale modern ma-chine production.

But Mao insists not only that it is necessary to bring about the socialist industrialization of the country—that is, press forward the socialist revolution on the economic front—but that the socialist revolution on the political and ideological (cultural) fronts has to be carried on no less energetically. Establishment of the new society needs socialist education for all strata of the population. As part of this socialist education, he warns that revolutionaries must remember that this social-ist transition stage will last a long time and that throughout this period class struggles will continue. The dispossessed classes (feudal landlords, capitalists) will constantly try to hold back the wheels of social progress, and turn them back if possible. This danger will be particularly great while China is surrounded by nations that are still capitalist and may be inclined to help capitalist-minded elements inside China. Out-of-date ideas, cultural values, habits, and customs created by the old exploitative societies will also act as brakes on social progress.

It is clear that such a long-term, planned advance needs

long-term, consistent leadership. Hence the insistence that once the long-range plan of the Party and its general line are laid down, there should be no deviation from them and there should be no factionalism (the setting up of rival headquarters with rival plans inside the Party). Every Party member is called upon to be active and enthusiastic throughout the course of the plan. But it is not expected that this ideal will be attained. Some who were active in carrying out the first part of the plan dropped out in the later stages. Men who were democratic and nationalist were well to the fore in the struggle waged for democracy and national independence against Chiang Kai-shek's Kuomintang dictatorship and its imperialist backers. They may have worked hard for post-liberation rehabilitation too, but found their enthusiasm flag when the country accomplished this stage of the Revolution (essentially the establishment of bourgeois democratic liberties) and embarked on the new stage of socialist transformation of society, a struggle to end private capitalist ownership and exploitation and to establish a planned socialist economy with public and collective ownership of all the means of production. The deposed President Liu Shao-chi and his supporters were such people. They wanted to hold back the socialist Revolution and, when they failed, tried to stop it halfway and divert the country onto a capitalist road of development. It was in the cultural field especially, in education, the theater, publishing, and the arts, that they were particularly active in preparing the ideological ground for such a reversal of the course of the Chinese Revolution. (Hence the need for the Cultural Revolution of 1966—to win the whole cultural field for socialism.)

Because of the danger posed by such antisocialist forces, Mao Tse-tung insists that under present-day world conditions, the new-democratic and socialist revolutions must be carried out under the leadership of the country's industrial working class and its political Party, the Chinese Communist Party. Only this class has the innate interest to carry through a revolution that will eventually be of universal benefit.

As a class, the feudal landowners are for obvious reasons opposed to these revolutions. The capitalists or bourgeoisie (middle classes) naturally wish to establish capitalism and not socialism. The social strata of the intellectuals, the technicians, and intelligentsia side with whichever class they serve. The exploited working class, the industrial proletariat, is impelled to socialist solutions of its problems by its whole way of life and the class struggles it is forced to wage in its own defense. It owns no property; it has no attachment to capitalism. Discipline and a sense of organization are inculcated into it as a class by its role in society, through the discipline of factory routine and in the struggle for its wages and rights carried on by its trade unions and political party. It develops a scientific outlook through constant participation in technical and scientific work. It learns humanity and mutual aid through its constant struggle for survival and vindication of its human rights.

The Chinese proletariat finds its natural ally in the other most exploited class in society—the peasantry. These two classes, workers and peasants, comprise 90 per cent of the nation. But the peasantry is not a homogeneous mass. There are the landless farm laborers and the poor peasants. They want revolution. The land reform frees them from the landlord's yoke and gives them land. They soon learn that socialist cooperation will lead them to prosperity. Beyond these are the middle peasants, who can more or less make ends meet, and the rich peasants, who can augment their farm incomes by renting out land, hiring and exploiting laborers, and engaging in usury. So not all the peasants are equally revolutionary. The staunchest allies of the proletariat, for obvious reasons, are the landless laborers, poor peasants, and the lower strata of the middle peasants. But these peasants lack the disciplined revolutionary qualities and revolutionary theory of the proletariat. They need socialist education and the organized leadership of the proletariat. Numerous peasant uprisings and revolts against the feudal order in China all failed for lack of proper leadership and merely resulted in the establishment of new feudal imperial dynasties. Only the struggle of 1946–49 led by the Communist Party of the working class ended in the victory of people's rule.

The middle peasants tend to waver in the revolutionary struggle. They will not lose from the Revolution, but they are not sure that they will gain. It is the same with the petty bourgeoisie in the cities, the small shopkeepers and self-employed craftsmen. But when they see the general trend of events moving in favor of the Revolution and socialism, these middle-of-the-roaders under proper leadership come in on the side of the Revolution.

The rich peasants just as obviously tend to prefer a free enterprise system that leads to capitalism. They see their interests best served by a so-called free-for-all economic system with free markets in which the law of supply and demand operates to set prices, and "free" laborers can be hired and exploited. Rich peasants thrive in the spontaneous trend to capitalism which a small peasant economy generates when left to itself.

The proper handling of the complex peasant question is clearly of key importance in creating a socialist economy and state. Bit by bit all the peasants have to be won over to a socialist way of thinking and doing things. As early as 1943, when the Communist Party and the liberated areas it led were battling for their lives against the invading Japanese armies, Mao stressed the need for the peasants to organize along cooperative lines. In his article "Get Organized!" he wrote:

> Among the peasant masses a system of individual economy has prevailed for thousands of years, with each family or household forming a productive unit. This scattered, in-dividual form of production is the economic foundation of feudal rule and keeps the peasants in perpetual poverty. The only way to change it is gradual collectivization, and the only way to bring collectivization, according to Lenin, is through cooperatives.*

* "Get Organized!" (1943), *Selected Works*, Vol. III, p. 156, FLP.

These thoughts were constantly in mind. A man of peasant stock himself, Mao deeply understands the importance of this problem. In March 1949, not long before the founding of the People's Republic, he pointed out that "scattered, individual agricultural and handicraft units, which make up 90 per cent of the total value of output of the national economy, can and must be led prudently, step by step and yet actively, to develop towards modernization and collectivization; the view that they may be left to take their own course is wrong."* If the peasants do not develop in a socialist direction, then they will go capitalist.

In guiding the peasants to socialism Mao stressed that in the political sphere the alliance between the workers and peasants is essential for the continued success of the Revolution. That alliance enabled the Chinese people to throw out the Chiang Kai-shek regime and its Great Power backers and establish the new-democratic People's Republic. It enabled them to rehabilitate the war-torn country and carry through the land reform that ended feudalism in China. But the transition from new democracy to socialism—that is, the establishment of a socialist state founded on public and collective ownership of the means of production and the elimination of capitalist ownership and capitalist tendencies in society—also depends on that alliance.

The alliance of the workers and peasants is the basis of the people's democratic dictatorship that rules China today. This is the form that the Marxist dictatorship of the proletariat takes in China. It takes this form because Chinese industry was and is relatively weak in relation to agriculture (peasants account for over 80 per cent of the population). Hence the working class can exercise its leadership of society only in alliance with all the other revolutionary elements among the people who oppose the comeback attempts of the landlords, rich peasants, and counterrevolutionaries of various kinds. In

* "Report to the Second Plenary Session of the Seventh Central Committee of the Communist Party of China" (March 1949), *Selected Works*, Vol. IV, p. 368.

this alliance the poor and lower-middle peasants are naturally the main revolutionary force in the countryside.

Since this state system is led by the workers and peasants, the most revolutionary strata of the population, it is possible to carry the bourgeois democratic revolution forward without pause into the socialist revolution that transforms ownership of all the means of production into public and collective and thus stimulates a rapid advance of the national economy.

Of its very nature this people's democratic dictatorship is democratic, in that it is designed to defend the people (the working class, peasantry, and urban petty bourgeoisie), the vast mass of the population, and uses democratic methods of debate and persuasion to settle differences (contradictions) among them. It is a dictatorship because it is prepared to use force to defend the people against their internal and external enemies. Naturally, methods of dictatorship must on no account be used to handle contradictions among the people. For this reason, in this later stage of the continuing Revolution, the working class and its Party has to do a massive job of re-education of the peasants. "The serious problem," Mao wrote in 1949, "is the re-education of the peasantry. . . . Without socialization of agriculture, there can be no complete, consolidated socialism."* In other words, socialism cannot be said to have triumphed in the countryside until the peasants have voluntarily chosen the socialist road and completed the establishment of socialist collective farms.

In line with this policy of collectivization and maintenance of the worker-peasant alliance, the Party, immediately after the land reform gave land to the peasants, began to help them organize first labor-exchange brigades, then mutual-aid teams, and then farm, loan, and supply and marketing co-ops.

In the farm co-ops, the peasants pooled their land as shares and received part of the pooled land's output as a dividend on their land share. This method of distribution of the co-op's

* "On the People's Democratic Dictatorship" (1949), *Selected Works,* Vol. IV, p. 419.

product had a drawback. A co-op member working harder than the rest would not get a fair share of the extra output his extra efforts produced. Another co-op member would get a larger share of output simply because he had owned and put in a larger share of land. This system gave insufficient incentive to labor. This was corrected when the co-op farms advanced in the mid-1950s to a higher stage: the collective farm.

In the collective farm, members set aside part of the annual output to pay the grain tax to the state, another part as operating expenses and reserve, and a third part as a welfare fund to care for widows and orphans, the sick and disabled, and mothers during childbirth. The rest—the work-point fund —was distributed to members as a return on the amount of labor they contributed to the farm. Each job was valued in work-points. The total number of work-points earned in a year by members was divided into the work-point fund. This determined the value of each work-point. This method of distribution takes care of the collective interests and the individual interests of members and provides adequate incentives too. The distribution method used by the brigades and teams of the communes today leaves the way open for members to express greater social consciousness and a lessened need for individual material incentives. They can determine by vote to increase that part of the output that goes to the public or collective sector, including cotton and general food allocations and welfare, and decrease that part that goes to the work-point fund.

Each move that the peasants made along this path of cooperation restricted and destroyed the economic and ideological roots of capitalism in the countryside. The next big move they made was the formation of communes, in 1958.

By 1957, nearly all the peasant households in the country were in cooperative or collective farms. By improving the organization of labor and land use, providing proper incentives to labor, and most of all by stimulating the socialist consciousness of the peasants, the Party had improved yields, output, and standards of living. But the peasants were discovering that the collective farms were not large enough and lacked the resources to solve various problems that had to be solved if the advance to prosperity was to be maintained.

A collective farm numbering a few hundred households could satisfactorily handle such problems as planning more efficient use of land and manpower, but sometimes problems of irrigation or drainage demanded resources and a scale of planning that encompassed a whole river valley system and needed the labor of tens or even hundreds of thousands, or millions, of people. Networks of collective farms began to be formed to solve these and other large problems such as re-structuring the land, building terraces on hillsides, reforesta-tion, reclamation, mechanization, and electrification. These networks finally evolved from temporary amalgamations into permanent organizations for large-scale cooperative effort. In 1958, one such network in Chayashan in Suiping County, Honan Province, formally amalgamated to form the first rural people's commune in China. By the end of that year prac-tically all of China's cooperative and collective farms had joined together to form some twenty-five thousand communes. It was in this way that Upper Felicity Collective Farm joined and became a production brigade of the Great Felicity Com-mune in Honan Province. Its system of distribution remained the same as when it was a collective farm. The gross income, however, was distributed in different proportions, and it steadly increased.

The communes developed as large-scale, socialist collective economic organizations of an entirely new type. They not only run diversified economic activities such as farming, forestry, animal husbandry, fisheries, and various side occu-pations, but also industrial, mining, and commercial under-takings. At the same time they are the basic organs of state power in the countryside, the basic level of local government.

None of these developments took place without opposition and conflict. Mao Tse-tung, as Chairman of the Party, sup-ported them at every stage. He has immense prestige and authority as chief architect of the defeat of the Kuomintang and the establishment of the People's Republic. Nevertheless, the policy of farm cooperation had to be carried out in the face of various kinds of opposition both within the Party and outside it. Despite rigorous screening of new members, the Party after all necessarily reflects the various social forces and pulls of conflicting class interest in the country. The Party must live in close contact with the social forces outside it, and these exert pressures on all Party members. When the Party called for land reform, it was opposed by the landlords and rich peasants who would lose by it. Those who could tried to exert pressure on Party members, some of whom, in consequence, failed to carry out Party instructions conscientiously. Some Party members even tried to help their landlord relatives evade the land-reform laws. Later, when the call came to organize co-op farms, the same elements tried to get peasants to opt out of the co-ops. Certain Party members, reflecting the opinions of feudal and capitalist elements in society, have a bad record of opposing or sabotaging Party decisions on rural cooperation. Ex-President Liu once Chairman Mao's designated successor, was one of those who consistently worked against agreed Party policy.

In 1950 when the Party was preparing for land reform and advocating a subsequent rapid advance to mutual aid and cooperation, Liu Shao-chi was saying: "The type of peasant household which owns three horses, a plow, and a cart should increase." Such a household in Chinese conditions necessarily meant a rich peasant household. Liu was thus advocating exactly the sort of development that would prevent the growth of cooperation and strengthen a rich-peasant economy. The confusion of his thinking was even greater when he declared, "When peasant households each owning three horses make up 70 per cent [of the total number of rural households] collective farms can be set up in the future." Any economist knows that it would be utterly impossible for 70 per cent of the peasants working on their own to become rich peasants. What Liu was really saying, therefore, was that China should take the road of developing a free-enterprise capitalist agriculture and postpone indefinitely the whole program of rural collectivization.

It was this type of thinking that Mao Tse-tung had in mind when he wrote in 1953:

> After the success of the democratic revolution some people stood still. Failing to realize the change in the character of the revolution, they continued with their "new democracy" instead of undertaking socialist transformation. Hence their rightist errors. As far as agriculture is concerned, the socialist road is the only road for our country. The development of the mutual-aid and cooperative movement and the constant growth of the productive forces in agriculture are the heart of the Party's tasks in the countryside.*

Liu's insistence that capitalism must precede socialism in China's villages was a complement to his theory that "mechanization must precede cooperation." Had this latter policy been followed, China would still be wallowing in insoluble economic difficulties. Cooperation in agriculture would have been waiting for mechanization; mechanization would have been waiting for industrialization; industrialization would have been waiting for a backward agriculture to produce more funds for industry and raw materials; and agriculture would have been waiting for machines and chemicals and power from industry. It would have been a vicious circle of waiting and frustration.

Liu Shao-chi's way would have led to the indefinite postponement of both socialist agricultural cooperation and the socialist industrialization of China. Fortunately Mao's ideas prevailed in this continued struggle between two policies, two ways of social development. The peasants in the mid-1950s poured into the cooperatives and went on enthusiastically to organize collective farms. In the struggles to overcome the

---

* From a speech in 1953 quoted in *The Struggle Between Two Roads* by the editorial department of *Renmin Ribao, Hongqi*, and *Jiefangjun Bao* (November 23, 1967), p. 10, FLP.

difficulties in their way, numbers of intelligent, capable, fair-
minded, and keen young leaders sprang from their ranks.
The peasants learned that the new ways of doing things
needed new leaders and that the advice of rich peasants was
more likely to be wrong than right. Without waiting for the
big machinery, tractors, and combines that Liu thought indis-
pensable for collectivization, they went ahead with what they
had and created miracles of engineering, building great dams,
reservoirs, canals, and dikes with their primitive tools, picks
and shovels, carrying poles and baskets, will power and in-
genuity. They increased yields and output and provided
products for export, capital and raw materials for industrialization.

This was in the latter part of 1955. In just over a year
from then the cooperative movement had swept ahead with
such momentum that practically all the peasants entered cooperatives.

Socialist transformation of the urban economy went ahead
at the same time. While state-owned enterprises forged ahead
in the general upsurge of the national economy based on a
booming agriculture, private capitalist enterprises in industry
and commerce were transformed into joint state and private
enterprises with the state injecting new capital into the joint
enterprises. The capitalist owners received 7½ per cent interest on their original investment. Those who were able
continued to manage the businesses or helped as technicians
appointed by the new joint managements. The individual
handicraftsmen were encouraged to go cooperative. They
either formed independent co-ops in the towns or villages or
merged into the cooperative farms as handicrafts teams. In
this way the private capitalist sector of the national economy
was swiftly reduced to negligible proportions and then eliminated. The socialist state and cooperative sectors based on
public and collective ownership dominated all national economic activities. The joint state and private enterprises will,
of course, be phased out gradually as the present capitalist
owners either go on pension like all senior citizens or, if they
wish to continue at work, live on salaries like other wage

earners. (All such enterprises were indeed being phased out in 1972–73. The capitalists received back their original invested capital. Most banked it in the People's Bank at 2½ per cent interest per annum.)

China's national economy thus went through the following transformations:

COMPOSITION OF CHINA'S NATIONAL ECONOMY

Types of Enterprises

Kuomintang Areas	People's Republic		
1948	1949	1953	1957
State Capitalist Enterprises	State Socialist Enterprises	State Socialist Enterprises	State Socialist Enterprises
Bureaucrat-capitalist Enterprises	Private Capitalist Enterprises	Cooperative Farms and Handicraft Co-ops	Farm and Handicraft Cooperatives
Foreign Capitalist-owned Enterprises	Feudal Land-holdings	Private Capitalist Enterprises	Joint State and Private Enterprises
Private Capitalist Enterprises	Individual Small-holdings	Individual Small-holdings	
Feudal Land-holdings	Self-employed Handicraft Enterprises	Self-employed Handicraft Enterprises	
Individual Small-holdings			
Self-employed Handicraft Enterprises			

Even at this stage Liu Shao-chi still tried to disrupt the advance of the socialist sector. Complaining that a number of cooperative farms had been rashly formed before conditions were ripe for them, he personally approved a decision to "contract the cooperative movement." Taking advantage of Chairman Mao's absence from Peking in May and June of

1955, he and Teng Hsiao-ping, then Secretary of the Party, disbanded two hundred thousand cooperatives. Fortunately, the leadership given by Mao Tse-tung and the Party and the good sense and enthusiasm of the peasants prevailed, and this setback to cooperation was soon overcome.*

The contest between the socialist cooperative movement and capitalist tendencies nevertheless continued. By 1958 the cooperative farmers had increased agricultural output by a third. They went on to establish collective farms, collective farm networks, and then communes. The communes, separately and in cooperation, undertook a series of new big public works projects for water and soil conservation involving the labor of tens of millions of peasants. Honan Province alone in that one year increased its irrigated acreage from 32 per cent of its cultivated area to 70 percent.

But the communes were hardly formed and the Great Leap in the economy had hardly started when the country was struck by an unparalleled series of natural disasters. The farm lands were ravaged by flood, drought, tidal waves, hurricanes, and insect pests. Output dropped disastrously. The state and communes had enough reserves to tide the nation through this crisis, but it was a close shave. Without the People's state and the communes, millions would have starved.

This series of disasters was grist to Liu Shao-chi's mill. Party activists held that the economic crisis was 40 per cent manmade (because of mistakes made in running the new communes and in other fields); Liu called it 60 per cent. When the crisis was overcome in 1962 he said, "The peasants have gained nothing from the collective economy in the last few years." This was justification for the new measures that he had designed to boost the farm economy. These, the *San Zi Yi Bao* (Three Selfs and One Guarantee), called for

* In my book *New Earth* (Southern Illinois University Press, Carbondale, 1972), I have described in detail how the cooperative movement developed in one county in Chekiang Province, East China, from the land reform to the collective farm, and also how this Liu Shao-chi "compression" occurred and was overcome by the peasants.

the extension of plots for private use in the farms, the expansion of free markets, the increase in the number of small enterprises having sole responsibility for their own profits and losses, and the fixing of output quotas on the basis of individual households. When there were criticisms that these measures would lead to capitalism, he retorted, "Don't be afraid of capitalism running amok."

The extension of free trading on the markets and encouragement of individual effort and initiative in cultivating private plots during the three difficult years had given quick results in increased output. But this marked a retreat from socialist principles. Like Lenin's New Economic Policy to save the Soviet Union from famine in the 1920s, such measures might be justified as a temporary emergency operation, but Liu wanted to extend them further and institutionalize them. His *San Zi Yi Bao* would have expanded the elements of a capitalist free-market economy, strengthened private, small farming activities, and sabotaged socialist planning. They would have enticed the peasants away from cooperative farming, away from the collective fields of the communes, and restored individual, go-it-alone farming. Liu and Teng Hsiao-ping, who backed him up, saw nothing wrong in this. Teng even said, "So long as it raises output, 'go it alone' is permissible. Whether cats are white or black, so long as they can catch mice, they are good cats." The "big character posters" put up by the people during the Cultural Revolution criticized this pronouncement by Teng as rank opportunism.

Liu and Teng never succeeded in enforcing a national reversal of the Party's policy on rural cooperation, but they did get their *San Zi Yi Bao* implemented in a number of places. The results were predictable—weakening of the socialist, collective sector of the rural economy and strengthening of capitalistic trends. It was this type of covert and overt opponent of the Marxist program of rural cooperation who was denounced as "revisionist" during the Cultural Revolution. It was revisionist in a double sense: revising or emasculating Leninist revolutionary principles and also revising the Chinese

Communist Party's program for building a socialist country-side.

Events were now moving to a climax in the struggle be-tween the ideas and social forces represented by the Liu Shao-chi faction and those led by the Party and Chairman Mao. It was becoming clearer that Liu, who had been desig-nated by the Party to carry out agreed Party policy, was in fact more and more committed to carrying out his own poli-cies, which would manifestly lead not to socialism but to capitalism or a hybrid form of state-capitalism. To check this development, Chairman Mao convened the Tenth Plenary Session of the Eighth Central Committee of the Communist Party in the autumn of 1962. At this session he reminded the Party and the people that the opponents of socialism—the unregenerate landlords, rich peasants, capitalist elements, and other reactionaries—were continuing to wage a class struggle against socialism and were using their representatives inside the Party to do their work for them. To counter this attack he called for the launching of a nationwide movement for socialist education.

The instructions and directives for conducting this move-ment were set out in what is known as the Ten-point Decision —the *Decision of the Central Committee of the Chinese Communist Party on Some Problems in Current Rural Work* of May 1963, and the 23-Article Document of 1965—*Some Current Problems Raised in the Socialist Education Move-ment in the Rural Areas*. These documents were drawn up under Mao's personal guidance. They stress that the key struggle at this time in China is the struggle between the forces of socialism and of capitalism. They say that this is a class struggle between the social forces that want to go for-ward to socialism and those that want to take a capitalist road. The socialist forces are described as those of the work-ing people, the poor and lower-middle peasants and workers, supported by the progressive intellectuals, by the left wing of the middle classes, the middle peasants and urban petty bour-geoisie, and led by the working class, the proletariat. The capitalist-inclined forces are those of the small capitalist class, supported by the remnants of the landlord class, rich peasants, and various kinds of Kuomintang riff-raff remaining on the mainland.

In the Ten-point Decision Mao said that to "resolve the contradiction between socialism and capitalism" it was imperative "to grasp the class struggle as the key, grasp the struggle between the road of socialism and the road of capitalism." Previously he had warned that "if socialism does not occupy the rural front, capitalism assuredly will."*

Analyzing the current situation in China and the alignment of class forces in the countryside, he now stressed how necessary it was to rebuff the attacks of the feudal and capitalist forces against socialism, against the communes. To do this it was imperative to "rely on the working class, the poor and lower-middle peasants, the revolutionary cadres and intellectuals and other revolutionaries, and pay attention to uniting more than 95 per cent of the masses and more than 95 per cent of the cadres," in order to wage a sharp, tit-for-tat struggle against the desperate attack of the capitalist and feudal forces operating through the small number of leading Party members they had succeeded in influencing.

These documents are a remarkable expression of Mao's trust in the masses and confidence in the efficacy of mass action when led by the Party.

According to Mao the "main target" of the movement was "those within the Party who are in authority and taking the capitalist road." Some of these, he pointed out, were acting on the stage while others were operating from behind the scenes. Supporting them all were "certain people at the higher levels—at the commune, district, county, prefecture and even at the provincial level and in the central departments [of Party and government] who are opposed to building socialism."†

* Quoted in *Decisions on Agricultural Cooperation,* Sixth Plenary Session of the Seventh Central Committee of the Communist Party of China, October 11, 1955.
† The 23-Article Document.

At a time when most people saw only certain conflicts between personalities, and with bureaucrats and petty tyrants in public posts, Mao divined the shape of the conflict that would burst out clearly for all to see in the Cultural Revolution which exploded in mid-1966.

It is now plain that the socialist-education movement was carried out in an ambiguous way from the start. Had it been carried out in classic Party style it would have been conducted first in certain experimental areas; the experience gained there would have been summed up at Party headquarters; and then on this basis it would have been launched throughout the country. There would have been editorials and articles explaining it and the Party policy. At meetings and rallies the masses would have been roused to counterattack the main target: "those within the Party who are in authority and taking the capitalist road" and their henchmen. The whole Party would have gone into action with one mind.

This was not what happened. Part of the Party followed Chairman Mao's ideas and teachings and did attack the capitalist forces in the countryside. They exposed those who were fostering private capitalist tendencies at the expense of socialist collectivist tendencies. They checked the increase in the area of private plots and excessive growth of sideline production at the expense of grain and food production, that is, basic farming; they restrained the expansion of the free market. Work teams composed of urban cadres were sent out in large numbers to help the peasants carry out the socialist-education movement. The good ones joined with the peasants to reconstitute the Associations of Poor and Lower-Middle Peasants that had carried through the land reform as the reliable allies of the working class and the Party in the villages. They worked to prevent the growth of corrupt practices among rural cadres by making sure that they were ideologically and politically reliable, honest, and efficient, and criticized those who were not. The socialist-education movement was a success, wherever such work teams operated.

Cadres who followed Liu Shao-chi's and Teng Hsiao-ping's ideas did not dare oppose the Ten-point Decision directly, but they used the most ingenious methods to get around it and either abort the whole movement or switch its direction. They did not want it to succeed because they themselves would have been its targets—"persons in authority taking the capitalist road."

Liu Shao-chi had for years been busily surrounding himself with cadres who shared his ideas and were loyal to him. He was placing his men into key positions in preparation for the inevitable struggle between his faction and line and that of the Party as led by Chairman Mao. Full implementation of the Ten-point Decision would have smashed his strongholds in the countryside, so he got Teng Hsiao-ping to concoct a Second Ten-point Decision (Draft) just four months after the first and put this out in direct opposition to the first authentic Ten Points. The concrete instructions given in these new "ten points" have not been published in full, but they have been denounced for shifting the fire of the movement from those at the top directly responsible for taking the capitalist road in the rural areas and, on the pretext of conducting "socialist education," directing it against the poor and lower-middle peasant grass-roots leaders.

Liu himself produced a revised draft of Teng's new "Ten Points." He used as the basis of this the experience gained by his own wife, Wang Kuang-mei, leading a work team in an experimental area, the Taoyuan Production Brigade, near Beidaiho in North China. Working incognito in a closely guarded house and taking counsel from a shady, disgruntled character in the village, she insisted that the spearhead of criticism be directed against a loyal Party secretary well trusted by the local peasants and opposed to Liu Shao-chi's ideas. Far from strengthening socialist leadership in the brigade, her activities confused the issues and threw the whole place into political confusion. This enabled the antisocialist elements in the brigade to come to power with her assistance. Dressing up her activities in high-sounding phrases, Liu had this material printed and circulated in Party circles all over the country as the "Taoyuan Experience."

According to the second version of the new "Ten Points,"

the cardinal issue of the socialist-education movement was not
to expose the small minority of Party officeholders taking the
capitalist road but to solve the "contradiction between being
clean or unclean on the four questions" (of politics, ideology,
organization, and economy). Under these heads few grass-
roots leaders could escape some criticism, and as was Liu's
intention, the movement would exhaust itself in a witch hunt
"hitting at the many in order to protect the few" at the top—
himself included.

On the surface this program of Liu's seemed to be very
"left," in rousing the rank-and-file peasants to criticize the
grass-roots leadership in excessively brutal terms. In actual
fact it was, in Chinese Communist Party terminology, "right-
ist" because it diverted criticism from the real culprits, the
capitalist roaders at the top, the real opponents of the socialist
cooperative movement, the small number of Party members
in positions of high authority who were leading the peasants
away from socialism and toward a capitalist road of development. For a time, in a number of places, the Liu Shao-chi
Ten Points program resulted in aborting and discrediting the
socialist-education movement. This phase of the movement
was reflected in Upper Felicity. Instigated by a work team
from the county town, the peasants there carried criticism of
the Party secretary to excess and in effect drove him out of
the brigade.

Similar efforts by Liu Shao-chi and his henchmen to divert
and abort the socialist-education movement in the urban areas
as well led to the outburst of the Cultural Revolution. As
Chairman Mao said in February 1967: "In the past we waged
struggles in rural areas, in factories, in the cultural field, and
we carried out the socialist-education movement. But all this
failed to solve the problem because we did not find a form,
a method, to arouse the broad masses to expose our dark
aspect openly, in an all-round way and from below. Now the
form was found—the Cultural Revolution."*

Chairman Mao put out the slogan: "It is right to rebel

---

* Quoted in the Political Report to the Ninth Party Congress, 1969.

against reactionaries!" Under his leadership the Party called on all members to boldly rouse the masses so that they could liberate themselves from those who were leading them astray. Mao called on the "proletarian revolutionaries," those truly dedicated to the socialist revolution, to "unite and seize power from the handful of Party persons in power taking the capitalist road!"

It was not only a question of Liu and Teng and a handful of other persons. These men represented a trend of thinking that was quite widespread in China at that time and that they had fostered and turned into a revisionist Party faction and a policy in every field of work: economics, politics, culture, art, education, public health. It was possible to dismiss these persons from their posts by administrative means, but it was not possible to dismiss this trend of thought from people's minds by administrative means. That could only be done by the people themselves, each man being roused to judge what ideas were correct and what were not, what ideas served the people and what ideas did not, and himself discarding wrong ideas, revisionist and capitalist ideas, selfish ideas, so that the correct ideas of public service should prevail. That is why the Cultural Revolution had to be a gigantic process of mass action, based on debate and reasoning.

This was one of the most extraordinary revolutions in history. It was a revolution led by the Communist Party against itself to clean up, or as they phrase it, "rectify," its members' thinking. It was a revolution largely waged by debate in speech and writing in which the weapons were posters in large characters (ideographs) posted up on countless walls; broadcasts and newspapers; in which the contending sides mobilized and rallied their supporters by meetings, demonstrations, marches and countermarches. In a period of three and a half months Chairman Mao and his supporters reviewed thirteen million Red Guards, students, and other youth on the Tien An Men Square in Peking.

It was not unexpected that in some places social turmoil erupted into violence; debates ended in fights and even in armed conflict. In the famous Sixteen Points—the *Decision of*

the Central Committee of the Chinese Communist Party Con-
cerning the Great Proletarian Revolution of August 8, 1966—
such violence was expressly prohibited. "When there is a
debate, it should be conducted by reasoning, not by coercion
or force." But Kuomintang agents and all sorts of antisocial
riff-raff naturally tried to take advantage of the situation to
stir up trouble and fish in troubled waters. "Persons in
authority," jealous of their privileges, resorted to violence to
protect them. Once these "ghosts and monsters," as the Chinese people call them, surfaced, they had to be exposed and
rendered harmless by being pulled down from their posts of
authority or, if they were criminals, put under restraint.
Chairman Mao himself says: "A revolution is not a dinner
party."

In the countryside such turmoil and violence were the exception. Many worrisome problems had already been solved
during the first, socialist-education phase of the Cultural Revolution. On December 10, 1966, the Central Committee of the
Party had also published its directive specifying that during
the Cultural Revolution the farmers, while criticizing revisionist policies and bourgeois ideas, should at all times stress
production. As a result, farm production continued to climb
throughout these years of revolution.

In a series of such unexampled struggles from 1966 onward,
the revolutionary masses led by the Party headquarters of
Chairman Mao exposed and drove out of power the capitalist-
oriented followers and colleagues of Liu Shao-chi. These
included men like Teng Hsiao-ping, the Party Secretary;
Peng Chen, the Mayor of Peking; Wu Han, the Vice-Mayor;
Lu Ting-yi, the Minister of Education; Chou Yang, the man
who had actually controlled the Ministry of Culture, and
who, as the big character posters said, had let loose a horde of
ghosts and monsters on the stage and screen in the other arts
and literature.

In January 1967, the workers of Shanghai, supported by
the peasants, revolutionary cadres, intellectuals, students, and
urban people and by the People's Liberation Army, threw
out the capitalist-roaders who held power in the Municipal

Party Committee and the Municipal People's Council and took power in the city. This example was followed all over the country by the revolutionary mass organizations supporting Chairman Mao. By mass action of the people on the spot, the capitalist-roaders were ousted from their posts in factories, farms, commercial and transport organizations, schools, universities, theaters and film studios, and scientific institutions and from provincial, district, and county governments and communes. In place of the former administrations and managements they set up their tripartite revolutionary committees pledged to implementation of the Party's and Chairman Mao's revolutionary policies.

By carrying out the Cultural Revolution, the Chinese Communist Party pioneered a method by which a socialist state under the dictatorship of the proletariat can prevent itself from being subverted by any new privileged group or vested interest, and continue the revolutionary advance to a classless communist society.

The victory of the Cultural Revolution had several important results. That part of state power which had been seized by the revisionists, particularly in the fields of culture and propaganda, education, and the arts, was restored to the hands of the revolutionary forces led by Mao. This ensured that the new generation would not betray the revolutionary ideals of their fathers. The Cultural Revolution was a gigantic education in revolution for that younger generation and for tens of millions of adults too. It educated, tested, and purified the Party. The widespread dissemination of the scientific ideas and teachings of Chairman Mao and practical knowledge of Mao's revolutionary methodology, and the wholesale jettisoning of outworn ideas, attitudes, and habits, were the most significant achievements of that revolution. The Revolution unleashed new forces of leadership, enthusiasm, and initiative among the masses, both urban and rural. They brought about a great upsurge in production. They have carried China's economy forward at a bound.

By restructuring the land and solving the problems of drought and flood in the communes, by creating areas of stable, high yields, China in 1970 harvested its ninth successive bumper crop of 240,000,000 tons of grain. It went on to harvest its tenth bumper crop in 1971. Industrially it stood firm on its own feet. With textile output at eight and a half billion meters, it was not only able to feed and house but clothe its 750 million people adequately. It was building giant power generators and 25,000-ton ships. Every province could produce motor vehicles including tractors, and this in a country that twenty years ago could hardly make a bicycle. It was sending artificial satellites around the earth. It was producing 18,000,000 tons of steel. With oil production at 20,000,000 tons it was self-sufficient in this fuel and developing nuclear reactors. It was producing 14,000,000 tons of chemical fertilizer for its farms (half of this in small local plants). It calculated its total value of agricultural production at thirty billion dollars and industrial production at ninety billion dollars.

On this material basis of sufficiency—an astonishing achievement for a country that was chronically starving only two decades ago—there were other achievements that might well be the envy of developed countries. It had eliminated unemployment and beggary, prostitution and venereal disease, drug addiction and alcoholism. The health service had eliminated smallpox, cholera, and typhoid. The country was free from internal indebtedness and its foreign-trade balance showed a surplus. Currency and prices had long been stable. It was an extraordinary fact that, though by no means affluent itself, China was yet able to provide assistance to other countries amounting to $709 million. One hundred million dollars of this went to Pakistan, and most of the rest went to Tanzania and Zambia to build the 1,100-mile Tan-Zam Railroad.

All of us who participated in the Cultural Revolution, both the *hsia fang* cadres and the peasants of Upper Felicity, lived through the events I have described above. We in the cities had been more concerned with the debates, discussions, and struggles in politics, culture, and in striving to ensure that the leadership wherever we worked was in the correct revolutionary hands. The peasants had been naturally more concerned with the struggle between the revisionist line of Liu Shao-chi and the revolutionary, socialist line of Chairman Mao in relation to the farms. While we were living through the events themselves we were sometimes so deeply involved that we couldn't see the forest for the trees, but in the later stages of the Revolution in 1970 we had spent many hours, we in our study groups and they in theirs, going over and analyzing what had happened and what remained to be done to carry the struggle to completion. What I have written in the preceding pages is what I have come to understand of the struggle. All this was part of the education given us by the Cultural Revolution in how to apply Mao's methodology to the current situation in China and ensure successful continuation of the Revolution.

When I thought over all these achievements of China, I saw in them the modest dedicated work of millions of ordinary citizens like our Lao Man and Ta Sao. Mao Tse-tung hails the people in many of his famous quotations: "The people and the people alone are the motive forces in the making of world history."* "The masses are the real heroes."† In discussing agricultural cooperation, he says, "The high tide of social transformation in the countryside, the high tide of cooperation . . . is of extremely great, or worldwide significance."‡

The Cultural Revolution in Felicity 🏵

*T*he Cultural Revolution reached Felicity Commune in the autumn of 1966. News of the exciting events in Peking, Shanghai, and other cities was coming in thick and fast, and

---

* "On Coalition Government" (April 24, 1945), *Selected Works*, Vol. III, p. 257.

† "Preface and Postscript to *Rural Surveys*" (March and April 1941), *Selected Works*, Vol. III, p. 12.

‡ "On the Question of Agricultural Cooperation" (July 31, 1955), p. 1, FLP.

finally there came Chairman Mao's call to "bombard the headquarters" of the revisionists. As in other communes, the peasant rank-and-file, the local intellectuals, and cadres spoke out at meetings and wrote a barrage of posters against various manifestations of Liu Shao-chi policies that had been followed by the old commune leadership. What came in for particular criticism were the so-called "Four Freedoms"—the freedom to buy and sell land, engage in private enterprise, hire labor and lend out money at interest, which Liu had advocated in the early fifties, and the San Zi Yi Bao. Public opinion indignantly rejected those who appealed to people's selfish instincts by "putting work-points in command" and relying on material incentives as the main means of increasing production.

They also criticized the style of work of cadres who divorced themselves from the rank-and-file and became bureaucratic, dogmatic, or dictatorial and insensitive to public feeling.

Quite a number of youngsters went off to Peking and took part in the big reviews of Red Guards held by Chairman Mao on Tien An Men Square. They came back determined to "rebel against the reactionaries." The chairman of the commune happened to be away at the time, working in another area, so Hsu, then vice-chairman (and present vice-chairman of the commune revolutionary committee), had to bear the brunt of the criticism. He was the target of broadsides in the "big character posters" pasted up on the walls of Great Felicity, and he was also called to account at a big meeting of commune members in the assembly hall. This was the first stage of the Cultural Revolution.

In the second stage, toward the end of 1967, it was generally accepted that the leading cadres had understood the points criticized and had been "touched to the soul." The new revolutionary committee of the commune was established. Activists in the movement were elected to the committee, along with the best of the old cadres and representatives of the people's militia. Following that, in January 1968, all the commune's forty production brigades formed revolutionary committees, and the new leading groups of the production teams were set up. Then came the stage of struggle, criticism, and transformation, continued struggle against revisionism of all kinds, criticism of all reactionary ideas, and transformation of everything that negates socialism.

As part of this stage, all leading cadres of the commune went down to work at the grass-roots level and regularly thereafter took part in manual labor with the rank-and-file commune members for at least fifty days each year. At the same time, as part of the work of transformation, bad or irrational rules and regulations were discarded.

The commune then took up the task of "purifying the class ranks," a general process of criticism and self-criticism, discussion and analysis of events in the Cultural Revolution. With that preparation, the task of "rectifying the Party" started. Every Party member was considered by his peers and the rank-and-file of the commune members and they judged whether he or she was worthy to remain a Party member. At the same time, the Party recruited as members those who had proved themselves staunch revolutionaries during the Cultural Revolution. When I returned to Felicity in 1972, all forty brigades had completed this work of checking over the Party membership. The Party branches had been reestablished.

"What was the role of the Party members during the Cultural Revolution?" I asked.

Hsu put it this way: In the socialist-education movement, the campaign for the Four Cleans put the emphasis on solving problems at the grass roots and the medium levels of the state and management apparatus. The upper levels of the Party sent work teams down to the lower levels to help carry out the movement. Due to Liu Shao-chi's bogus "Ten Points" directive, some mistakes were made but these were corrected later, either when the new 23 Points drafted by Chairman Mao came out in 1965 or by the Cultural Revolution in 1966.

The Cultural Revolution was also led by the Party but in a different way. The main emphasis was on solving problems at the upper levels. These dealt mainly with the problem of revisionism in the top leadership, that is, Liu Shao-chi's "bourgeois revisionist headquarters." In this case therefore it was not possible for the higher levels to send work teams down to the lower levels to guide and direct the movement. Those higher levels of the administrative and management and Party structure were themselves to be criticized by the rank-and-file. Under these conditions the normal leadership manned by Party and non-Party members on down through the regional, provincial, and county and district or commune levels had to be prepared to stand aside if necessary and consider all criticisms in a humble spirit. Rank-and-file Party members and government and management cadres took part in the great debates and joined the revolutionary mass organizations formed in the Cultural Revolution either as rank-and-file members or leaders. Both Party and government structures were fractured and unable to function normally. Orders, instructions, and reports could not circulate up and down in the normal way. Under these circumstances the policies of the Party led by Chairman Mao came direct to the masses, the rank-and-file, in the form of instructions or directives published in the press, broadcast by radio and television, or simply distributed or handed down in the form of written communications. This was the time of the "great democracy." The revolutionary people exercised power and carried out the instructions of the "proletarian headquarters" led by Mao.

The Cultural Revolution was mainly concerned with the big questions of the orientation of the country in general. It only touched on economic questions in the communes insofar as these concerned that general orientation toward socialism or capitalism. This problem of orientation could only be solved by exposing the fallacies advanced by Liu Shao-chi under the guise of "socialism," and this could only be done by the great public debate conducted by the masses of the rank-and-file. Not only was it necessary to overthrow Liu Shao-chi and his relatively small clique of henchmen at the top. It was necessary to criticize and remold a host of lesser figures. Some were unwilling or unwitting accomplices of Liu or his dupes, and they not only had to be shown the error of their ways but helped to make good. Furthermore, everyone was expected to "make himself a target of revolution" and examine whether his own thinking and activities had been influenced by ideas of selfishness and revisionism.

Since the village people know each other pretty well, the course of the Cultural Revolution was much smoother and less complicated than it was in city institutions such as the translation bureau. But the Cultural Revolution was, in fact, a vast movement of socialist political and ethical education and action. Its lessons were not learned so easily. For instance, socialist ideology, proletarian politics, and service to the people and the Revolution should have been the fulcrums of debate, but in Felicity it too often happened that family ties were more powerful arguments when it came to criticism of individual cadres. This was why it had been necessary to make such a sharp criticism of clan feeling and firmly prohibit youngsters from kowtowing to their elders during the 1970 Spring Festival celebrations.

The struggle here also had its regrettable moments of violence. Here, too, hostile elements besides Liu Shao-chi's followers tried to disrupt the movement. Some of the younger people were led astray by ultra-leftist elements. At the expense of political issues, they tried to force debate on economic questions involving the very structure of the communes. This would have diverted the movement from its main aims. They tried, for instance, to force a change in the relations of the teams within the brigades. They wanted by administrative action to compel the teams to pool their incomes and share everything equally. This would have stirred up friction among the teams because many commune members are not yet ready for such extreme egalitarianism. It was these same hotheads and extremists who in some cases, carried away by an excess of zeal, tried to settle their differences with their opponents with fisticuffs and not reason. This played into the hands of those reactionary elements who sought to make use of the situation to stir up trouble and discord in the commune. In Hsi Yen Brigade two ex-landlords, Ko Wen-tso and Hai Lien-ying, together with eight other men whom they had managed to influence, stirred up a riot during which a crowd attacked a number of cadres with hoes and cudgels and beat them unconscious. When this incident was investigated, the landlord instigators were exposed. They were subsequently tried by the People's Court and sentenced to five years in jail. I was present at one of the big meetings near the commune center where the eight lesser fry were publicly criticized and called upon to criticize themselves as the first step to their remolding and reformation.

This was a lesson for the whole commune, and no further incidents of this kind occurred. When the commune and brigade revolutionary committees were formed and the Party committees reestablished, the work of transformation went full steam ahead. (In the postscript to this diary I describe their achievements in the following months.)

Farewell to Upper Felicity 🌿

*W*e could have stayed. Ta Sao had everything worked out. Ching Chun would be getting married in a year or two, but that would not cause any big change in household arrangements. We would split our big cottage in two by bricking up the inside doorway. We could retain the large room with the stove, and Ching Chun and his bride would live for the time being in the small room. They naturally wouldn't do their own cooking—the bride would become part of the big family and eat with them all together—so that was no problem.

We were standing by the compost pit with Ta Sao and Lao Man. He had just come in from work and still held his spade. He thought for a moment and deftly flicked a pig dropping into the pit. "We'll build another couple of rooms or three if need be. The team will help!"

"Lao Chen," he said meditatively. "We have lived very well together in the past year. Like one household. We haven't done enough for you, but you have done a lot for us. [Here Lao Man was letting his imagination run away with him.] You sweep the courtyard. You help me dig out the manure. No one in the hamlet has ever had a word to say in criticism of you. [Here Lao Man might have added, "They are all too polite to do that."] So you mustn't forget: This is your home if you want to stay here or whenever you want to come back to it!"

But time was getting on. Winter was coming in. November 8 would be *Li Tung*, Winter Begins. The leaves began to fall, red, brown, and yellow, and scamper away in the cold wind. Every day I or someone else was busy with the bamboo broom, sweeping the leaves into the compost pit. Truly I had learned that nothing should be wasted, not even a leaf.

The day we left Upper Felicity was quite an occasion. We knew only a couple of days beforehand when we could get the truck to take our things back to the city. That day and the next we were completely immersed in packing, only breaking off in the evening to make the rounds of our friends and say good-by. The next morning, the day of our departure, we were up at four. The bed had to be taken down and packed, our quilts and pillows folded and packed in plastic sheets. After we had eaten, the stove had to be dismantled and wrapped around with straw rope, while the last bowls and saucepans had to be stowed in the big wooden box we had readied for this last-minute packing. We nailed it down.

A stream of friends came in to help: Ta Sao and Ching Chun, members of our OSD Team, and young chaps from the nearby May Seventh Cadre School, which had supplied the truck. With all these willing hands we cleared the cottage and put everything on the truck in less than half an hour. When I had seen that everything was loaded and properly tied down I could finally raise my head. I found that practically the whole brigade had gathered to say good-by. Ta Sao and Yuan-tsung embraced each other like the sisters they had become. Their eyes were wet. The children, as children will, scampered around excitedly and climbed on the truck to "take a look." Ta Hsiang was too shy, even after all the months we had lived together, to stand and have her hand shaken. She hid herself blushing behind her mother.

"We must be off!" called the driver.

We clambered up among the beds and chairs, boxes and easels, suitcases and quilts. Everybody shouted good-by and waved. The motor roared and we were off with a jerk and a bump. We waved and shouted, "Good-by! Good-by!"

"Come again!" cried the massed voices of our friends in Upper Felicity.

"We will! We will!"

We waved and waved until we turned the corner at the end of the hamlet lane. We shouted our last good-bys as we lurched up the narrow lane and met some neighbors coming belatedly home for the morning meal.

It is nice to know that in Upper Felicity we always have a home and a warm welcome awaiting us.

As we left Upper Felicity behind I mulled over two related questions: Had I been remolded and learned from the poor and lower-middle peasants? And how were they doing?

Whether I was remolded, whether I had become a better man, I would not venture to say. I had learned enough modesty from the peasants of Upper Felicity to leave that to the future to decide. But it was certain that I had learned much from them. In thinking of China I would always think of men and women like Lao Man and Ta Sao, the millions who toil and produce the food the nation eats and the clothes it wears, who have stood up to the rages of the elements and enemy invaders and have emerged triumphant through five thousand years of turbulent history. Who have the patience and stamina now to undertake to break new ground in the history of man, and who will surely succeed.

Every normal, honest cadre who has been *hsia fang*—gone down to the countryside from the city to live and work with the peasants—must feel an obligation to them and mentally pledge as I did: "Lao Man and Ta Sao, I won't let you down."

Postscript

Felicity Revisited 🎏

I left Upper Felicity in the autumn of 1970 and returned to Peking. As I began to prepare my diary for publication, I realized that I should gather my thoughts about the Cultural Revolution. I found it difficult to analyze some aspects of it (this was before the revelations about Chen Po-ta and the treachery of Lin Piao), so my friends suggested that I visit places other than those I already knew and other areas besides Peking in order to get a clearer picture of it all.

For several weeks I visited factories, schools, universities, and other institutions in Peking, Shanghai, Soochow, and Canton. Later I left on a lecture tour to eighteen universities in the United States and Canada. After a brief stay in Hong Kong I went to California—to Stanford and Berkeley and to Santa Cruz, a beautiful place of châlet-like college houses perched on the mountains of the Bay area above the plain and the ocean. I flew down to Texas—to Austin, Houston, and Arlington; I went to the heart of the Midwest, to Southern Illinois University in Carbondale. I addressed the Rotary Club there and told them what I had learned about China's Revolution. I spoke at Columbia, Princeton, Yale, and Cornell, at Michigan, Chicago, and, up in Canada, at York and Toronto universities. When President Nixon was visiting China in February 1972 I spent busy days at the University of California in Los Angeles and again in the Bay area. I ended the tour in lovely, sun-drenched Hawaii, where I completed my manuscript about Upper Felicity. I had traveled 30,000 miles, and wherever I went there was the keenest interest in my story of Lao Man and Upper Felicity. After an elegantly served dinner in Harvard's august Faculty Club, what the professors wanted to know about was how the Lao Mans of China live. They were right. If you know how Lao Man fares, you know how China and one-fifth of the world fare.

Finally, in August 1972, I was back in Upper Felicity. In the green of high summer the land was at its best. The saplings in the courtyard of the commune center stretched tall to the roofs. There were cool pools of shadow under their foliage. Here Party Secretary Kuo did the honors. This time he told me many things about the commune that I had not known before. Like all good leading cadres in all communes, he was full of figures either in his head or notebook and ready to pass them on.

Great Felicity Commune had 40 brigades, 116 production teams, 5,242 households, 27,800 people, and 72,000 mu of land.

"Look at this," he said, showing me his production chart. "In 1965 we still only averaged 90 jin. Next year we brought in electric power lines and dug deep wells, and we raised 160 jin a mu for a total of 12,400,000 jin. This year we'll raise 29,000,000 jin."

Kuo showed me the main granary. We waited a bit to get the keys. It was double locked, and two men held the keys. While we waited, crowds of Great Felicity folk came to clap and welcome their "foreign guest." Inside, the granaries were filled to the rafters with wheat and corn stored against natural calamities and war. The commune was well ahead in the battle against need. The state grain tax (unchanged in amount from year to year) was now only 3 per cent of output. The

villagers had put aside millions of jin of grain. In 1971, besides selling the state 3.5 million jin of grain, they had stored
5 million jin and added another 3.5 million jin to this from
the 1972 spring harvest alone. Every household had its own
reserves, and many had savings in the bank. This year (1973)
they will average 450 jin a mu. This triples their yield before
the Cultural Revolution and is above the yield of 300–400
jin prescribed by the national agricultural plan for farms
north of the Yangtze River. In this respect Felicity is holding
up its end in the province.

Up to two years ago Honan Province did not grow enough
food grain for its 50 million population. But in 1970 it not
only supplied itself with all the wheat it needed but also
exported grain. Thanks largely to its 1,666 people's communes
and the Cultural Revolution, the province has more than
doubled its preliberation grain output.

The general picture in the province parallels that in
Felicity. It has ended the disasters brought by drought and
flood. It has built reservoirs, ordered the course of its rivers,
dug wells, drainage, and irrigation canals and ditches. It now
has 100,000 kilometers of power lines, 97 local fertilizer
plants, 800,000 members of peasant scientific research teams.
It irrigates 40 million mu, ten times as much as before liberation. It has mechanized farming on 40 per cent of its
arable land. It too has pacesetter farms, and Felicity still has
quite a way to go to catch up with them. The Yuehtan
Brigade in Yenshih County raises an average of 720 jin of
wheat per mu and, on some plots, 1,000 jin.

Farming is the basis of Felicity's prosperity, but its revolutionary committee has followed Party instructions to back
this up with other activities.

I went to see the tractor park and repair works. The yard
was larger than before and a bit chaotic-looking, but it was
a hive of activity. Besides a truck, a combine harvester, and
other implements, it has seventeen Loyang caterpillar tractors
that plow and cultivate 30 per cent of the commune's land.
The repair shop has expanded to produce many things needed
not only in this but in other communes. It has made and

sold 1,000 pumps and also trailers and pneumatic cart wheels, 350 kinds of cutters and threshers, and 75,000 hoes, mattocks, and sickles. In 1972 the workers there produced 800,000 yuan worth of goods. I was glad to see some of those formerly shy girls from Upper Felicity there, clad in overalls and running machines like veterans.

It is surprising how much can be done with even the most modest mechanical means. In the foundry of the repair shop I found the lathes were made either in Chihsien County or out of old parts by the workshop itself. In the pump-making shop they were busy molding parts out of metal scrap which they melted down in a homemade furnace. The only machines this shop had were a large drill, a hand-me-down from some larger plant, and a small drill which they had made themselves. They were using scrap metal to make their trailers.

The pride of the commune is the new flour mill. This three-storied grey brick building is the tallest and most imposing structure in the whole commune. It dominates the village from the place where ponds and hillocks once made a semiwasteland at the back of the school. The story of how it came to be built is typical of how such things happen in a commune. The suggestion to build it was first voiced at one of the meetings of commune members. The peasants' livelihood had improved, and they wanted better flour than they had been getting from their old millstones or even the electrically powered mills run by their brigades. These saved time and effort and animal traction, but the mills heated up and the flour was "half-baked." So the idea of a really modern mill quickly gathered support. The time was propitious. The tractor repair works was making a tidy profit, so this was saved until there was enough to start building the mill. It was completed in eight months in 1971 and cost 120,000 yuan. Milling 80,000 jin a day at full capacity, it serves not only Great Felicity Commune but other farms as well. The first commune-run mill in the county, it is rated better than that run by the county itself. It is well designed and so mechanized that only seven people are needed on a shift. As it is collective property, its profits go to the commune as a whole, and this has helped increase the commune's accumulation fund from 800,000 yuan (42 yuan per capita) in 1958* to more than 4 million yuan (177 yuan per capita) in 1965 and over 17 million yuan (607 yuan per capita) in 1971—a fifteen-fold increase over 1958 and a 4.6-fold increase over the year before the Cultural Revolution.

Thanks to this combination of farming and growth of local industry, Felicity has become a real millionaire commune. Turnover in its thirteen supply and marketing co-ops is running in excess of a million yuan a year (not including farm products). Side-occupations produced nearly a million yuan in 1965 and nearly 3 million yuan last year (1971). An able Felicity farmer can expect to earn 500 yuan a year in money terms.

All elementary school-age children in the commune go to school. Junior and senior middle school education is available for 1,500 students. It provides a reasonably adequate health service to its members for an annual 1.50 yuan a head. Smallpox, cholera, and malaria have been wiped out. Children take an oral antimalaria vaccine for four months once a month from the age of two.

"We were ashamed that we still could not produce enough grain for ourselves. That was in 1958. Now we've changed all that. We grow enough and to spare. We've doubled our herd of livestock. Every brigade is breeding horses now, and some are even buying their own tractors. We make our own bricks. We have thirty-one food processing plants. We make our own cooking oil and noodles, and we have more than a million and a half fish fry in our ponds." So said Secretary Kuo.

"We took Tachai as our model and we did not ask help from others. We relied on ourselves. We strung up 200 kilometers of high- and low-voltage power lines and made a

---

* I give these and the following figures as they were quoted to me. If there appear to be discrepancies, this is because the number of people involved or the area varies as new members join the commune or the population grows or new land is brought into cultivation or is allowed to lie fallow.

socialist plan of mechanization. We leveled 50,000 of our 72,000 mu of land so we could use tractors to plow deep —over 30 centimeters. We dug more than 40 wells and two canals 16,000 meters long with another 17,000 meters of supplementary channels. With our irrigation pumps and channels we can handle any drought or rainfall we are likely to get. In case of drought we can irrigate nearly all our land from deep wells or the River Wei.

"We have reclaimed 27,000 mu of land. That marsh at Lao Yu Wu is now growing corn and melon. Not even a tree could grow on the southern end of the alkaline flat. We are cultivating 12,000 mu of it now. Our people sift out the alkali by hand. You can see the mounds of salt as you drive by. By that method and proper irrigation and drainage, manuring, rotation of crops, and leaving the land to lie fallow every other year, we raise fair crops on it. We learn as we work. We trained 830 agrotechnicians and in the process bred six good strains of corn and four of wheat. These new strains will help other farms grow more and better grain. I think we can say we are carrying out Chairman Mao's revolutionary line.

"Now we are concentrating our attention on mechanizing farming and other activities," he added in an important afterthought.

Secretary Kuo is a heavy man with a bearlike gait. His tough, wiry hair rises straight up from his skull like a brush. He would not rest until he had taken me around to see every new thing on the commune. Finally he gave me a farewell meal that floored me and all the cadres and peasants who attended it. We ate *chiaotze,* pork and *baba fan,* chicken and fish from a local reservoir and topped this off with corn and local apples . . . all Felicity fare.

What about Lao Man and his family and my OSD Team?

I wanted to walk over to the hamlet from the commune center but Secretary Kuo, who does not get an overseas journalist to visit the commune every day (in fact I was the first to go there), insisted on taking me over by car. We drove up to Lao Man's cottage in a cloud of sunlit dust.

They expected us, so everyone was at home: Lao Man,

Ta Sao, and the children. For a few minutes it seemed that everyone was talking at once. Neighbors came over and pumped my hand in the modern way. The young wife next door (she who had spoken with my wife about family planning and the opposition of her old mother-in-law) hovered shyly by the wall. I went over to her and congratulated her on the new little grandson she cuddled in her arms.

Lao Man and his family had prospered in these two years. They were now a labor-rich household with four able-bodied adults and a very competent little housewife in Ta Hsiang. Their team's increased output gave them 500 jin of food grain each a year. That was much more than ample. All their big earthenware grain jars were full, and they had sold grain to the state and banked the proceeds. Lao Man credited this increase in yields to better irrigation and field management, to the deep plowing and increased use of fertilizer. The brigade had dug fifteen deep wells now and owned four pneumatic-tired carts. They had bred an improved strain of wheat. They had more manure. With more foodstuff available, every household in the team was raising two pigs, whereas one had been the rule before. Number Two Team, the best of the three in the brigade, was even raising five sows collectively as the start of a collective piggery. Yields were 400 jin a mu.

By this time everyone knew that I was writing a book about the hamlet, so Lao Man tactfully gave way to Kao from Number Two Team who was bursting to tell about his team's successes. He had brought along his account book and gave me these figures:

OUTPUT AND DISTRIBUTION IN NUMBER TWO TEAM
(in terms of jin of grain)

	1970	1971	1972
Output	150,000	170,000	78,000 summer harvest 220,000 estimated total
Tax	17,000	17,000	17,000
Distributed to members	70,000	85,000	
Reserve	40,000	40,000	

The rest of their output had been used for current expenditure, fodder, seed, and welfare. Kao told me that in 1971 a work-point had been worth 7 mao 1 fen. In 1972 he reckoned it would be worth 9 mao 2 fen. As we had driven in, I had seen his team out harvesting the corn, collecting greenstuff, and building compost heaps. He was sure they could raise 250,000 jin in 1973 and 280,000 in 1974.

He and Lao Man agreed that the brigade could fulfill its plan of growing 720,000 jin of grain in 1973. All of its land was now well irrigated. It had withstood an eight-month drought in 1972, and there was little likelihood of things getting much worse than that. Such an occurrence in the old days would have sent most of the village off begging. Now it had hardly slowed down their growth, though naturally it had cost them more to raise their crops both in terms of money for power and in extra labor. Today they took all this in their stride. Everyone in the brigade had prospered. Since I had left, they had built an additional 150 rooms. This meant a big improvement in their comfort and a useful extension of individual privacy. They had 50,000 fish fry in their ponds. Two of their youths had gone to college.

I asked a question that had previously slipped my attention: How had they decided how to divide their gross output?

They told me that, give or take a few points' difference for special reasons decided on by members (in view of difficulties because of drought, for instance, or the need for especially large investments), the proportions were more or less uniform throughout the country. After making a survey of the desires of the peasants and general practice, the Party and People's Government recommended that the proportion of output set aside for distribution among commune members as work-points, per capita food allotments, pensions, maternity grants, etc., should be around 50 to 55 per cent, while from 30 to 35 per cent should be set aside for the collective reserve (the production fund for investment, reserves, etc.). These proportions were pretty generally adhered to unless there were very good reasons to diverge from them. The grain tax and welfare accounted for the other 10 per cent, with welfare (health, education, sports, and culture) taking around 5 per cent.

It was felt that these proportions were a reasonable reflection of the claims of the state, the collective, and the individual commune members. The same considerations governed the decision on how to divide the distribution fund. Here the Party and People's Government recommended that 60 per cent of that fund should be divided equally among all members as their basic food ration, while 40 per cent should be set aside as the work-point fund, to be allocated among working members depending on the number of work-points they had earned. This proportion is clearly based on an assessment of the level of socialist consciousness among the peasants. That assessment is manifestly high. There is, after all, a certain element of material incentive in the concept of the work-point. Here again there are certain variations of a few points in the 60:40 proportion, depending on the conditions of team or brigade.

I asked about my other friends.

Our OSD Team had dissolved. Everyone had returned to Peking and resumed work. Most of the cadres and their families in the other Felicity hamlets had also returned to the city. So had the first group of cadres in the May Seventh Cadre School. Most of these had gone back to the translation bureau and were doing the work of a second group who replaced them in the cadre school. Later a third and last group would come down so that finally everyone in the bureau would have had the experience of living and working in the countryside with the peasants. No one yet knew if the cadre school would continue after that. I heard that quite a number of cadres were now going to do similar stints of work in industrial enterprises to integrate with the industrial workers. This seemed to me a good idea.

After that we all paused for breath. The Mans and I went into our old cottage for a quiet chat. The big room was bare except for farm tools and a table and chairs and stools. The doorway into our little bedroom was now covered with a

wedding curtain of emerald green and red. Ching Chun had
married. I suddenly realized that the sturdy and homely young
woman I had shaken hands with was the bride. Little Pig,
I now learned, had been sold at the time of the marriage
and had more than paid for the festivities.

Au Chiu was a gangling nine-year-old. Hsiao Ching was
again coy with me, but I could see that she was really just
as cheeky as before. Ta Hsiang wore her broadest smile but
kept modestly in the background. Ta Sao looked well, unchanged. Lao Man was as tough as ever.

Too soon it was time to go. I had 15,000 miles to go to my
new home in Albany, New York. I gave Lao Man the hammer I had brought him as a present, with a scarf for Ta Sao
and books for the children. As we said good-by, Ta Sao, as
generous as ever, hurried out and returned with a present
for me—a big plastic bag filled with a dozen eggs and dates
from the tree in the farmyard.

Would I see them again? I felt that it would not be long.
Since I had last seen them I had traveled 30,000 miles to
and around America. I could be in New York in a couple
of days if I wished. I would like to introduce them to my
new friends in America and elsewhere overseas. Distance no
longer separates them to any great extent. It is other things,
far more intractable. As I left Felicity, I hoped and was confident that we humans who had made those obstacles could
overcome them and soon, too.

After I had looked over those green acres and saw those
tree-bowered villages, I made a new entry in the red notebook that Great Felicity Commune had presented to me:
"Felicity is definitely no longer a lower-than-average farm. It
is average now and on the way to better than average."

Appendix A

The Huang Fu Brigade 🌿

I was able to get rather complete figures about the production and distribution arrangements of the Huang Fu Brigade in Great Felicity. I print them here for those readers who would like more detailed information on these matters.

The 99 households in the area of the Huang Fu Brigade numbered 530 people before liberation. They farmed 3,100 mu of land. Six of these households were landlords or rich peasants. They owned a total of 1,800 mu. Seventy-five of the other 93 families were poor peasants who regularly had to flee from either drought or flood. During one of the last dispersals before the People's Government was formed, 15 families disappeared without trace. Eight other families were forced by starvation to sell either sons or daughters. "We lived little better than beasts," they say bitterly. "We starved regularly every winter."

What is extraordinary is that the Huang Fu peasants, who now number 173 households with 960 people, still farm those same 3,100 mu of land but are universally well-to-do. Taking all things into consideration, they are living better than they ever dreamed they could in the old society. In the old days they reaped less than 100 jin a mu. But in 1958 after land reform and forming their commune, they reaped 500,000 jin and, in 1966, raised this to 540,000 jin, that is, 177 jin a mu. This was enough to provide every member with a basic allocation of 278 jin. Even allowing that the children and babies would not eat all that allocation, it was still not enough. They still had to buy grain from the state. But in 1968 they did still better. Their total output was 790,000 jin of grain. Out of this they allocated 460 jin to each member as basic grain ration, 40,000 jin for reserve, 300,000 jin to be sold to the state, 11,000 yuan in cash to be shared among members.

By 1971 they were well ahead. Their total output was 1,140,000 jin. Out of this they allocated 580 jin to each member as basic grain ration, 220,000 jin for reserve, 120,000 jin for welfare and investment, 300,000 jin to be sold to the state, 14,000 yuan in cash to be shared among members.

That year the brigade bought a Loyang tractor, pneumatic-tired carts, horses and mules, set up two pumping stations with 14-inch- and 12-inch-diameter pipes, dug eight mechanized wells and acquired fifteen motors, three diesel engines, five milling machines for grain, seven water pumps, and six threshers. By this time every family enjoyed electric light in its home, 140 had bought loudspeakers to hook into a radio diffusion system, 20 sewing machines for their personal use, and 55 handcarts. They planted 80,000 trees. (These are on public lands. They planted another 20,000 on their own home plots, and so these are privately owned.) The brigade has an elementary school and middle school, a clinic and cooperative medical service, and its own brick kiln.

In 1972 the summer harvest was 750,000 jin, and the autumn harvest was estimated at 600,000 jin, a total of 1,350,000 jin. The brigade plans to raise a yield of 500 jin a mu within the next three years. This will be ahead of the quota set by the national agricultural plan for farms south of the Yangtze which enjoy a much longer growing season than farms north of the Yellow River. They are also going to plant more trees, orchards particularly, and buy another tractor.

One team of this brigade is composed of sixteen young men and women, middle school graduates who have come here to work from Chihsien County town. They are welcome guests. In 1971 they produced 2,000 jin of grain per capita for a total of 32,000 jin. This year they expect to do better and reach 35,000 jin. One of them has been recommended by the team for a college education. He may return here. The decision depends on his own choice and the recommendation of the state board that assigns graduates to jobs awaiting them all over the country.

A happy, lively bunch, they crowded round me when I arrived, eager to introduce themselves and show me their dormitory (spotless), and granary (bulging). They lived in one compound, girls in one cottage, boys in the other, and did their own cooking and accounting for their part of the farm. These were products of the Cultural Revolution's educational reforms. Throughout their latter school life they had grown accustomed to working in factories and farms as part of their education. To come to Felicity for a life of farming was nothing new to them. These were the type of youngster that Chairman Mao said would be warmly welcomed by the peasants.

Appendix B

1 li	0.5 kilometer	0.3107 mile
1 jin	0.5 kilogram	1.1 pounds
2,000 jin	1 ton	
1 mu	0.0666 hectare	0.1647 acre
15 mu	1 hectare	2.4771 acres
1 yuan	10 mao	U.S. $0.40

NOTE: The Chinese people's currency has remained stable since the early 1950s. Prices of daily necessities too have remained stable or been reduced. The exceptions have been agricultural products. Prices of oil seeds and animal products, for instance, have been raised by the state to benefit the peasants.